D1506687

TRAVELS IN JEWRY

" Israel in Italien " (Berlin, 1909).

Jewish Life in Modern Times (1st edit., 1914; 2nd edit., Revised, 1929).

The Ruhleben Prison Camp (1917).

The Journal of a Jewish Traveller (1925).

A Ghetto Gallery (1931).

Britain's Nameless Ally (1942).

The Jews in the War (1st edit., 1942; 2nd edit., Revised, 1943).

History of the Jews in Vilna (Philadelphia, 1943).

The Zionist Movement (1945. American and French editions, 1946. Spanish edition, 1947. Hebrew and Italian editions, 1952).

The Progress of Zionism (8th revised edition, 1946. French edition, 1945).

Contemporary Jewry (1950).

Revised and enlarged edition of Paul Goodman's *History of the Jews* (1951).

A Short History of Zionism (1951).

THE AUTHOR

TRAVELS IN JEWRY

By

ISRAEL COHEN

New York

E. P. DUTTON & CO., INC.

1953

LIBRARY OF CONGRESS CATALOG CARD NUMBER: 53-6068

TO THE MEMORY
OF MY
JEWISH FELLOW-WRITERS
WHOSE LAST JOURNEY
ENDED IN
THE NAZI DEATH-CAMPS

PREFACE

THE studies and sketches in this book are of some thirty Jewish communities in different parts of Europe, which I visited on various occasions between the two World Wars. Some of them I visited several times, some I knew even before the First War, and others I revisited after the Second War. In two of them, Cologne and Berlin, I lived for some years, and in all of them my stay was long enough to familiarise myself with all salient factors in the life of the local Jewry. These studies cover a wide range geographically, extending from Paris to Salonika, from Lisbon to Lemberg, and from Budapest to Rome. They also embrace a manifold variety of communities, whose distinguishing features present striking contrasts in the social, political, and cultural fields. Some of them, such as Berlin and Vienna, Warsaw and Vilna, once played important and leading parts in Jewish life, exercising influences in the intellectual and spiritual domains that reached to the most distant parts of the Jewish world. Now they have been reduced to mere names, nor are they likely ever—or at least within any foreseeable space of time—to rise from their ruins and gain the proud stature and honoured status that they formerly enjoyed.

It is just because of the unparalleled calamity that has overtaken these and other once populous and pulsating centres of Jewish activity, that it is desirable to have, both as a reminder for the present generation and for the enlightenment of future ones, a portrayal by a contemporary of the conditions that existed before Hitler destroyed so large a part of European civilisation. Most of the communities in Central and Eastern Europe, especially those in Poland and Rumania, suffered continually from disabilities, discrimination, and recurring violence, but all their hardships were trifling in comparison with the barbarities of extermination to which they were subjected during the war, nor does the recollection of their inter-war ordeal serve in any way to assuage the post-war agony.

With few exceptions, these studies were written at times when the experiences and impressions resulting from each visit were still fresh and vivid; but, despite the colossal catastrophe that has supervened, no attempt has been made to point a moral or adorn a tale, although, wherever necessary, a paragraph or note has been added to indicate the nature or the magnitude of the tragedy that has occurred. Fortunately there are still Jewries on the Continent, which, although they have sustained enormous losses in population and grievous deprivation in leadership, have nevertheless retained a semblance of their old structure and are working bravely and hopefully towards a gradual restoration. On the other hand, I have also included some places of historic interest, such as Avignon and Cordova, which were spared the affliction of the Nazi scourge, but which have endured their own tribulations in a previous age, and whose survival, with their wealth of mingled memories, still attracts the pilgrim and accentuates the varied destiny that characterises the Jewish people.

All three kinds of communities—those that have been blasted out of existence, some that are recovering (either under a continuation of the old régime, or under a new form of government) from relatively minor disasters, and others that are now merely the resorts of the scholar and the historian—have in different measure, but with equal right, contributed to this record of travel.

I.C.

CONTENTS

9

LIST OF ILLUSTRATIONS

*Acknowledgments are due and gratefully tendered to the
Forward Association, New York, for the reproduction of the
illustrations facing pages 64, 65, 97, 129, 160, 192, and 193.*

Chapter I

COLOGNE AS ZIONIST CENTRE

THE CAPITAL of the Rhineland, so sorely devastated by the War, once figured very prominently in Zionist affairs, for the Central Office of the Zionist Organisation was situated there from 1905 to 1911. It achieved this distinction because it was the home of David Wolffsohn (1856–1914), the successor of Theodor Herzl in the leadership of the movement. The political insignificance of Cologne in comparison with Vienna, then the important and teeming metropolis of a great Empire, was urged as one of the reasons why the Zionist headquarters should not be transferred there. But as, failing Dr. Max Nordau (1849–1923) who would not accept the leadership, there was no other choice but Wolffsohn, the provinciality of the city was not allowed to form an obstacle. There were indeed some countervailing advantages. After the political deadlock had been reached in the negotiations both with Sultan Abdul Hamid and with the British Government, the removal of the seat of the Executive to the tranquil seclusion of the Rhineland was regarded by many as a tactical measure, for there seemed little prospect, for some years to come, of any possible development outside the sphere of organisation and propaganda. Besides, Cologne could conveniently be reached by the members of the Executive who lived in Paris, London, The Hague, and Berlin; and Wolffsohn could continue to pay visits to the Jewish Colonial Trust in London, of which he was Chairman, without absenting himself too long from his presidential chair.

I was at the Central Office in Cologne from March, 1910,

until September, 1911, when it was transferred to Berlin. My appointment was due to two main reasons. In the first place, Wolffsohn wanted to establish an English department for correspondence with the Federations in English-speaking countries. Ever since Herzl opened his office in Vienna in 1896 all communications with these countries were sent out in German, and as they were usually long and often presented difficulties of construction and interpretation to those who were unfamiliar with the language, they were sometimes misunderstood and not seldom ignored. Having become acquainted myself, in the office of the English Zionist Federation, with the long-winded lucubrations, which always began with *Sehr geehrte Herren Gesinnungs-genossen*, and contained sentences in which the subject was often separated from the predicate by a dozen lines, I could sympathise with the secretaries in remote British Dominions who doubtless found it necessary to consult a dictionary to unravel the meaning of these puzzling despatches, and I could understand the increasing resentment against the monopoly maintained by the German tongue in the official correspondence of the Zionist Executive. The complaints gradually grew into a sort of revolt, and Wolffsohn there-fore decided to remedy the situation in the interests of the movement in general. He entrusted me with the task of creating and directing an English department of the Central Office for correspondence with all bodies in English-speaking countries. The new department was also at the service of the Head Office of the Jewish National Fund, which was presided over by Dr. Max Bodenheimer, a leading lawyer in Cologne, and an intimate friend of Wolffsohn.

The other reason for my appointment was the change in the personnel of the Central Office necessitated by the with-drawal of Mr. Nahum Sokolow. He had held the position of General Secretary for a few years, together with the editorship of the official organ *Die Welt*, and conferred on both offices the distinction of a gifted and versatile personality. But as he sided with the " practical " Zionists, who failed to secure control of the Organisation at the Zionist Congress in Hamburg, in December, 1909, continued co-operation with Wolffsohn, the leader of the "political" Zionists, was obviously impossible. The gap caused by his departure and that of other officials was filled by the engagement of other men, of whose sympathies with the policy of the Executive there was no shadow of doubt. The Office was placed under the direction of Mr. Siegfried Hoofien[1], a kinsman of Mr. Jacobus Kann (a member of the Executive), of The Hague, and he was assisted by Dr. Martin Rosenblueth, from Berlin, who had played an active part in a Zionist students' organisation. The editorship of *Die Welt*, which, since its transfer to Cologne, had been conducted successively by Dr. Coralnik, Dr. Berthold Feiwel, and Mr. Sokolow, was entrusted to Dr. Jacob Klatzkin (1882–1947). The latter was not particularly happy in his editorial job, as he already felt drawn to those problems of philosophy, the exposition of which in critical tomes afterwards brought him recognition and fame; and as we took our walks in the Volksgarten, a well-wooded park in the neighbourhood, he often complained of the deadening influence of the city. The Hebrew organ of the Executive, *Haolam*, which first appeared in Cologne in 1907, was published there for only about a year. It was transferred in 1908 to Vilna, which was the headquarters of the Central Committee of the Russian Zionists, and was continued there until the outbreak of the First World War.

My principal work consisted in conducting the correspondence of the Central Office and of the Jewish National Fund with all English-speaking organisations, which embraced not only the affiliated bodies in England, the United States, Canada, and South Africa, but also the individual societies in Australia and New Zealand, Shanghai and Singapore. An undue amount of attention was claimed by disputes of a purely local character, which loomed large at a time when

---

[1] Mr. Hoofien, in 1911, went to Palestine as an official of the Anglo-Palestine Bank, of which he afterwards became Managing Director.

15

there was no really great question to engage the interest of
the Zionist world. There were disputes, for instance, between
the English Federation and the Order of Ancient Macca-
baeans concerning the latter's recognition as a Separate
Union, and also between the Canadian Zionist Organisation
and a disgruntled individual who tried to set up a rival body.
It is difficult nowadays to imagine how so much heat could
have been generated over matters that had no vital bearing
upon the ideals of the movement, although they touched
upon principles of discipline. The normal routine was
relieved every now and again by an English letter from
some out-of-the-way place, where nobody had dreamed that
there were any Jews, still less Zionists. One such place was
Nagasaki, where there was an ardent Zionist, who kept up a
regular correspondence, but the little Jewish community of
which he was the president, as well as himself, had passed
away before I visited Japan in 1920. I then learned that the
Scrolls of the Torah and other ritual appurtenances of the
Nagasaki Synagogue had been taken possession of by the
Shanghai Jewish Community. Another remote town from
where a request came in English for information about the
movement was Volo, in Greece. This epistle caused quite a
sensation, and a map was consulted to discover the exact
whereabouts of the city. Salonika, it should be added, was
at that time within the frontiers of Turkey, and Zionist
activity there would not have been tolerated.

Apart from correspondence, it was necessary to supply
Zionists in English-speaking countries with current news of
the movement. All the Federations and many individuals
received *Die Welt*, but few people read it, and nobody considered it his business to translate and communicate items
of interest to the local Jewish Press. I therefore began to
issue a weekly English Bulletin, containing all important
news as well as summaries of the leading articles in *Die
Welt*, which was sent not only to the offices of all English
organisations and societies, but also to all the principal
Jewish papers in English throughout the world and a

number of selected individuals. I also began to develop some publicity for the cause in the English Press, an effort in which I was helped by the personal connections that I had previously established in the course of my journalistic activity in London. It was necessary, moreover, to increase the supply of literary matter, for at that time the whole of Zionist literature in English consisted only of translations of Herzl's *Der Judenstaat*, Pinsker's *Auto-Emancipation* (which nobody could get), and a pamphlet by Max Nordau. I therefore brought out a book, under the title of *Zionist Work in Palestine* (published by Fisher Unwin), consisting of translations of articles by leading authorities in a special Palestine number of *Die Welt*. This publication, which was profusely illustrated, received widespread and very sympathetic notice in the English Press. It had been considered a risky venture from the financial point of view, as it was sold at a shilling, but it yielded the Jewish National Fund a handsome profit. I also wrote a thirty-two page pamphlet describing the aims and achievements of the Zionist movement, which was likewise favourably received, particularly in the British Dominions, where there had long been a demand for Zionist literature.

The Executive during my stay in Cologne consisted of a triumvirate—Wolffsohn, Jacobus Kann (the Hague banker), and Professor Otto Warburg (the botanist, in Berlin). Wolffsohn had a flourishing timber business, which occasionally took him to Slovakia, and he usually stopped *en route* at Budapest, for the purpose of trying to get official sanction for Zionist activity in Hungary. He spent the early morning hours at his business office, and arrived at the Zionist office about mid-day, often returning in the afternoon. He took a keen interest in all current matters, especially in the conduct of *Die Welt*, and although the political situation did not call for any great activity on his part he was kept busy by the agitation of the Opposition in different countries. Articles criticising him for the policy he represented appeared in Jewish papers in Vienna, Berlin,

Vilna, and elsewhere, and he seldom allowed them to go unanswered in his own organ. Meetings of the Executive were not frequent, nor was there any need at the time that they should be otherwise. When a meeting was held in the summer Wolffsohn took his colleagues, Kann and Warburg, to the picturesque surroundings of Bad Godesberg, where they could sit and confer, after a pleasant repast, on the terrace of a restaurant overlooking the Rhine—thereby setting a precedent for a far more momentous conference over a quarter of a century later.

The principal political activity at the time was occasioned by the opposition of the Young Turks to Zionist aspirations. After the overthrow of Abdul Hamid in 1908 and the establishment of a constitutional Government in Constantinople it was hoped that the new régime would look more favourably upon Zionist proposals; but it was not long before it was realised that the Young Turks were just as jealous of the integrity of the Ottoman Empire as the old Sultan had been. They were firmly opposed to the fostering of separate nationalisms within the confines of their Empire, and their antipathy to Jewish nationalism was stirred up by a small clique of assimilationists, who misrepresented and maligned the aims of Zionism, not only in their own Judaeo-Spanish papers, but also in the Turkish Press. It thus became necessary to take effective measures for dispelling the misunderstandings and misrepresentations current in political circles in the Ottoman capital, as well as for enlightening the public in general. For this purpose a branch of the Jewish Colonial Trust was opened there under the name of the Anglo-Levantine Banking Company, and it was placed under the management of Dr. Victor Jacobson, who was thus able to act as a diplomatic agent without holding such a title. He devoted particular attention to the Press, and, with funds provided by the Zionist Executive, he founded two French papers—*Le Jeune Turc*, a daily for the general public, which advocated autonomy for the nations in the Ottoman Empire, and *L'Aurore*, a Zionist weekly. Vladimir

Jabotinsky was connected for a time with the editorial direction of the daily, but owing to a critical review that he wrote of Jacobus Kann's book on Palestine, as well as a conflict of views on other matters, his association with the paper was brought to an abrupt close.

The Wolffsohns lived in a medium-sized villa in the Sachsenring, furnished with taste and comfort, about five minutes' walk from the Zionist Office, which was at the corner of the Karolingerring. They were childless; they were—perhaps on that account—very fond of entertaining guests, and they were charming hosts. Wolffsohn was at his best on a Friday evening, when, after grace (for which he provided Turkish fezzes) had been said with all the traditional melodies, he loved to talk and relate incidents from his store of experiences. He was fond of referring to his visit to South Africa, which he had undertaken (a couple of years earlier) in the interests of his health, and which developed into a triumphal tour. Sometimes he would ask me to translate an article dealing with Palestine published in an English paper. I remember in particular explaining to him the main points of a trenchant article by Israel Zangwill, in the *Fortnightly Review*, which drew a dismal picture of the prospects of Zionism.

It was at Wolffsohn's house that I first met a number of people, who, each in his particular sphere, played an important part in the Movement. Among them were Leo Motzkin, who was then engaged on the monumental history of the Russian pogroms, which was issued under the auspices of the Zionist Organisation; Aaron Aaronson, then known only as the discoverer of "wild wheat" in Palestine, and later associated with the British Intelligence Service in the First World War; Dr. Arthur Ruppin (1876–1943) who had not long opened the Palestine Office in Jaffa; and Dr. Osias Thon, the Cracow Rabbi, who was a staunch supporter of Wolffsohn. It was there, too, that I first met Dr. Ignaz Zollschan (1877–1948) who had made a great reputation with his scholarly work on *Das Rassenproblem*, and who was delegated to represent the Zionist Organisation at an International Congress on Races in London in 1911.

Wolffsohn was an easy man to work with, for he was always natural and frank, conscious of his limitations, which he made no attempt to conceal, since these were outweighed by his undoubted gifts and qualities. He was without the intellectual training enjoyed by most Zionist leaders, but he had acquired the capacity to deliver an effective speech, and during his presidency he was certainly, after Nordau, the best speaker in the galaxy of Zionist orators. His voice was somewhat gruff (due, perhaps to a throat affection), but he had a lively humour, a dominating figure, and a charming manner, which compelled the attention and earned the applause of the public. The last service I was able to render him was in connection with the preparation of his opening speech for the Tenth Congress, which was held in Basle, in August, 1911. Two months before that event he invited me to take a walk with him one morning, in the course of which he mapped out all the leading points and ideas that he wished to embody in his address. It was evident from the sequence of his suggestions and the facility with which he made them that he had given them careful thought. He asked me to draft the speech in English on the basis of his outline, and when my draft was ready it was translated into German by a colleague. But this German version was then thoroughly revised and carefully amended by himself, and subjected to various deletions and numerous amplifications before he was satisfied with it, for it was to form not only his opening speech at the Congress, but also his valedictory address as President.

The Zionist Office was housed in a large flat, in the residential part of Cologne. It included the office of the Jewish National Fund as well as the " Juedischer Verlag ", which acted as the publication department of the Organisation and issued a number of literary and instructive works on current Jewish questions. The only room in the Office that was available for me was the one in which were stored

all the personal belongings of Herzl—his books and book-
case, desks, pictures and busts; and although little space was
left in which to work and move about, my discomfort was
more than compensated by the inspiration of the surroundings. On one occasion I was visited there by Hans Herzl,
who was visibly moved as he fingered some of his father's
books. Twenty-five years later I had the pleasure of seeing
all those treasured objects installed in a worthy and dignified
resting-place in a special room of the Head Office of the
Jewish National Fund in Jerusalem.

The change that has taken place in the Jewish community
of Cologne is indicated by two figures. Before the advent
of Hitler the city had nearly 15,000 Jews, now it has only
about six hundred. Many emigrated before the war, but far
more were deported to the death-camps in Poland.

Chapter II

MEMORIES OF BERLIN

I FIRST VISITED the once arrogant capital of the now
desolated German Empire in the summer of 1906. I was
on the way to Galicia, then part of Austria-Hungary, to
enquire into the underground workings of the Polish
revolutionary movement for the great but short-lived Liberal
paper, *The Tribune*, of whose editorial staff I was a
member. It was at a time of halcyon peace in the world of
international politics, when the Jews in Germany seemed
little perturbed by the anti-Semitic ferment that had so long
been a normal feature of its national life. Even during that
first brief stay I was offered a postcard with an anti-Jewish
caricature, which was sold outside the Café Bauer in Unter
den Linden. My next visit was at the end of 1909, after the
Zionist Congress in Hamburg, the only one ever held in
Germany. I was then struck by the vital part that Berlin
played as a source of information about the persecution of
the Jews in Tsarist Russia, which figured so often in the
world's Press. An important bulletin, *Russische Korres-
pondenz*, containing accounts of repressive decrees and
officially incited pogroms, was edited there by Leo Motzkin
(1867–1933)[1], who was regularly supplied with this depressing news by a band of Zionist friends beyond the Vistula.
My third journey to Berlin was in the autumn of 1911, for
the purpose of becoming a resident, as I accompanied the
Central Office of the Zionist Organisation on its transfer
from Cologne, in order to continue my duties as secretary of

[1] Later President of the " Comité des Délégations Juives ", in Paris, and
Chairman of the General Council of the World Zionist Organisation. (See
Chapter XX, v.)

22

the English department. I had intended remaining not more than a few years, but my sojourn was prolonged, against my will and to my more than serious inconvenience, until the middle of the First World War.

The removal of the Zionist headquarters to the German capital gave the movement a much-needed stimulus, although it misled some newspaper correspondents into decrying it as a secret instrument of German policy. The new Office was located in the Sächsische Strasse, a quiet residential thoroughfare in the West End, off the Kurfürstendamm. It consisted only of the Central Office, the "Jüdischer Verlag" (publication department) and *Die Welt* (the organ of the Zionist Executive), as the office of the Jewish National Fund (for the purchase of land in Palestine) remained behind in Cologne, under the continued control of Dr. Max Bodenheimer, one of the earliest supporters of Theodor Herzl. But the Berlin Office soon expanded under the direction of Dr. Arthur Hantke, a member of the new Executive, who took charge of the work of organisation, to which he devoted himself with zeal and energy. A special department was created at the Office for the purpose of correspondence with the Zionist Central Committee in Russia (whose headquarters were in Vilna), and it was placed under the care of Dr. Simon Bernstein, a Russian Zionist scholar, who helped to improve the organisation of the movement in the vast territories of the Tsar. Another official, engaged to look after Zionist work in Poland, was Dr. Philip Korngruen, who came from Warsaw and some twelve years later became a leading magistrate in Tel Aviv.

Mr. Nahum Sokolow (1861–1936), who had settled in Berlin after giving up the post of General Secretary of the Zionist Organisation at the end of 1909, naturally took the political affairs of the movement under his wing, but that did not amount to much in those days, since the Young Turks were just as hostile to a large Jewish settlement in Palestine as the old Sultan had been. A close watch, however, had to be kept over the political scene in Con-

stantinople, and this continued to be done by Dr. Victor
Jacobson (1869–1934), a Russian Zionist of political ability,
with the subsequent assistance of Richard Lichtheim.
Thanks to the political calm Sokolow was able to absent
himself from Europe in 1912. He went to America, where
he achieved a striking success by his speeches and lectures
in many cities and infused new vigour into the movement.

Dr. Shmarya Levin (1867–1935), another member of the
Executive, specialised in propaganda. He had formerly been
a "Crown Rabbi" in Russia and also a member of the
Duma, and he united in his style of oratory the learning and
fervour of a Rabbi with the practical outlook of a politician.
He was a tempestuous speaker, never at loss for words or
ideas, which flowed and spurted from him in an unceasing
stream; and he concerned himself much more with the
problem of the Jewish "psyche" in exile than with the
question of material restoration. He was in regular demand
for public meetings; he toured all parts of Europe, except
Russia, to which he could not return without serious risk;
he seldom spoke for less than an hour and a half, by which
time he was bathed in sweat, for his hands worked all the
time as vigorously as his lips; and at the end of the meeting
he liked to be accompanied by a band of admirers to a café,
where, after some refreshment and witty talk, he would be
absorbed in a game of chess until long past midnight.

The President, Professor Otto Warburg (1859–1938), as
an authority on botany, devoted himself to questions of
agricultural colonisation in Palestine, and showed a
particular partiality for the cultivation of the olive-tree
under the auspices of the Jewish National Fund. Affable
and unassuming, he did not attempt to dominate either the
Executive or the Office and was of a retiring disposition
long before he actually retired. Having emerged from an
assimilationist milieu, the position that he had acquired in
the movement was both a testimony and a tribute to his
own convictions and an example to the host of ultra-
Germanised Jews throughout the Reich. After the Vienna

Congress of 1913 the Executive was increased by the addition of Dr. Tschlenow (1864–1918), one of the leaders of the Russian Zionists, but as he was unable to give up his home and his medical practice in Moscow, he attended only occasional meetings in Berlin.

The Zionist Office was a regular hub, for not only did we have as close neighbours the headquarters of the German Zionist Federation, with its organ, the *Jüdische Rundschau*, appearing cheek by jowl with *Die Welt*, but there were much more frequent meetings in the conference room and a much larger stream of visitors, both from Germany and foreign countries, than had been possible in Cologne. Moreover, whenever the Executive wanted to address a public demonstration, they could do so more effectively, and with the certainty of a more distant and resounding echo, than could have been expected in the Rhineland. It even became possible to get an occasional news item about the movement printed in the *Berliner Tageblatt* or the *Vossische Zeitung*, an event that aroused all the more surprise and gratification because of the general indifference and the hostility of German Jewry to the Zionist cause.

In those days Berlin seemed almost a paradise in comparison with the depressing change that overtook it after the First World War, not to speak of the inferno ushered in later by Hitler. It was perhaps because of the greater measure of tolerance that the Jews then enjoyed and the absence of any violent anti-Semitic agitation, that Zionism did not make any greater progress. Only rarely was it referred to in the leading papers, even though—or perhaps because—some of these were owned and edited by Jews. The Jewish question was, indeed, discussed, and it even formed the theme of public lectures by Professor Werner Sombart, author of a big book on *Die Juden und das Wirtschaftsleben*, who, although critical of Jewish ability, posed as a friend and did not betray any symptoms of the Nazi ideology which he afterwards expounded. On the other hand, Maxmilian Harden, Germany's most redoubtable political writer, being of Jewish origin (his father's name was Witkowski), studiously avoided all references to Jewish matters in his lectures, which always attracted a crowded audience, who paid for admission. Berlin offered me the opportunity, which I welcomed, of extending my journalistic activity, and I became the correspondent of the *Glasgow Herald* as well as of the *Globe* (a London evening paper long since defunct). It was there, too, that I was able to collect much of the material for my book, *Jewish Life in Modern Times*, which, although planned before I went to Cologne, was written entirely in Berlin.

The general tranquillity in the Zionist world was rudely shattered by the language conflict that raged in the schools of Palestine in the years 1912 and 1913. This was caused by a change of policy on the part of the leaders of the German Jewish philanthropic organisation, the *Hilfsverein*, who, although at first in favour of Hebrew as the medium of instruction in their schools, gradually sought to replace it by German. This attempt was firmly resisted by the great majority of the teachers, with the result that there were strikes and dismissals, followed by the opening of new schools, which were immediately staffed by the teachers and attended by the students who were determined that Hebrew should triumph. Matters were brought to a head through the struggle in connection with the Technical Institute at Haifa, the building and equipment of which had been largely financed by Russian and American Jews. The support derived from America was almost entirely due to the personal efforts of Dr. Shmarya Levin, who had carried out a propaganda tour in the United States in the interests of Hebrew culture.

The President and honorary secretary of the *Hilfsverein*, James Simon and Dr. Paul Nathan, had also provided a certain amount of money for the Haifa Institute, and they were the principal officers of the Board of Governors, which included representatives of the leading contributors. Levin, Tschlenow, and "Ahad Haam", the expounder of "Cultural Zionism", represented Zionist interests. The

German members insisted that instruction in all scientific and technical subjects should be given in German, and that Hebrew should be taught only so far as to enable the students to read Hebrew literature in the original. The Zionist members naturally demanded that Hebrew should play a greater part in the curriculum. They addressed public meetings in Berlin, wrote articles in the Jewish Press, and issued a vigorously worded pamphlet. The fight raged long and furiously before a compromise favourable to the Hebraists was reached eventually. It was not clear at the time why the *Hilfsverein* leaders had suddenly become such zealous champions of German *Kultur* in the Holy Land. When the war broke out in 1914, it was commonly said that it was due to secret pressure that had been exercised by the German Government in pursuance of their *Drang nach Osten* policy. No other explanation seemed so reasonable or convincing.

Apart from this *Kultur-Kampf*, the other questions with which the Zionist Executive in Berlin were concerned were the continued conflict—though in greatly modified form—between the "practicals" and the "politicals" and the control of the financial institutions. The meetings of the "Actions Committee" (as the Zionist General Council was called in those days) were attended by David Wolffsohn, Herzl's successor, who loyally respected the new leadership while candidly criticising it, but he firmly insisted on the management of the Jewish Colonial Trust and the other banks, as well as of the Jewish National Fund, remaining in the hands of himself and his friends.

When the First World War broke out in 1914 the Zionist Organisation was reduced to a state of suspended animation. In order to maintain relations with the constituent Federations, which were sundered by the two groups of warring Powers, a special bureau was established on neutral territory, in Copenhagen, which was at first under the control of Dr. Tschlenow and afterwards under that of Dr. Jacobson and Leo Motzkin. The head office of the Jewish National Fund was removed from Cologne to The Hague, where it was directed by Jacobus Kann (1872–1944)[1] the banker, and from where it was transferred after the war to Jerusalem.

The war made me, as a British subject, an enemy alien, and as I wanted to be able to communicate with my family and friends in England I was advised to call upon Dr. Franz Oppenheimer, whom I had known for many years. Oppenheimer, who was a distinguished economist and sociologist, was first introduced to the Zionist world by Theodor Herzl at the Congress of 1903, and afterwards drew up the plans for the first co-operative settlement in Palestine, at Merhaviah. He gave me a letter of introduction to Dr. Matthias Erzberger, one of the leaders of the Centre Party of the Reichstag, and the head of the German Censorship Bureau. Dr. Erzberger received me without any ado and promised to be helpful, and as I left his office I little dreamed that he was destined to perform the historic act of signing the Armistice for a defeated Germany at the end of the war, and to be assassinated a couple of years later by a German fanatic as the price of his courage. But shortly after my interview I was imprisoned as an enemy alien in a Berlin jail (the *Stadtvogtei Gefängnis*) and then put into an internment camp near Spandau for nineteen months—a distressing yet instructive experience that I have fully described in my book, *The Ruhleben Prison Camp*. My internment was interrupted by a further fortnight's confinement in the same jail, where I made the acquaintance of a number of interesting characters, all enemy aliens and nationals of different countries. The happiest memory that I retain of that strange experience was the solicitude displayed by a special department of the Jewish *Gemeinde* in my physical rather than spiritual welfare. It was Passover during the period of my imprisonment, and the communal authorities made it their business to supply me, as well as some Jewish fellow-prisoners, with an appetising hot meal of the traditional

[1] Died in the German concentration camp at Theresienstadt (Czechoslovakia).

dishes twice a day. I passed through Berlin again in June, 1916, when I was allowed to return to England in connection with a system of exchange of prisoners.

It was not until five years later that I saw the German capital again, looking much sadder and frowsier than in the days of the Kaiser. I was on my way to the first Zionist Congress after the war, which was held in the then congenial atmosphere of Carlsbad. I was struck by the increase in the numbers of Jews in Berlin, many of whom had migrated from Poland and other parts of Eastern Europe to what had become a region of freedom, although some thousands had been deported to Germany during the war for forced labour. Zionist activity underwent a considerable expansion in Germany, as in so many other countries, in consequence of the Balfour Declaration, and the Zionist Federation soon found that the old offices in the Sächsische Strasse were not adequate. A large house was therefore taken in the Meinecke Strasse, also off the Kurfürstendamm, which became the lively headquarters of the German Federation, and provided a convenient meeting place for meetings of the Zionist General Council. Many members who lived on the Continent, particularly those who lived in countries stretching from the Baltic to the Balkans, found the journey to London tiring and were not fond of crossing the North Sea. So Berlin sprang into favour as a rendezvous of the General Council, especially as it was better equipped with all the requisite facilities and amenities. The meetings usually took place in the Meinecke Strasse, but occasionally, when there was an exceptionally large attendance, they were held on the commodious, well-designed, and well-furnished premises of the Bnei Brith Lodge in the Tauentzien Strasse. Many momentous debates, some lasting into the small hours, on the burning questions of the day, were conducted in both places, not infrequently attended by stormy scenes and generally with results that affected the evolution of the movement.

Of all the many incidents that I recall, two are particularly vivid in my memory, one connected with Vladimir Jabotinsky (1880–1940), before he founded his Revisionist Party, and the other with Dr. Stephen Wise (1874–1949), the American Zionist leader. At the meeting in January, 1923, the differences between Jabotinsky and the majority of the Executive on questions of Palestine policy suddenly became overshadowed by a question that had nothing whatever to do with Zionism. This was the part that Jabotinsky had played in negotiations that he had been reputed to have conducted with General Petlura, the organiser of pogroms in Southern Russia in 1919–1921, or with an agent of Petlura, named Slavinsky, concerning a Jewish self-defence corps in connection with the Ukrainian army. Upon the urgent demand of the Labour Party the General Council appointed a Committee to investigate the incident, and Jabotinsky was requested to appear before it. He responded by immediately sending in his resignation from the Executive and was thus able to ignore the summons.

The meeting at which Dr. Wise played a conspicuous part was held at the end of December, 1928. The principal item on the agenda consisted of resolutions approving of the understanding that had been reached with Louis Marshall, President of the American Jewish Committee, and his associates in New York a couple of months earlier concerning the fundamental principles of extending the Jewish Agency for Palestine. Dr. Wise had been a leading opponent of the extension during all the years of its discussion, and was resolved to fight it to the end. He therefore travelled specially to Berlin to make a last stand, braving the Atlantic gales in an exceptionally stormy week. He arrived after the debate had already been in progress and evoked general admiration by the courage and zeal he displayed. He delivered a passionate speech, which was applauded for its eloquence, but he failed to influence the majority, and the vote in favour of taking the necessary steps to extend the Jewish Agency was overwhelming.

The last time that the Zionist General Council met in

Berlin was in the summer of 1930. The local political atmosphere was becoming overclouded, and it was thought prudent not to run any risks. When I passed through the city two years later on my way to Poland, and again on my return, I noticed a marked deterioration. The Swastika was gaining ground. The Nazis had become more numerous and bellicose, and the processions of their uniformed toughs, with bands blaring and banners flying, sent a shudder through anxious onlookers.

My last visit was at the end of March, 1938, five years after Hitler had been in power. I travelled through Berlin on my way to visit Zionist friends in Vienna just after the German invasion of Austria. The office in the Meinecke Strasse, which had reduced its activities under the growing terror, confining them mainly to emigration to Palestine, now wore a subdued and melancholy aspect. The *Jüdische Rundschau* had been suppressed for some time, and various departments were closed. All the leading personalities in the movement had already left the country, and their young successors were bravely holding the fort until they, too, would have to leave.

Before the advent of Hitler Berlin had a Jewish population of 160,000, now it has been reduced to about 7,000. As in the case of Cologne, many fled before the beginning of the war, but far more were deported to the death-camps in Poland.

Chapter III

THREE DECADES OF VIENNA

I—1913

MY EARLIEST MEMORIES of Vienna go back to 1913, when the capital of Francis Joseph's Empire, with its motley mixture of contending nationalities, was in the heyday of its power and glamour. It had an atmosphere of prosperity and good living, and a feeling of light-hearted gaiety was diffused by the sprightly music wafted from scores of cafés and by the gorgeous uniforms of military officers, who strutted about with clinking swords that seemed to be obsolete ornaments. My visit was occasioned by the Eleventh Zionist Congress, which was held in this city primarily for the convenience of the Jews in Central and Eastern Europe, who used to complain about Congresses taking place in Switzerland or farther west. For even though the overwhelming majority of the Jews in the neighbouring lands could not be expected to travel to Vienna, and the building in which the gathering took place could not accommodate more than a couple of thousand people, the mere fact that it was held there gave some eight millions of Jews the feeling that the deliberations were taking place in their vicinity. Besides, the Jewish community of Vienna, the largest and most important in Central Europe, whose members had contributed so substantially both to the economic development and the cultural advancement of Austria, provided a worthy meeting-place and a resonant sounding-board for Israel's biennial parliament.

The Congress was attended by over five hundred delegates, including a record number from the United States and

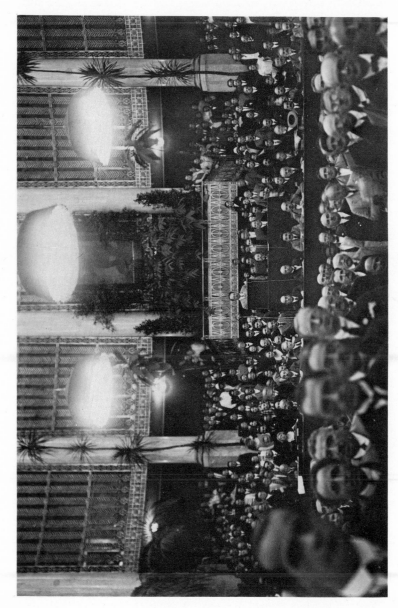

The XIVth Zionist Congress in Vienna
August 1921

LE GRAND SYNAGOGE DE BERLIN.

The Oranienburger Strasse Synagogue
in Berlin

Canada, besides a vast host of visitors. One of the most distinguished of the delegates was Professor Solomon Schechter (1850–1915), the head of the Jewish Theological Seminary in New York, who had some time before created a sensation in American Jewry by formally declaring his adherence to the Zionist movement. He looked rather older than his age, which was then sixty-three, owing to his shaggy grey beard, and was more a studious observer than an active participant, as he did not speak throughout the political discussions. I was particularly pleased, however, to meet this venerable and independent-minded scholar, as I had been one of his first students when he held the Chair in Hebrew at University College, in London, some fourteen years previously.

The proceedings at this Congress were marked by various differences that distinguished it from all previous ones. For the first time that which had been the most attractive feature of the opening sessions was missing. The famous Max Nordau, the outstanding figure at so many Congresses, second only to Herzl during his lifetime, was absent, and instead of his eloquent and trenchant survey of the Jewish situation we listened to the reading of a letter, in which he uttered a warning against any reckless handling of the Zionist financial institutions. It was addressed primarily to the " practical " Zionists, who had been very caustic critics of Herzl's policy, and stressed the need of practical work in Palestine being given priority to any political schemes. It sounded more like an admonition than a friendly greeting. His place was taken by a member of the Executive, the urbane Nahum Sokolow, who gave an able and critical review of the international Jewish scene. For the second time Hebrew played a conspicuous part in the deliberations: at the opening session a Hebrew address was given by that fiery and inexhaustible orator, Shmarya Levin, who had been a member of the Russian Duma during part of its brief, inglorious career; and later on an entire session devoted to Hebrew cultural matters was held mainly in that language.

The wildest enthusiasm was aroused by a speech in which Dr. Chaim Weizmann advocated the establishment of a Hebrew University in Jerusalem, partly in furtherance of the Jewish cultural renaissance and partly in the interests of the Jewish students of Central and Eastern Europe, who had already become victims of harsh discrimination at various universities. It was announced that a fund for the purpose had already been started with a substantial gift from an anonymous friend. The donor was David Wolffsohn, who had been Herzl's successor as President of the Zionist Organisation for six years. He had been elected President of the Vienna Congress and presided with exemplary impartiality, although he had to listen to some strong criticism of his previous régime. The determined stand that he made on the question of the financial institutions proved victorious: he and his friends remained in control of the banks and the Jewish National Fund. Little did he dream that it would be his last Congress, for within twelve months, shortly after the outbreak of the First World War, he passed away at the age of fifty-eight. Little did all others dream that there would not be another Congress for another eight years.

II.—1918–19

When I visited Vienna the second time, a few weeks after the end of the First World War, I found the city completely transformed. Gone was all the gaiety and glamour. Although not battle-scarred, it had lost its air of opulence, its grandeur had faded, and it looked poverty-stricken, bedraggled, and disconsolate. I had been sent by the Zionist Executive on a special mission to Poland, because the Poles had been celebrating their newly-won independence by indulging in widespread pogroms, and I had to pass through Vienna in order to reach my destination. During the few days that I had to stay there, while making preparations for the completion of my journey, I got into touch with various friends and also with representatives of the new Polish Government for the purpose of collecting such information as they had already received about the anti-Jewish excesses.

The Jews in Austria, like those in several other countries in Central and Eastern Europe, had, immediately after the war, created a National Council (*Jüdischer National Rat*) to represent their political interests, and I therefore first wended my way to its office in the Tabor Strasse. Outside the building was a blind old fiddler playing "Hatikvah." Within I was greeted by Dr. Robert Weltsch, who gave me an account of the worst of the pogroms, that in Lemberg (as Lwow was still commonly called), where seventy-three Jews had been killed, and also showed me photographs of victims and of scenes of plunder. He took me to the neighbouring Café *Zum Roten Turm*, where we found a crowded meeting of Zionists being addressed by the leader, Robert Stricker, who intended standing as a candidate for the Austrian Parliament (to which he was elected). After the meeting was over I had supper with the local Zionist leaders and gave them the latest news from London. I was then conducted to the Residenz Café, which was likewise full of an animated Jewish throng. There I was introduced to Dr. Emil Schmorak, who had been sent by the Jewish Relief Committee of Lemberg to confer with the Jewish National Council in Vienna on the question of relief measures. Dr. Schmorak told me that four Zionists—Leon Reich, Michael Ringel, Alexander Haussmann, and Josef Tennenblatt—had been arrested by the Polish authorities as hostages for the "good behaviour" of the Jewish population, and interned at Baranow, and he asked me to send a telegram to London for the purpose of securing their liberation. Several weeks later, when I was in Cracow, I met the hostages, who had meanwhile been released, though they were still kept under a sort of surveillance in that city.

Of the Polish representatives whom I saw in Vienna I particularly remember Dr. Wladislaw Gumplowicz, because I had made his acquaintance in 1906 in Cracow, where he was connected with the Polish revolutionary movement. He was a son of the famous sociologist, Professor Ludwig Gumplowicz, who, after achieving an international reputation by his brilliant works, which were translated into many languages, created a sensation by taking his life, and persuading his wife to take hers, on his seventieth birthday. Dr. Gumplowicz, who was an official of the Polish Legation, gave me his version of the Lemberg pogrom, tried to exculpate the Polish authorities, and assured me of his Government's fair and favourable attitude to its Jewish subjects.

As soon as it became known that I was staying at the Hotel Bristol, I had a succession of visits and telephone calls from a variety of people, who wished to impress upon me the desperate situation in Vienna and to learn about the prospects of emigration to Palestine. The Balfour Declaration had conferred upon the local Zionist Federation an enviable prestige and a fictitious influence. I was told that the Government of the new Austrian Republic had been discussing with Zionist leaders the question of their approaching the Entente for the purpose of sending food supplies to Vienna so as to avert a riot, which, it was feared, would be directed primarily against the Jewish population. Indeed, a Jewish self-defence corps had already been formed in the Leopoldstadt; but fortunately everything passed off quietly.

Among the Zionist veterans who came to see me were Johann Kremenetzky and Adolf Stand. Kremenetzky, a wealthy industrialist, who had been a member of the small Zionist Executive presided over by Herzl until his death in 1904, was anxious to undertake an important project in Palestine. Stand, who had been elected as a Jewish national member of the Austrian Parliament before the war, was particularly interested in the political implications of the Balfour Declaration. Another visitor was Dr. Max Rosenfeld, a young political writer, who had just published a very scholarly work on *Die Polnische Judenfrage*, in which he attempted a solution on the basis of minority rights, but he was prevented from following up his ideas, as he fell a victim a few months later to the influenza epidemic then raging in Central Europe.

Leaving Vienna, at the end of December, 1918, for Cracow proved almost as difficult a feat as getting to the Austrian capital had been. So large was the number of people who wished to travel and so few were the trains, that it was necessary to buy a railway ticket at least three days beforehand, and this could be effected only by that important functionary, the principal porter of the Hotel Bristol, who had special relations with the booking-clerk and naturally expected a handsome tip for his services. Dr. Schmorak and I were enabled to enter the train an hour before it was due to leave, otherwise we would have been condemned to stand in the crowded corridor all the way. For when the barrier was removed for the "unprivileged" passengers, such a surging mass besieged the train that it was densely packed from end to end, and there were even people clinging to the roof. We at least had seats, and therefore could not complain, although we were wedged in our compartment for nearly twenty hours, without heat, light, or drink.

III.—1920

My next visit was also occasioned by an eruption of Jew-baiting. This time the scene of action was Budapest, which had likewise to be reached through Vienna. I was about to set out in May 1920 for Australasia and the Far East, in the interest of the Palestine Restoration Fund, when I was requested by the Zionist Executive to go to the Hungarian capital *en route*, in order to investigate reports about the anti-Jewish terror conducted there by the "Awakening Magyars", a local breed of Nazis. On arriving in Vienna I called upon Chief Rabbi Chajes and Robert Stricker to inform them of my mission and to seek advice and informa-

tion about the people in Budapest with whom I should get
into contact. Neither of them was pleased to hear of my
proposed journey; on the contrary, they tried to dissuade me
from going, on the ground that it was dangerous for a Jew
to appear in the streets of Budapest, and that there were
some well-informed and reliable refugees from that city in
Vienna who could furnish me with a sufficiently detailed
account of what was happening. I decided, however, that I
must go. They thereupon advised me to keep the object of
my journey a secret, to take only a handbag with me, and
to leave all the rest of my luggage in my Vienna hotel, so as
to be able to move about more easily. I went to Budapest
and returned without encountering the perils that had been
feared, and remained in Vienna another couple of days to
write a report.

During the sixteen months since my previous visit there
had been some improvement both in the economic position
and in the organisation of the Jewish community. The Jews
in the Austrian capital, whose numbers had been greatly
increased by an influx from the territories that had been
assigned to Poland and Rumania (particularly Galicia and
the Bukowina), had adjusted themselves to the new situation.
Thanks to the *National Rat*, the Council of the Vienna
Community, which had hitherto been dominated by a
majority of assimilationists, was converted into a democratic
body, with a proportionate Zionist representation. Some
Zionists had also secured election on the Municipal Council.
Dr. Chajes, whom I had first met many years before in
Florence, when he was a lecturer at the Rabbinical Seminary
conducted by Chief Rabbi Margulies, soon became popular
and influential as spiritual leader of the community, in
which he had some famous predecessors. When I went to
the Synagogue in the Seitenstettengasse for the Sabbath
evening service, I was astonished to find a queue waiting for
admission, a phenomenon that I have never come across in
any other part of the world. His sermons enjoyed such
popularity, largely because he spoke simply and directly,

without a manuscript, that there was always a crowded congregation to hear him.

Robert Stricker had meanwhile been elected a member of the Constituent National Assembly, although, owing to changes in the electoral regulations, he did not retain his seat very long. But he was able to exercise his influence through the *Wiener Morgenzeitung*, which he had founded in 1919. It was the first Jewish daily paper in German to be established in Central Europe, and was edited with much ability, but amid recurring financial difficulties, by Stricker throughout its career, which came to an end in 1927. It was succeeded in the following year by a weekly *Die Neue Welt*, which Stricker likewise edited until the Nazi invasion caused its immediate suppression, and he began his long period of martyrdom.

IV.—1925

The next notable occasion on which I visited Vienna was to attend the fourteenth Zionist Congress in 1925. The city was again chosen primarily in the interests of the Jews of Central and Eastern Europe, among whom there had been a considerable increase of Zionist sentiment. Before coming to a definite decision, the Zionist Executive discussed the matter thoroughly with the heads of the Austrian Zionist Federation, as the *Hakenkreuzler* movement, under the leadership of Hitler's "spiritual" comrades, had become unusually troublesome in Vienna, and it was feared that there might be disturbances during the Congress and even in the Congress building itself. The local Zionist leaders consulted their Government and also the Police-President of Vienna, and were promised that every precaution would be taken to ensure that the Congress would take place without any risk. The authorities were prompted by a twofold motive in welcoming the event. The first was purely material and economic: they looked forward to the visit of a few thousand Jews from other countries who would bring their pounds,

dollars, and other valuable currencies to a city now largely
dependent for its solvency upon the tourist traffic. The other
motive was political: they wanted to be able to give proof
to the outside world that law and order prevailed in their
capital and that they were thoroughly in control of it. Had
they declined to be responsible for the safety of Congress,
or had they left it an open question, the Congress would not
have taken place; and then the city would have been all the
poorer and the correspondents of foreign newspapers would
have cabled their obvious comments, with the result that the
prestige of the Government would have sunk.

But after the preparations had already begun and the large
Konzerthaus had been hired, the *Hakenkreuzler* threatened
that they would prevent the Congress from being held.
There were further anxious discussions in Government
departments and at the *Polizei-Präsidium*. The authorities
remained firm. They would protect the Congress and the
delegates from any possible danger. They assured the
Zionist representatives that there was nothing to fear. They
realised that the Jew-baiters were bent upon violence and
they took concerted measures to avert the possible attack.
On the eve of the Congress they not only strengthened the
police, but also mobilised the army. Seven thousand troops
were employed in completely surrounding the district containing the Congress building and the numerous hotels at
which delegates and visitors were staying. Had the invasion
of an enemy been expected, it would hardly have been
possible to organise more elaborate and effective counter-
measures. But despite this, some delegates in taxis on their
way to their hotels were attacked, though they suffered only
slight injury. Suddenly, only a few hours before the
Congress was to begin, there was a rumour that a bomb had
been placed in the basement, and panic spread. Everybody
was immediately ordered out of the building, all committees
had to suspend their meetings, all offices had to be cleared;
and then the military and the police made a thorough search
and declared that they had found nothing. But the

authorities did not relax their vigilance a moment. There was a military guard in and around the building during all the time of the Congress, both day and night; soldiers ate and slept in a large room in the basement. There were also troops who bivouacked in the streets, with their guns ready in case of a surprise assault; but there was no need to fire a single shot.

Fortunately nothing happened. The Congress was able to follow its traditional course without any interruption (except from delegates themselves) and without any alarm. And Leo Motzkin, who was President of Congress, was able to indulge his love for an all-night session by protracting the concluding part of the proceedings until six o'clock in the morning, when we returned to our hotels in broad daylight.

V.—1938

My last visit to Vienna took place just a week after the Nazi invasion of Austria. The Zionist Executive were anxious to know what had happened to our friends and the Jewish community in general, and sent me to find out. I arrived at mid-day on Friday, March, 25th, 1938, without notice, and took a room at the Hotel Metropole, the large establishment near the Francis Joseph Quay, purposely avoiding the more fashionable hotels near the Opera House, as they were known to be occupied mainly by German officers. I first called upon Dr. Siegfried Schmitz, the journalist who used to edit the *Kongress-Zeitung* (the official report of Zionist Congresses) and who lived near by. In response to my ring at his flat an eye peered through the peep-hole in the door before I was admitted.

Schmitz was surprised to see me. He whispered to me to speak as softly as possible, and then gave me news of all the evil happenings that had already taken place. He told me that all Zionist offices had been closed and all Zionist activities suspended by order of the Gestapo. All Zionist officials had to present themselves at eight o'clock that morning at the Palestine Office, where they were interrogated individually by a Nazi official named Eichmann. This functionary, who was in charge of all Zionist affairs in Germany, was an expert: he was born in the German colony of Sarona in Palestine, knew Hebrew, and had made a special study of all aspects of the Jewish problem. He questioned the Zionist officials not only about their respective activities and hours of work, but also about the party to which they belonged. On hearing that one was a General Zionist, Eichmann asked to which Group he belonged, and on being told that it was Group B, he said: "I see: Ussishkin[1]." Among those present at this personal examination was Adolf Boehm, to whom Eichmann said that he was pleased to meet him, as he had already read the first volume of his *History of Zionism*, but had not yet found time to read the second. There were also four Revisionists[2] present, whom Eichmann called "*Greuelhetzer*" ("atrocity-mongers"). He was surprised that there were so many different Zionist bodies and offices, announced that in future they must all be co-ordinated under a central direction, and instructed Boehm and Schmitz to draw up a plan and submit it to him at eight o'clock on Monday morning. The Nazis could not begin their oppressive activities too early in the day.

On the following day Schmitz accompanied me on a visit to Adolf Boehm, but thought it prudent that we should not enter his flat together. Boehm showed me the plan that he had already drafted, but would not give me a copy in case it should be discovered that he had been in touch with me. He told me that he had at first refused the request to undertake the work of reorganisation, on the ground that he had no time and was inexperienced in such matters, whereupon Eichmann insisted, saying that if he had usually worked

[1] Menachem Ussishkin (1863–1941), born in Russia, a Zionist leader who settled in Palestine in 1919 and was Chairman of the Jewish National Fund from 1923 until his death.
[2] The Zionist Party which, before the Second World War, advocated a Jewish State on both sides of the Jordan.

fourteen hours a day until now, he would have to work sixteen hours in future. Never shall I forget the look of sorrow
and dejection with which Boehm told me that the Nazi
Commissar for Jewish Affairs had curtly declared that the
monthly *Palästina,* which he had so ably and devotedly
edited for many years, must now cease. No reason was given,
nor was any considered necessary, for it was assumed that he
understood full well that the continuance of Jewish publications was contrary to Nazi policy. Schmitz and I left as we
had entered, with an interval of five minutes between us.

· In the evening Field-Marshal Goering delivered his widely
advertised speech to inaugurate the campaign for the
German plebiscite to settle the future of Austria. He spoke
in the hall of the disued North-West Railway Station, which
easily held a few thousand people, and the newspapers
announced that the speech would be relayed to all restaurants
and cafés. As I had no desire to hear it I deferred my supper
until half-past nine, by which time I expected that it would
be over. But as soon as I entered a somewhat deserted eating-
establishment, I heard a thunderous voice, to which about
a dozen guests were listening with tense faces. A waiter
sidled up to me, whispered that the speech had already
lasted an hour and a half, and took my order. For the next
half-hour I was condemned to listen to the concluding part
of the furious tirade: it was the most menacing part.

"All Jews must leave Austria!" shouted Goering.
"Vienna no longer has a right to call itself a German city ...
It has to fulfil tasks in the cultural and economic fields, and
in neither can Jews be employed. The Jews must get out,
not because of hatred, but because of necessity. The Jews
must get out quickly, and take notice right now . . . The
Jews should understand that we do not care to live with
them . . . The elimination of the Jews must be carried
through after due consideration. But let the Jews take note
that by the end of the four-year plan Vienna will be a
German city again. Jews are in control of trade, finance,
art, everything. But I am going to alter that. We don't like

Jews and they don't like us. We will make them glad to go away. Vienna shall be free from Jews! "

It sounded like a death sentence, and it proved to be one. Even if Goering had not pronounced their doom, the Jews of Vienna saw too many evidences of Nazi might and malignity around them to be doubtful of their fate. The city was plastered all over with swastikas in all sizes. The black and red hooked-cross was on flags and banners on every public building, in shop-windows and over house-fronts, on military lorries and taxi-cabs. Large portraits of Hitler were on every advertisement hoarding, and smaller photographs of him, as well as of Goering and Goebbels, stared at you from most of the shop-windows in the Ring and the Kaerntner Strasse. Kerb-side hawkers were doing a busy trade in the Nazi emblem, and most of the people in the streets were wearing it, if not from conviction, at least as a protection against molestation.

The invaders had apparently come prepared with exact lists of those whom they intended arresting, so that they were able to carry out their plan within a few days. Jews engaged in the jewellery trade had been particularly singled out for arrest, and almost all of them, including the heads of the firm that had supplied the Austrian Imperial Court, were imprisoned. An order was issued requiring the registration and surrender of all foreign exchange, and in cases where the officials were not satisfied with the amount delivered by a Jew they kept him under arrest to extort a further sum. The Gestapo even sent telegrams in the names of their Jewish prisoners to banks or business-firms abroad to secure money, and the fact that they proved so well informed about the financial position of many Jews seemed to show that they had carried out a system of espionage at many leading banks in foreign countries. As the results of this confiscation did not come up to expectations, the Storm Troopers were allowed to raid the houses and shops of Jews and stole everything of value that they could lay their hands upon—money, jewellery, furs, securities, bank-books, motor-cars, typewriters. While I was in Vienna at least a few thousand Jews in the city were plundered in this way, apart from thousands in the provincial districts.

Not only were all Jewish employees dismissed by Christian firms, but all Jewish firms were compelled to discharge their "non-Aryan" employees, even if they were members of their own family. The places thus vacated were filled with Nazis, quite regardless of their qualifications. Every "non-Aryan" concern had to appoint a member of the Nazi Party as "Commissar," who received a salary; and in the case of a shop that could not bear such a burden, it was handed over to a Party member for nothing, who sold the goods at wholesale prices "on commission." In the case of big concerns the Jewish owner was either compelled to sell out at ridiculous prices, or he was charged with having abused the Nazi régime before the invasion, and consequently, as "an enemy of the State," he was deprived of all his property without any compensation. The victims were unable to obtain the help of Jewish lawyers, as these were no longer allowed to practise, and "Aryan" lawyers could not plead on behalf of Jewish clients. The wholesale robberies and physical ill-treatment of the Jews caused an epidemic of suicides, which were already said to number over six thousand, and owing to their number burials were allowed only at night.

The leaders of the Jewish community had been arrested for taking part in the collection in aid of the Schuschnigg plebiscite. They included Dr. Desider Friedmann, the President, and Robert Stricker, who were doomed to suffer nearly seven years of agony before meeting their end, like millions of others, in a death-camp in Poland. Not content with these arrests, the Gestapo insisted that the Jews should raise for them an amount similar to that which they had contributed to the Schuschnigg Fund, 800,000 schilling (about £32,000), as proof that they were equally well-disposed to their new masters, and after some weeks they got it. Those who were allowed to administer the affairs of the

Jewish community were ordered to expedite the emigration of poor Jews and of those with scanty means, while the Gestapo pursued their ruthless measures for despoiling those who still had some possessions. There were about 10,000 Polish Jews in Vienna, besides some thousands from Czechoslovakia, Hungary, and Rumania. All Polish Jews who went to the Polish Consulate for visas to enable them to return to their native country had their passports withdrawn if they had been away from Poland for over five years. The Gestapo threatened that they would gather those Polish Jews together and drive them over the frontier into Poland, in the same brutal manner in which they had expelled hundreds of Austrian Jews from the Burgenland into the neighbouring countries.

Thousands of Jews were besieging the Embassies and Consulates of different Governments in frantic efforts to obtain visas. Their state of despair was evidenced by the fact that they began queuing up at midnight, members of a family relieving one another, so as to make sure of being admitted into the coveted presence the following day. At the British Consulate I found the courtyard, the staircase, and the waiting room crammed with anxious-looking men and women; and I was told that over 6,000 had already applied for permits for Palestine and the British Dominions, especially Australia. The feeling of terror could be sensed most keenly in the cafés, where the light-hearted hubbub of conversation of former days had sunk to a timid whisper, for everybody suspected his neighbour, and nobody spoke without first glancing over his shoulder.

After five days of what seemed to me a prelude to the inferno, I was handed by one of the hotel clerks a cyclostyled note requesting me " most politely " to vacate my room by the following midday " as the Gestapo were coming in." I was not surprised that the Hotel Metropole was to become their headquarters, as I had noticed a gradual infiltration of arrogant-looking German officers about the place. I decided not to wait until the last moment.

Before leaving the city I went with Dr. Schmitz to the Doeblinger cemetery, to pay a silent tribute to the memory of Theodor Herzl. His grave had been the scene of imposing pilgrimages for over thirty years, and it was feared that some Nazi vandals might have desecrated it. We were relieved to find that it had not been touched, and as we walked away we could not help thinking how different the fate of Vienna Jewry, and, indeed, of many other Jewries, might have been if only Herzl's appeal had met with greater understanding and more extensive support.

Early the following morning I took the first train to Prague. When we neared the frontier, and after all customs and passport formalities were over, two plain-clothes officials went from one compartment to another, carefully comparing passengers' names with the entries in a little black book that one of them carried. I breathed more freely after they had gone. I presume that my name was added to the Gestapo's black list at a later date.

Before the advent of Hitler the Jewish population of Vienna was 180,000; by August, 1939, it had fallen to about 80,000; now it is about 10,000. Of those who were still in Austria at the outbreak of war the overwhelming majority were exterminated in the death-camps.

Chapter IV

DIARY OF A MISSION TO POLAND

(December, 1918—January, 1919)

THE NEWS that reached London in November, 1918, immediately after the end of the First World War, concerning pogroms in what had been Russian Poland and in Galicia, aroused so much alarm that the British Government issued a warning against further excesses. The newly formed States in Eastern Europe were solemnly admonished that if they indulged in bloodshed at the birth of their independence they could not reckon upon the help of the Western Powers in the task of their construction. But despite this warning, further messages arrived of more serious outrages against the Jews in Galicia. The leaders of the Zionist Organisation in London thereupon resolved to send a Special Commissioner to investigate the situation. Owing to the difficulties of travel at the time and also to the nature of the intended mission, the consent of the British Foreign Office was necessary. Dr. Weizmann interviewed Sir George Clerk,[1] Secretary to the Foreign Secretary, Lord (then Mr. Arthur James) Balfour, on the subject and proposed that I should undertake the mission. Sir George approved of the proposal, and Lord Balfour agreed to provide the requisite facilities.

I had visited Galicia previously in 1906 and had since then closely followed the Jewish position in that country as well as in Russian Poland, so that I was not altogether unfamiliar with the sphere of my projected enquiry. From the day that I left London, December 6th, 1918, until my return in the

[1] Died June 18, 1951.

48

following February, I kept a detailed Diary in view of the importance of my mission. I have omitted various passages from the original that are unnecessary for an understanding of the events of the time, and have added a few footnotes.

1918.

December 6.—Left London for Southampton and Havre.

December 7.—Arrived in Paris. Had supper at Grand Hotel with Nahum Sokolow, who was very pleased at my going to Poland to inquire into the pogroms. He suggested that I should propose to the Zionists in Vienna, Warsaw, etc., to hold Conferences for the purpose of giving mandates to him and Weizmann to represent them at the Peace Conference, the authorisations to be by letter as well as by telegrams.

December 9.—Swiss Consulate asked me to produce Zionist authorisation, countersigned by a British authority, before issuing Swiss visa. Sokolow agreed that there was no object in keeping my mission secret, though I should have to act discreetly.

December 10.—Sokolow had luncheon to-day with Foreign Minister, Pichon. Expressed himself delighted, as he sat close to Pichon and was introduced to Thomas Masaryk and other notabilities. Gave me a letter of introduction to Masaryk, in case I visited Prague. Left Paris.

December 11.—Arrived Lausanne: called on Dr. Chaim Tschernowitz,[1] to whom I conveyed greetings from Sokolow.

December 12.—Arrived Berne. Called at British Legation, saw the Minister, Lord Acton, who read to me telegraphic message received from Foreign Office in regard to my mission, which agreed with the terms of Balfour's letter to Weizmann. Advised me about getting visa for Austria. Met August Zaleski[2] in hotel: as though divining my mission he asked me if I was going further East. I said " Yes." " To Poland? " " Yes." He at once volunteered to procure me all

---

[1] Appointed in 1923 Professor for Talmud at the Jewish Institute of Religion in New York. Died 1949.
[2] Later Polish Ambassador in Rome and Foreign Minister in Warsaw.

facilities: would give me Polish visa, also letters of introduction to Polish authorities. He tried to exculpate Poles from guilt for pogroms: said much damage caused through fighting in streets of Lemberg between Poles and Ruthenians. The Polish Government would welcome investigation, anxious to arrive at friendly understanding with Jews. Said it was in interests of Allies to recognise Polish Socialist Government, as attempt to establish Conservative Government (or monarchy) would play into hands of Bolshevists. Told me that French Government, recognising Polish National Committee (Dmowski's party) in Paris, which was opposed to Warsaw Government, refused to let him pass through France to England. Outlined to me general demands of Poles in regard to territory. At present their greatest enemy were Bolshevists: unfortunately many Jews among them, though he admitted far more Jews among anti-Bolshevists. As for boycott of Jews in Poland, he personally had always been opposed to it, as he was a Liberal, not Socialist.

December 13.—After calling at Austrian Consulate for visa, visited Mission Polonaise, where saw Zaleski, who introduced me to Count Szembek and other colleagues. One of them explained to me geographical demarcations desired by Poland, and gave me some literature on Poland and the Jewish question.

December 14.—My passport viséd at Polish Mission. Sent telegram to Adolf Boehm,[1] Vienna, announcing my mission and urging hastening of Austrian visa.

December 15.—Received express letter from Dr. Berthold Feiwel,[2] Zurich, announcing internment of Zionist leaders in Galicia, Michael Ringel, Leon Reich, Alexander Hausmann, and Josef Tennenblatt, asking me to wire Sokolow to take immediate steps to secure their release. Wired Sokolow.

[1] Prominent Zionist and historian, died 1943.
[2] Zionist politician and author, later Director of Keren Hayesod. Died Safed, 1937.

50

December 16.—Called Austrian Consulate: still no reply from Vienna.

December 17.—Zaleski gave me seven letters of introduction to people in Poland. Suggested I should approach Madame Rosika Schwimmer, Hungarian Minister in Berne (representing Karolyi's Government), staying in same hotel, who might get me visa for Austria immediately. Called on Madame Schwimmer,[1] alert, amiable, middle-aged lady with spectacles; speaking English correctly and fluently. On question of pogroms in Hungary, said she had no information except Press telegrams. But she knew that whilst war was still on, an appeal was made by Catholic Party in Hungary for a Press Fund of 3 million kronen, so as, ostensibly, to establish rival papers to Jewish Press. Real object of Fund was to organise pogroms as means of diverting wrath from Church and magnates, when the people realised that even victory (as expected) had brought them nothing but losses, suffering, and starvation. The real object of Fund being known, as much as 12 million kronen had been raised. Even gypsies in outlying villages had given freely for extermination of Jews. Fortunately for the Jews, the outbreak of the Revolution had upset the calculations of the organisers. Madame Schwimmer exacted a promise that I would never disclose the source of my information on this matter. She promised to get me a visa for Austria, also to give me *laissez passer* up to Budapest, and letter of introduction to Count Karolyi.

December 18–20.—In bed with "flu."

December 21.—Got Austria visa.

December 22.—Zaleski told me he had not yet heard from Polish Government about internment of four Zionist leaders. Said feeling between Jews and Poles reported still to be very bitter: hoped I would have tranquillising influence.

December 23.—Left Berne for Zurich; met by Dr. Berthold Feiwel. Later met Dr. Felix Pinkus and H. Cohnheim (American citizen), who had also intended going to

[1] Died New York, 1948.

51

Galicia to investigate pogroms, but prevented by passport difficulties. After buying stock of food, left Zurich, travelling with Phillpotts, British Commercial Attaché in Vienna, returning to his post.

December 24.—Travelled from Buchs *via* Feldkirch to Innsbruck. No light in railway carriage, only in corridor. Many windows boarded up, panes having been smashed. Upholstery of compartment shabby, plush cushions replaced by straw mattress. Stayed at Innsbruck over-night: city in Italian occupation.

December 25.—Continued journey from Innsbruck *via* Salzburg to Vienna. At night carriage in complete darkness, had small wick-lamp for short time. Young Austrian lieutenant came into carriage: had joined up at beginning of war, made prisoner in Russia, fled from Tomsk to Petrograd, then got back to German lines.

December 26.—Boy came into carriage with small basket of horse-sausages, 3 kronen each. Arrived Vienna midday, took room at Hotel Bristol. Went to *Jüdischer National Rat*, Taborstrasse, welcomed by Dr. Robert Weltsch, who spoke to me about pogroms and showed me collection of photographs of victims and scenes of plunder. Took me to Café Zum Roten Turm, where I attended meeting of Jewish nationalists addressed by Robert Stricker.[1] Afterwards went to Residenz Café, where was introduced to Dr. Emil Schmorak, lawyer from Lemberg, who undertook to accompany me there, as he would be returning in a few days. Asked me to send another wire to London, appealing for intervention on behalf of interned Zionist leaders.

December 27.—Sent telegram to Feiwel for London on behalf of interned Zionists. Visit from Dr. Schmorak, who gave me detailed account of situation in Lemberg before pogroms. He had left Lemberg just after pogroms and came to Vienna on behalf of victims, to get funds, etc.

December 28.—In morning Solomon Herz, from Lem-

---

[1] Austrian Zionist leader, for short time member of Austrian Parliament, arrested by the Nazis in Vienna in March, 1938, murdered in Nazi camp at Oswiecim, 1944.

berg, described to me political conditions in Galicia. In afternoon Dr. Moses Waldmann, journalist, also from Lemberg, gave me critical account of relations between Jews and Poles. Afterwards went to Polish Legation, had one hour's talk with Dr. Gumplowicz (whose acquaintance I had made in Cracow 12 years ago). *December* 29.—Visited this morning by Dr. Max Rosenfeld,[1] who brought me copy of his book, *Die Polnische Judenfrage*. Solomon Herz came again, gave me further particulars of Lemberg pogrom and became hysterical as he described various incidents; mentioned names of persons whom I should look up in Lemberg.—Dr. Weltsch told me Austrian Government wanted through Zionists to persuade Entente to send food to Vienna: it would be in Jewish interests, as continued distress might lead to riots in which Jews would be chief victims. Visited office of Israelitische Allianz, whose Secretary, Dr. A. Kaminka, told me of measures taken for relief of pogrom victims in Galicia, mentioned amounts he had received and so far distributed. He was robbed of gold watch in Cracow and wouldn't go there again without official escort. After dinner visited Dr. Gumplowicz at his *pension*: gave me his version of Lemberg pogrom and of Polish attitude towards Jews. On returning to hotel visited by veteran Zionist, Johann Kremenetzky,[2] who told me that great number of Polish and Galician Jews were anxious to reach Palestine at earliest possible moment: many had already sold up home and property to Poles for ridiculous price; some had come, partly on foot, to Vienna and gone to Trieste, where they awaited favourable opportunity to go to Palestine. After supper went to Café Zum Roten Turm, where Dr. M. Waldmann told me that young man just arrived from Lemberg reported that Ukrainians still fighting around the city, grenades bursting in streets. Waldmann also informed me that he had been condemned to death *in contumaciam* by Poles on ground that he had

[1] Dr. Rosenfeld died in February, 1919.
[2] Wealthy industrialist, who was a member of the first Zionist Executive under Herzl's presidency.

helped Ukrainians and sent telegram to President Wilson. He had been informed of this by Jewish girl typist employed at Polish Military Headquarters, who had written out death-sentence and then fled to Vienna.

December 30.—Dr. Schmorak accompanied me to Hotel Habsburg, where Waldmann gave me connected account of Lemberg pogrom. Visited *Jüdischer National Rat*, where met Adolf Boehm, Adolf Stand,[1] and others. Dr. Otto Abeles[2] promised to get me official permit to enter train for Cracow in advance.

December 31.—Ordered ticket for Cracow three days in advance from hotel porter, who got it through Commissionaire (who asked 10kr. for his trouble), as impossible for private individual to get ticket at booking-office owing to great demand. After lunch packed up, and with Dr. Schmorak went to Nord Bahnhof, arriving 3 p.m. for the 4.45 train. Only one 1st Class compartment, with window broken, which we avoided. Went into 2nd Class which was marked 1st: seats stripped of plush covering, lining visible, windows could not be opened. All carriages and corridors crowded; no heating or light; some people even on roof.

1919.

January 1.—Long stop at Lundenburg. Two girls entered our compartment: one, a Jewish girl, said *numerus clausus*[3] prevented her from entering Cracow University, so had registered at Prague University. Arrived Cracow 11.30 a.m. Went to dozen hotels all full of fugitives from East Galicia. Jews and Poles; at last by bribing porter at Hotel Krakowskie with 20 kronen got dirty shabby room with two beds. Called on Rabbi Dr. Osias Thon, who told me he had been a few times to Count Lasocki, President of the Polish Liquidation Commission (Provisional Government of Galicia), who had promised to telegraph to Military Authorities at Lemberg that the four interned Zionists should be sent to Cracow,

[1] Zionist politician, member of Austrian Parliament. Died 1919.
[2] Author and Zionist official. Died in Nazi camp, 1944.
[3] Restricted admission of Jewish students to universities.

where Polish Liquidation Commission would be responsible for them. At house of Dr. Thon met Dr. Obstler, Rabbi of Friedental (Austrian Silesia), who told me that in this town about 160 Jews formed militia, stronger than the Christian. Went to public meeting in Kahal (community) building, addressed by Dr. Thon in connection with his candidature for Polish Constituante (Parliament). On the way met Jews with guns (militia), even orthodox men wearing flat hats and caftan also with guns. Building packed. Jewish officer, Dr. I. Schwarzbart, forced way for us. Dr. Thon dealt with war, Palestine, Jewish national autonomy in Poland. Interrupted by Socialists. A P.P.S. (Polish Socialist Party) Jew caused booing when he called himself a Polish nationalist.

January 2.—Called at Polish Liquidation Commission. Young officer took my letter of introduction from Zaleski and conducted me to Count Lasocki, who received me in friendly manner denounced pogroms, deprecated seizure of hostages. Told me he had telegraphed again to Lemberg for transference of interned Zionists to Cracow. Promised to get me room at good hotel by ordering Director of Police to see to it. Also promised me letter of introduction to other Polish authorities and military permit for Lemberg. Introduced me to Zuk, Director of Polish Press Bureau, old man with grey hair who took me to office of *Naprzod* to see Ignaz Daszynski.[1] Reminded latter of my interview with him 12 years ago. He spoke for an hour on general Polish situation and on Jewish question in particular. At Hotel Saski for dinner: Count Lasocki told me he had got room for me in this hotel, so I moved in. Went to Polish Press Bureau, where Zuk gave me Count Lasocki's letters of introduction and added note from him on Jewish position in Galicia. Told me that communication between Przemysl and Lemberg again stopped. Invited me to have supper with him. Drove to Thon, asked him on behalf of Count to make *Novy Dziennik* (Jewish paper) more moderate. Thon told me that *numerus clausus* introduced only in medical faculty of

[1] Later Speaker of Polish Parliament.

Cracow University and preference given to assimilators. Advised me to seek interview with Professor Godlevsky, of Medical Faculty.

Called at Press Bureau for Zuk, who took me to his house for supper. His wife English. Zuk said he knew of no Government order against sale of *Novy Dziennik*, presumed it was case of hostility of individual railway officials. He repeated charge that Jews sided with Ukrainians, also with Russians and Germans—always against the Poles. Afterwards Prof. Marchlevsky (with English wife) came in: continued discussion about Polish and Jewish nationality. I explained to them difference between nationality and citizenship, that Jewish nationals could be good Polish citizens. Prof. Marchlevsky said that a Jewish nationalist was for him a foreigner and would be treated accordingly. He advocated *numerus clausus* at Medical Faculty because Jewish students shirked military service during war, and so many Polish students killed and wounded: hence limitation of Jewish students to 10 per cent. When a student inscribed himself of Jewish nationality he could not expect equal treatment with Polish nationalist. Asked Professor why the Jews living in East Galicia, where Poles fewer than Ukrainians, should be expected to declare themselves Poles rather than Ukrainians? He couldn't answer the question: only said it was complicated and hoped Peace Conference would settle it satisfactorily.

January 3.—Called on Dr. Zimmermann, lawyer, who showed me pile of documents relating to pogroms in Poland; told me about formation of Jewish Defence Corps. Went to Polish Liquidation Commission, where saw Zuk, who told me, in name of Count Lasocki, that no Government order was issued against sale of *Novy Dziennik* at railway stations. While having lunch at Hotel Saski, Count L. came over to me and spoke again about *Novy Dziennik*: said the paper had once remarked that there was a Jewish legion in Palestine which could be used in a land that formerly belonged to Central Powers! Such remarks, he said, irritated the Polish population. Told me railway connection with Lemberg again in order. With Dr. Schmorak visited Dr. Thon, who told us he had long conversation with Prof. Javorski (Conservative), who had been asked by Polish Government to prepare a paper on Jewish question in Poland for Peace Conference. Javorski agreed to advocate cultural autonomy for Jews in Poland, but rejected idea of political autonomy. Dr. Thon highly gratified at his success with Javorski.

January 4.—At office of Dr. Zimmermann met Dr. Span, of Tarnow, who told me Jews arriving at station were repeatedly molested and robbed. Station-master at Tarnow kept crowds of hooligans out of station, but as Jews left station were attacked: one man had part of his beard plucked away. He showed me three tickets Tarnow–Olmuetz bought by Jews so badly bruised that tickets stained with their blood. The Mayor had no power to maintain order: Jews forbidden to organise self-defence. Went to Polish Liquidation Commission, but Count Lasocki had gone to Lemberg. Informed that train from Lemberg this morning hit by Ukrainians and several killed. Told Zuk about latest pogrom in Lemberg: he was displeased at this fresh manifestation of Polish culture. Said Professor W. Nathanson and Dr. Diamant (politician) would like to speak to me. Returned to Zimmermann, asked him to get me all pogrom reports and protocols translated into German or English. Went to Dr. Thon, who told me that pogrom had been expected in Cracow between Christmas and New Year, so he went to police to ask for measures of protection. Many Jews had packed up belongings, ready for flight, and taken door-keys away from house-porter. Whilst having supper at Hotel Saski an officer announced that Paderewski [1] would arrive in Cracow the following morning. Great applause and buzz of conversation and comment.

January 5.—Young law student, Seidener (sent by Thon),

[1] The celebrated musician became Poland's first Prime Minister, holding office from January 17th to November 27th, 1919. Died 1941.

came to accompany me to Chrzanow, where pogrom had taken place November 6–7. At 9 a.m. band of musicians (railway-workers) went playing through Slavkovska to station, to welcome Paderewski. Near station civil militia (including large number of Jews in caftans) drawn up with guns; inside enormous crowds, band playing. Saloon car drew up, from which descended on to platform Madame Paderewski, then Paderewski, old, tired, ill, bowed. We looked on through window of waiting-room, then entrained for Chrzanow.

Arrived Chrzanow 11.30 a.m. Almost only Jews visible, outside station Jewish cabmen with droschkies and carts. Driven in droschky through dirty muddy roads, noticed chalk inscriptions on some houses; "Here lives a Pole", "Here lives a Catholic" (as protection from attack). Went to Dr. Zipper, lawyer, who told us of painful situation, following pogrom, in regard to reconstitution of Town Council, and fraud and terrorism carried on to secure return of Pole for Chrzanow and district to Constituante. Zipper told me that Jews again fearing pogrom, half of them had not slept all night. Also told me that at Trzebinja peasant who had stolen Scroll of Torah had papered his wall with it: refused to give it up until Prefect of Chrzanow sent couple of gendarmes to recover it and return it to synagogue.

Went to Dr. Rieser (physician) who gave us many details about pogrom. Told us that most stolen things were heaped up in front of his house, where soldiers kept guard, thus his house was saved. Several pogromists stole from one another, also hurt one another in melée. Knew two days in advance pogrom would take place. Jewish defence corps came from Cracow (Nov. 14) and saved a great deal. On pogrom night Dr. Rieser was called out to attend to wounded bandit. Peasants came with wives and children, carts, sacks, bags, to take things away, also motor-lorries. After lunch Dr. Zipper came and told us that Jews holding big meeting in Communal Chamber expected me. Decided not to go but to receive small deputation. Then went out with Dr. Rieser to visit some damaged houses and shops: saw broken windows replaced by boards, iron shutters battered, torn away. Visited restaurant where everything looted: big supplies of meat, bread, cake, wines, spirits, etc. (bought in Vienna for expected celebration of Polish independence); everything destroyed, curtains, mirror, tables, safe. Restaurant formerly patronised by officials, lawyers, etc., now boycotted for shame. Also saw former confectionery shop plundered, everything smashed, floors covered with débris; general shop of widow also demolished and ransacked. Went to other small shops, owner of one, brawny, broad-shouldered man told me he had been 4½ years in army, 1½ years on Russian front: this was his reward. As we walked through main street passed groups of Jews. From lighted hall came stentorian voice of Daszynski preaching liberty, while Jews went in fear and trembling.

Soon after returning to Dr. Rieser's house came deputation of four Jews from Javorzno, who told me Jewish members of Town Council compelled to resign and all Jews threatened with expulsion within 14 days. One old man showed me bruise on head, another told us saw Rabbi of Javorzno pulled by beard by Polish soldier sent to protect Jews. Mrs. Rieser told me that photographs were taken of damaged shops by young Jew, but plates smashed by his Christian landlord. Young girl, niece of Ahad Haam,[1] gave me letter for London to post in Switzerland. Members of Jewish Community Council, headed by President, then came in all excited, gave hysterical account of experiences during pogrom. Dr. Rieser accompanied us to station: we travelled in first-class pitch-dark carriage to Cracow, arriving 8.45 p.m. Saw trams beflagged in honour of Paderewski's visit.

January 6.—Called on early by distressed lady, who told me that her husband, Dr. Rossberger, Medical Officer for Jaroslav for 25 years and President of Jewish National Council, was arrested 3 weeks ago without charge, and

---

[1] Pen-name of famous Hebrew writer, Asher Ginsberg, creator of Cultural Zionism (1856–1927).

brought to Cracow yesterday for internment. Promised to intercede. Went to Polish Liquidation Commission: as Lasocki absent had interview with his deputy, Noel, on various matters—second pogrom in Lemberg on December 29 and incidents at Javorzno, Jaroslav, Tarnow, and Chrzanow. Noel got into telephonic communication with Tarnow and Chrzanow: told me that prohibition was only against German papers and tried to make out that Yiddish was German; that Jews at Javorzno had voluntarily resigned and were boycotting Council; would see that Jews remained there in safety; would inquire into case of Dr. Rossberger and let me know to-morrow; no pogrom intended at Chrzanow, where Jews were free to vote in elections as they wished. As for reconstitution of Chrzanow Town Council with 8 Poles and 4 Jews in a town with 65 per cent Jews, he said Jews agreed to this: I replied they had no alternative.

As I walked across Ring Platz special edition of *Naprzod* being sold, announcing attempted *coup d'état* in Warsaw against Pilsudski, also that Paderewski had left Cracow early this morning. Met Frau Dr. Rossberger and told her result of my intervention for her husband. Received two visitors from Javorzno, who told me of attack on Jewish shops and general insecurity in town. Both had fought in war; one had wound in forehead, another in foot, and lost sight of one eye: said that all Jews wanted to go away immediately, even without demanding restoration of goods stolen or of debts.

January 7.—Received this morning telegram from Colonel Wade, head of Allied Mission, saying he would be in Warsaw for some days, so I asked porter to get me seat in sleeping-car of to-night's train to Warsaw. At Polish Liquidation Commission had one and a half hour's interview with Noel on various aspects of Jewish question in Poland. Noel apparently sincere and liberal, a friend of Dr. Ringel, one of the Zionist hostages. Told me had just received reply from General Rozvadovsky, agreeing to transference of the four Zionists to Cracow, where they could live at liberty provided they don't leave the city. Went to office of *Novy Dziennik*, where Dr. Thon explained programme of Western Galician Jews for national autonomy. Gave me letters and telegrams to take to Warsaw Zionist Central Committee.

Went to Professor Wladislaw Nathanson, baptised Jew, natural physicist, who had studied at Cambridge under Joseph Thomson. Discussed pogroms: he said Jews were to blame as much as Poles, because they had dealt dishonestly. and the Poles at first opportunity resolved to wreak revenge. He pleaded the ignorance of Polish peasants, easily egged on to attacks. He argued that Jews had all rights: I instanced several wrongs. He maintained attacks on Jews could be explained by historical conditions, also said Jews were cowards, which I indignantly disproved by referring to Jewish cases of heroism in Great War. Tried to hedge by saying he wasn't politician, but scientific student. Could not understand how anybody could claim rights in Poland who didn't declare himself Polish nationalist. Taunted me with recent study of the question, which I refuted. Then he admitted Poland at present in state of anarchy, unable to maintain proper order. Left him rather heated: at last realised how anti-Jewish the converted Jew is. Returned to hotel, packed, supper, settled, drove to station. No sleeper, but uncomfortable seat in first class coach.

January 8.—Arrived in Warsaw 7.30 a.m., and got room at Hotel Bristol. Went to Zionist Office, Granishna, where I met Heschel Farbstein [1] and others. Farbstein took me to Izchak Gruenbaum [2] (Secretary of Jewish National Council): it was arranged that pogrom material should be prepared for me within few days. Had lunch at Hotel d'Angleterre, where Napoleon I once stayed. Later returned to Gruenbaum, who gave me historical explanation of rise of Anti-Semitism in Poland. Farbstein came in, reported

[1] Later Member of Polish Parliament, Mizrachi leader settled in Jerusalem. Died 1948.
[2] Later Member of Polish Parliament, subsequently settled in Jerusalem, was member of Executive of World Zionist Organisation.

result of his interview with Vice-Minister of Interior about fixing elections (for Town Council) in many towns on Sabbath: he got no satisfaction. As it was seven o'clock, Farbstein advised me to leave the house, as shooting would soon begin in the neighbourhood and it would be impossible to walk through the street. Told me that the synagogue opposite (Tlomackie) was guarded by two soldiers constantly. Rabbi Dr. S. Poznanski[1] had difficulty in getting through gate to reach his house behind the synagogue.

Farbstein took me to his home, top flat in Krolewska: large, well-furnished rooms. Told me all kinds of Jews always came to him for help and advice, showed me masses of material about Lemberg pogrom. Said that at time of Russian advance 100,000 evacuated Jews came into Warsaw! —distress enormous: called meetings of students and college-boys, each of whom was to find lodging for one family. Also told me he was standing for 9 constituencies in forthcoming Parliamentary elections. Deputation of two Mizrachi representatives came to ask Farbstein to stand for Warsaw.

In hotel vestibule noticed Englishman in khaki: spoke to him and found he was J. M. N. Jeffries, *Daily Mail* correspondent. Told me he thought pogrom stories were exaggerated and that Bolshevik danger was now of greater importance than Jewish question. He suggested I should interview Paderewski. He took me upstairs and introduced me to his colleague, Hyatt, American Associated Press, then to Paderewski's secretary, who made appointment for later. Had friendly talk in English with Paderewski, who received me in his private suite in Hotel Bristol. Assured me he would keep his promises given to the Jewish leaders in America, that he would do all in his power to improve the Jewish position in Poland. Protested that he was philo-Semitic and that the stories about his being anti-Semitic were untrue. He had not been back in Poland long and it would take him some time to make thorough study of all

[1] Died 1921.

aspects of the situation. He expressed a desire to see Farbstein, and I undertook to inform latter of Paderewski's wish.
Interview cut short by Paderewski's wife.

January 10.—Received by Minister of Foreign Affairs,
Wassilevsky (tall, ascetic-looking, about sixty), with whom I
spoke German. He said that no members of the Government were anti-Semites: they were all opposed to the
National Democrats, who were anti-Semites. They were
against all persecution on religious or racial grounds. There
had been no pogroms, and the reports were exaggerated. He
heard shooting also in his own neighbourhood and had
spoken to the military authorities about it; they said that
the soldiers were young recruits, who didn't know how to
manage their guns. He then referred me to head of Political
Section of Ministry, Dr. Jodko. I reminded Jodko of my
interview with him in 1906 at Cracow: he recalled it and
asked about our mutual friend, W. M. Voynich.[1] He also
made protestations of philo-Semitism, determined to whitewash Government. A Commission of officials had been sent
to Lemberg to investigate, and he hoped to publish their
report. He agreed that Jews should receive compensation
for damage sustained, but Government's finances not
brilliant.

Went to Farbstein and told him Paderewski wanted to see
him. Several Zionist friends, including Dr. Poznanski, were
there to meet Colonel Wade, who was adorned with red tabs
and coloured ribbons. Wade (speaking German with bad
accent and grammar) emphasised that no word about interview should appear in Press. Dr. Joshua Gottlieb[2] urged
that Polish Press should stop anti-Semitic attacks, that clergy
should preach tolerance, that teachers should set better
example to pupils; deprecated the idea that problem would
be solved by Jews emigrating. Poznanski reiterated opening remarks of Wade—that lands that blessed Jews would

[1] Antiquarian bookseller in London, who employed August Zaleski as
assistant about 1905–6.
[2] Yiddish journalist and prominent Zionist, murdered in Nazi death camp
in Poland.

themselves be blessed and *vice versa*. Dr. Waschitz (Lemberg) complained of persecution of Jewish Press. Wade replied in English (myself acting as translator): he believed Jewish demands would find fulfilment in election of Jews to Parliament, even making allowance for Polish attempt to reduce Jewish voting strength. Wade, before leaving, asked me to call upon him next morning. Returned to hotel, arranged with Paderewski's secretary for interview of Farbstein next day.

January 11.—Called upon Colonel Wade: he asked me who sent me out to Poland, whether it was Sokolow. He said question of national rights in Poland was difficult and compared it with demand of Ulster for guarantees in relation to Home Rule. He further said Poles reproached Jews for not identifying themselves with their cause, always going with the stronger power, Austrian or Russian. I replied that attitude of Jews was simply loyalty to sovereign power, Austrian or Russian, as the case might be.

Wade: "But Jews should have regarded themselves as being prisoners together under same gaoler."

"No," I said, "Jews were oppressed by Poles even before the war, although there were no pogroms. There was the boycott in Congress Poland, and subservience in many ways in Galicia, where Poles had political authority."

Wade: "The Jews helped the Ukrainians in the fight against the Poles."

Thereupon I read my report of the Lemberg pogrom from Moses Waldmann's notes. Wade intensely interested: said the thing was so grave and important that one should not make a noise about small matters, such as compulsory Latin transcription of Yiddish paper. Asked me for written report, and he said I couldn't accompany him to Lemberg, as he must preserve air of impartiality.

Went to War Office, saw War Minister, Colonel Wronchinski. I said that I heard the only Jewish paper in Poland, *Novy Dziennik*, was suppressed by order of General Rozvadovski and couldn't understand why in free Poland

Jewish Community Office in Warsaw

Jewish Market in Warsaw

a section of people should be deprived of liberty of expression. He replied, would telephone to Military Commander, Cracow District, to find out. He presumed *Novy Dziennik* had written against the Polish army. Sent for typewritten Polish translations of articles in Yiddish papers alleged to be attacks on Polish army: promised to let me see German translations.

Called on Chief of General Staff, Count Sczeptycki, tall, powerful, grey hair, asked me (in French) if I had anything agreeable to tell him. I referred to suppression of *Novy Dziennik* by General whose authority was limited to Przemysl. Count condemned anti-Semitism: would investigate, and if he found paper had been suppressed would issue counter-order. He then said Jews shouldn't meddle with Bolshevism, so informed him it was a Jewess who made attempt on Lenin. Then went to Rabbi Dr. Poznanski, who showed me 40 cartridge cases picked up in neighbourhood of synagogue on morning after Christmas in consequence of soldiers shooting recklessly on pretext they were being attacked by General Haller's troops. Wrote out long telegram for London Zionist Office, took it to Farbstein, leaving to-night for Vienna, to be telegraphed from there. Farbstein told me he had interview with Paderewski, who gave him greetings from Judge Mack of New York.

January 12.—At Zionist Bureau met Dr. Bychowski, nerve specialist, standing as candidate for Polish Parliament. Conducted me through purlieus of Ghetto: dirt, distress, depression everywhere. Countless little stalls kept in partnership, four women joint-owners of basket of apples: youths selling little sweets in paper by lottery, 5 pfennig a draw—sometimes a blank. Jewish cabbies, porters, coalheavers; beggars and tramps in rags of many colours. Old woman on door-step whined: " *Shenk mir a Nedovoh, bin an arme almonoh*" (" Give me alms. I'm a poor widow "). Entered several dwellings in Jewish house, many " dwellings " only of one room occupied by parents and four children. One tenant had room to let, but was particular

E

about lodger, as last one had stolen dinner out of pot. Everywhere damp, foetid smell. Long queue of women and girls waiting for bread with cards, kept in order by militia man with gun, who beat them with butt-end. Visit to Nalevki—dirt, mud everywhere. Strike of house-porters, who demanded at least two rooms for own dwelling.

January 13.—Visited Dr. Bychowski again: told me of interesting "Wonder-Rabbi" living short distance from Warsaw, who had 100,000 followers, none of whom took any step (as regards marriage of daughters, business, politics, etc.) without consulting him; he also prescribed for all illnesses, but when he saw patients getting worse he gave them a *Zettel* (note) for a doctor in Warsaw. Said there were about 30 such "Wonder-Rabbis" in Poland, all with large following. Told me of disease discovered only among Jewish children—the "Tee-Saxe" malady, diagnosed in America—arrested development, children dying at age of two: hardly any case among Christians: explained as product of old worn-out race.

Later went to War Office, where expected Captain Bouffarl to show me articles from Yiddish papers attacking Polish Army, but he showed me only extracts in Polish from Yiddish papers about assaults on Jews by Polish Legionaries and declared these items untrue. I replied that as names of Jews shot were given, he could prove stories untrue only if he could show the persons alive. Met Count Szembek, of the Polish Mission in Berne, who asked me my impressions of situation in Poland; he agreed to take letter for me to British Legation, Berne.

January 14.—Began draft of first article on pogroms for the London *Times*. At house of my friend Menachem Leibowitz met a Mr. Berlin who had just come from Riga. Berlin had been prisoner of war in fortress at Sebastopol and saw entire Jewish Communal Council murdered. At Yalta he saw 800–900 men and women stripped naked by Bolsheviks, their feet weighted with stones, driven into sea, so closely packed on beach that unable to drown, their hands forced upwards by waves. This spectacle lasted for some months until Germans took Yalta, then sent divers to recover corpses for burial—some divers went mad.

January 15.—In hotel lift met M. Grabski, leader of National Democrats, known to be adviser of Paderewski. Invited me to his room for talk. He said Poland now in difficult situation, having to fight against Ukrainians, Bolsheviks and Germans, therefore difficult to establish order at home. Declared that fighting around Posen provoked by Germans pulling down British flag, that Ukrainians were practically Bolsheviks, having proclaimed socialisation of land, and it was therefore necessary to drive them back. Ukrainians had terrible hatred for Poles, and mutual tolerance was necessary. I remarked this applied also to Jewish question. Grabski said Jews both in Poland and abroad were against Poland, although they had complete liberty in new State. I replied it was on paper only. He said Jews should unite with Poles to build up new Poland. I replied it was difficult for Jews to forget pogroms, especially as Government hadn't even issued protest. He said that nothing would be gained by inquiry or prosecution, that Jews had fought on side of Ukrainians, had poured boiling gruel on Polish soldiers, had caused 30,000 Poles in Galicia to be hanged and had greatly profited by war. (I questioned all these charges.) Situation embittered by Poles leaving land for towns and meeting with Jewish opposition! In a Great Poland this source of trouble would disappear. Admitted that he was formerly anti-Semitic, but declared he was no longer one. He proposed that Conference of representatives of all Polish parties should meet with Jews to come to understanding on condition that Jews in Poland and abroad declared in favour of a Great Poland including Dantzic and Vilna. He wouldn't demand that Jews should declare themselves members of Polish nationality.

It was now 1 a.m. and the Secretary of the Foreign Ministry, who was present, began to nod, so I left and went to my room. There I found card from Mr. Richard Kimens,

Assistant Commissioner, British Mission to Poland, saying he would call in morning at 9 a.m.

January 16.—Mr. Kimens called early, and I went to see him at midday. I told him of the helpless condition of the Jews in Poland, of the pogroms, assaults, robberies, etc., of the impotence of the Government and necessity of British troops coming here to give protection to Jewish lives and property. Approved of my having sent a telegram to London to this effect and promised to send another for me. Said he would like to have my report on Jewish conditions in Poland and that it was important I should remain another few days to discuss Jewish question thoroughly with his assistant, Rowland Kenney, arriving soon from Vienna. Schwalbe (journalist) took me to meeting of Workmen's Council at Kaminski's Theatre: had talk there in French with Communist leader, who was anxious to know if social revolution would take place in England!

January 17.—Took telegram to Kimens for despatch to London. Discussed forthcoming elections with Schwalbe. In the evening went to Opera, performance of *La Bohême* in honour of Allies. Ovation given to Italian officers, one of whom delivered fiery oration acclaiming Polish prowess and greeting Polish State. Italian and French national anthems sung.

January 18.—Visit of Sokolow's son. Long talk with Kenney (tall, serious, sympathetic); gave him rapid sketch of Jewish situation and promised him reports. He said if there was going to be a new Polish State, it might as well be founded properly. Went to Kaminski's Theatre, where was one of four big election meetings organised by Jewish National Council. About 3,000 present; Abraham Podlishevski in chair. Gruenbaum spoke of forthcoming Jewish National Assembly: said that if Government wished to prevent it, they would use their influence in Parliament to get it allowed. He criticised Jewish *Folkist* party, who wanted legislative power:—demanded that all Jews in Polish Parliament, irrespective of party, should work together as united Jewish party. Criticised *Folkist* party for making alliance with clerical Orthodox party simply to get a mandate: also criticised individual who wanted to get into Parliament on strength of his money. Ridiculed assimilators for wanting Jewish votes: if they felt like *Polacks,* let them go to the *Polacks!* (Loud applause). Following speaker was a *Folkist,* who invoked the dead of Lemberg, said that Jewish National Council represented only Zionists, not all parties: criticised position caused by so many different Jewish parties presenting different memoranda to Pilsudski, who naturally gave each less attention than he would give to united Jewish representation. Audience became restless and refused to give further speakers hearing: motion carried to limit further speeches to 5 minutes. A neutral speaker compared *Folkist* party to those who in time of Moses wanted to remain in Egypt: hence three days of darkness when many of them died out. He compared Poale Zion to Korah, who, while in wilderness, complained of Moses and wanted a "portfolio": warned Poale Zion of Korah's fate. (Great hilarity and applause.) Another Zionist speaker, J. Heftman,[1] followed.

Returned to hotel. Podlishevski called: chat about variety of Jewish parties. He suggested I should have a talk with Medem,[2] one of the most important leaders of the Bund and a founder of the Yiddish school system. Told me that Jewish Bolshevist also spoke at meeting, and that Gruenbaum replied, proving that Bolshevism would mean ruin for the Jewish people, as it abolished the middle-man and petty trader, and benefited only factory-workers, among whom Jews sparsely represented. Podlishevski said Jewish national autonomy in Poland necessary for schools and hospitals: Jewish boys were laughed at by Poles when Rabbi came to give lessons. Chassidim now willing to send children to school, but not to Polish school, owing to Sabbaths and festivals. Separate hospitals necessary for obvious reasons.

[1] Now President of Journalists' Association in Israel.
[2] Died in New York, 1923.

January 19.—Dinner with Farbstein: told me of Rabbi of small town travelling to Warsaw, attacked in carriage by soldiers who opened his bag, threw his *tallit* (prayer-shawl) and *tephillin* (phylacteries) on floor, and stamped on them. During dinner, about 3.30, messenger came to Farbstein to inform him of shooting going on in Jewish quarter Nalevki, asked him to go to local Military Commander about it. Went to Gruenbaum, who explained to me principles of different Jewish parties in Poland. He said Bund and *Folkists* were opposed to Zionists because they looked on them as "emigration party" fixing their gaze on Palestine and thus devoting less attention to *Golus* interests. If Zionists declared for Hebrew as Jewish national language, then Government would suppress Yiddish and do wrong to Yiddish-speaking people. The *Folkists* were foolish enough to demand Parliament of their own with legislative powers.

Went with Gruenbaum to meeting of young Zionist workers, where forthcoming election discussed. While there was informed by Schwalbe of violent shooting going on in Nalevki: machine-guns used since 3 o'clock; urged me to inform Paderewski. Journalist Tygel accompanied me: said he was dragged out of tramcar by soldiers who beat him on the face. Went to see Paderewski's secretary: informed him of affair in Nalevki: he inquired on telephone, was informed patrol had been shot at and three persons slightly wounded. (Story about firing at patrol pure fiction.)

January 20.—Called this morning at British Mission, discussed Jewish question with Kimens and Kenney, especially present terrorism, need of national rights (schools, hospitals, etc.). Whilst there Dr. Gumplowicz, of Polish Legation, Vienna, arrived with Polish friend. Returned to hotel and wrote out article on "The Pogroms in Poland" for the London *Times*.[1]

January 21.—Called on Kimens and Kenney in their room in hotel: gave them Report on Pogroms. Kimens told me courier would leave in afternoon. Went later to British

[1] This article was published in *The Times* of February 8, 1919.

Mission, handed in telegrams of Polish Zionists to Balfour and President Wilson: despatched by radio. Saw Paderewski's secretary, asked for interview. Then took tram to Belvidere Palace to see Marshal Josef Pilsudski, Chief of Polish State. From entrance an officer accompanied me to vestibule, taken to waiting-room, whence ushered in to large room with gaudy furniture, where official told me Pilsudski rather unwell, would perhaps receive me in his bedroom. He then returned and fixed interview for two days later. Spoke again to Paderewski's secretary, asked for interview: fixed for to-morrow.

January 22.—Inquired in morning of Paderewski's secretary about interview: asked to come again at 12: called at 12, told to come again at 2: called at 2, told to come again at 9 p.m. I said it was Paderewski's last opportunity, as I was leaving to-night. Went to Foreign Ministry, was told that telegrams to foreign newspapers were free from censorship. At 9.15 spoke again to Paderewski's secretary; who said he would inform me as soon as Paderewski was ready. Returned at 10.20. Paderewski now Prime Minister, having formed Coalition Ministry on the 17th. He was finishing supper with American Mission: came into ante-chamber (typewriter, beer bottles, etc.). Offered me cigarette: had animated conversation on Jewish situation. I regretted to note that Paderewski had become less conciliatory than at our previous interview. He said military raid on Jewish quarter Nalevki last Saturday and Sunday was necessitated by search for weapons in fighting against Bolshevism. I pointed out that no weapons had been found in Jewish houses, but soldiers had robbed and assaulted Jews. I asked whether Government would issue condemnation of pogroms. He replied there had also been pogroms in Whitechapel and Cardiff (a gross exaggeration), and those in Poland were caused by resentment against Jews for having sided with Germans. I reminded him of Prince Lubomirski's Government and of several prominent Poles who had also sided with Germany. Paderewski said Government would issue condemnation of pogroms, but could not appeal to Poles without also making similar appeal to Jews, as it would otherwise be one-sided. He complained of the part played by Jews in the Bolshevist movement, whereupon I observed that Jewish Bolshevists were small fraction of Russian and Polish Jews, that Jews had killed Bolshevist leaders, and all Jewish parties opposed to the movement. In reply to question whether Government would give Jews compensation, he asked whether Poland would be compensated for her losses in war, and concluded by assuring me he would keep his promise to Jewish leaders in America to do utmost for just treatment of Jews. As on the occasion of our previous interview, Paderewski's wife interrupted him, pulled him by the sleeve, saying he must go back to their guests. Went on talking till 11.15, leaving both of us dissatisfied.

January 23.—After breakfast took tram to Palace Belvidere for interview with Marshal Pilsudski.

I was received in a large and lofty ante-chamber by an officer in grey uniform, and then passed on to another officer wearing a grey tunic, blue trousers with a broad yellow stripe, and resplendent top-boots, who ushered me up a flight of stairs and through a series of apartments, until we reached a large drawing-room with a parquet floor and furniture covered with bright tapestry.

Marshal Pilsudski came in with a slow step, coughing. He was in military attire—with black trousers, grey tunic with high collar and white cuffs; and as he bade me be seated, I noted the resolute and furtive look, the drooping moustache, and the close-cropped hair, which picture postcards throughout the country had made familiar. He was obviously suffering from a cold, and had a couple of handkerchiefs peeping from a pocket in addition to the one that he was using for his nose.

I began by asking in what language we should speak—English, French, or German, and he replied: " In German." I said that I had come from England to study the Jewish situation in Poland owing to the unfavourable impression that had been created by the pogroms.

Pilsudski: "The pogroms were caused by the sudden collapse of Austrian rule and the absence of authority, and by the hatred of Jewish dealers—the only class who had profited in the war. It is true that dealers in all parts of the world have profited. But as so many Jews in Galicia were engaged in trade, hatred was easily directed against all Jews."

I.C. "Didn't the Polish landlords and peasants also profit by the war?"

Pilsudski: "If they did, it was through dealings with Jews. Anger was directed against the Jews because they were smugglers and worked as *Kettenhändler* (chain-dealers), forcing up prices."

I.C.: "Doesn't the Government intend issuing a condemnation of the pogroms?"

Pilsudski: "How can you expect that the Government would say that it disapproves of pogroms? That would suggest that the Government consists of pogromists. It is understood that the Government doesn't approve of the pogroms or of violence of any kind against anybody."

I.C.: "Then what about the shooting in the Jewish quarter Nalevki last Sunday, when several Jews were wounded?"

Pilsudski: "I don't think the affair was serious, and have not yet received a full report about it. I must enquire. So far as the situation in general is concerned, I must say that the Poles are not philo-Semites. That must be admitted. The Jews in Poland form a very large number and are a foreign body whom one would like to get rid of. On the other hand, it must be said that the Poles are by nature not a wild people, and the present violence cannot continue. Secondly, as soon as the independence of Poland was declared, equal rights were granted to all Jews exactly as in all Western democracies. There were no exceptional laws for Jews."

I.C.: "But the Jews are in an exceptional position, which makes their equal rights quite illusory. For example, in certain districts of the Kielce province Jews are not allowed to vote at the forthcoming election unless they sign a declaration that they regard themselves members of the Polish nationality."

Pilsudski: "Yes, I have heard something to that effect, but nothing very definite."

I.C.: "Then the Jews in the railway service in Poland, numbering over a thousand, have been dismissed."

Pilsudski: "I didn't know there were any Jews in the railway service, except perhaps in Galicia."

I.C.: "I am speaking of Congress Poland. I have been told on the best authority that Jews were in the railway service, that they were really dismissed, and that the Minister of Labour has received a representative deputation to submit their grievances."

Pilsudski: "I must make enquiries into the question. I presume that the Jews were employed by the Germans, and as all people who worked for the Germans are hated they were dismissed."

I.C.: "But Poles also worked for the Germans. Were they dismissed?"

Pilsudski: "The Poles worked on the railways before under the Russian régime, so they remained."

I.C.: "Yes, but there were other Poles too, who rendered Germany political aid, such as Prince Lubomirski's Government."

Pilsudski: "That was only a bluff."

I.C.: "And what about the pro-German Rector of the Warsaw University, and the Polish writers who wrote at German dictation?"

Pilsudski: "Those people had, of course, to disappear from public life as they had so compromised themselves, and they will not be able to resume their activity for some years."

I.C.: "Because a few Jews worked with the Germans, all

Jews in Poland are made to suffer; but as for the Poles, only those suffer who were the actual offenders."

Pilsudski: "In these confused times and our present disorganised conditions you can hardly expect strict justice."

I.C.: "If I can't expect justice for a large number, I hope that I can reckon on it for a few—for the four Zionists, Ringel, Reich, Hausmann and Tennenblatt, who were taken from Lemberg as hostages and are interned at Baranow."

Pilsudski: "I can't do anything in this matter at present, as it was a military measure designed to secure the tranquillity of the people in Lemberg. If I were to release the hostages it would cause considerable discontent among the Poles."

I.C.: "Is there any specific charge against the hostages?"

Pilsudski: "None; if there were, we should make short work of the matter. It is said that they were not neutral in the fight between the Poles and the Ukrainians, but whether they were so or not it is difficult to say. Besides, the hostages have nothing really to complain of. I sent my adjutant to Baranow to see how they were accommodated. They are in a castle and are quite safe. I have already issued an order that as soon as the situation at Lemberg is eased, all hostages —both Ukrainians and Jews—are to be released. The situation in Lemberg is, indeed, distressing—bombarding an open city! But it is difficult to evacuate 200,000 people."

I.C.: "Does the Government intend giving any compensation to the victims of the pogroms?"

Pilsudski: "In principle, I am in favour of such compensation being given, but I cannot yet say what the decision of the Government will be, as the whole question is still under consideration."

As our conversation ended I thanked the Chief of State for having received me so cordially, and wished him a speedy recovery.

I left Warsaw by night train for Cracow.

January 24.—Arrived Cracow, 8 a.m. Visited Rabbi Dr. Thon and went together to office of *Novy Dziennik*, now

Gazeta Zydovska. Met there Dr. Ringel[1] and Tennenblatt, two of Zionist hostages transferred from Baranow. Later met third hostage, Dr. Leon Reich,[2] who asked me to get General Rozvadowski to issue order releasing them from all restrictions.

January 25.—Left Cracow at night for Lemberg. Travelled in damaged compartment in crowded train, no light or heat and little sleep.

January 26.—Arrived Lemberg, 9.45 a.m. Jewish porter took my hand-bag and attaché case to Hotel Krakowski. No droschkies or trams. Roads thick with snow. Attended meeting of Zionist Committee. Eisler, Captain of Jewish Militia, took me through part of city where all buildings badly punctured and damaged by machine-guns, hand-grenades, etc. After dinner he accompanied me to house of Dr. Zipper, where many Zionists were gathered. Was welcomed as first visitor from Western Europe. Gave account of my mission up-to-date and stated what further information I required.

January 27.—Dr. Schmorak and two friends took me on tour through Jewish quarter to see damage caused by pogrom. All Jewish shops broken into, plundered: owners who resisted assaulted or shot. Most windows still broken, some covered with boards. Looting also took place in square around Town Hall. Visited streets where entire blocks of houses burnt out: on front of some houses round charred patch showing each house had been set on fire separately. Three separate attempts to set Liberal Synagogue on fire, as Poles declared machine-guns were there: three scrolls of Torah entirely destroyed, two damaged. In Rabbi's robing room five tin cases of benzine still lying on floor. Old *Vorstädtische* Synagogue (300 years old) burnt down, with loss of 36 scrolls, many of them originating from Spain. Big safe forced open, gold and silver ornaments stolen. One Torah scroll stabbed by bayonet in several places. A third

[1] Elected in 1922 to Polish Senate, died (perhaps murdered by Nazis) 1940.
[2] Later member of Polish Parliament and Chairman of Jewish Parliamentary Group. Died 1929.

Synagogue (*Chiddushim*) was complete ruin: charred fragments of prayer-books and Pentateuchs still lying about in
snow. Informed that machine-guns were used to command
streets, preventing Jews from escaping. After the big pogrom
on November 22–23, there was a smaller attack on December
29–30, 1918. The extensive destruction was mainly the result
of a punitive expedition by Polish troops, aided by rabble,
against the Jews because of their neutrality in this Polish-
Ukrainian war. There had been assaults, robbery, outrage,
murder, and arson. 73 Jews killed, a few hundred seriously
injured, 49 houses and one synagogue burned to the ground.
The estimated damage was 100 million kronen (over
£4,000,000). Collected evidence that pogrom was carefully
prepared.

January 28.—Had interview at Potocki Palace with
Colonel Wade and Colonel Smyth (of Allied Mission) on
pogrom and general Jewish situation. Wade expressed
agreement with principal Jewish demands regarding
national autonomy, but urged that word "national" should
be dropped. He agreed, at my request, to make out certificate
that the four Zionist hostages had been elected delegates
to Zionist Conference in London on February 11, so that
they might get permission to go to London. Our interview
brought to early end as Wade said he had to go and meet
the Ukrainian delegates to discuss question of armistice.
Went to Registration Bureau to fetch documentary and
photographic material on pogrom. Then to *Platz Kommando*
to get permit to return to Cracow.

January 29.—Went again to Potocki Palace to give
Colonel Wade letter from Galician Zionist Executive, notify-
ing that the four Zionist hostages were elected delegates to
Zionist Conference in London, and asking Polish Military
Commander for permission to let them go. Asked Wade to
write out official certificate to ensure that Polish permission
be given. Then drove through blizzard to station. Got seat
in first class compartment: very cold. Not far from Lemberg
(Grodek) we saw armoured train where General Rozva-

dovsky had his headquarters. Intended stopping at Przemysl, but was warned not to by Pole, who told me there was a sort of Workmen's Republic there, with armed militia who plundered. Reached Jaroslau 4.30 p.m., already dark, bitterly cold. Stayed at Hotel City: Jewish proprietor told me his cellar was plundered previous week (many bottles of wine stolen). Slept in sitting-room converted into bedroom: had to put overcoat over bed-covering.

January 30.—Left Jaroslau 1.30 p.m. Secured seat in first class compartment, but window of corridor-door missing, also window of side of train, causing terrible draught, which compelled me to put up my coat collar. At every station many Jews in long caftan, ringlets, top-boots, running in all directions. Several got into my train: one stood praying *Shemoneh Esreh* [1] in corridor. Later a doleful fiddler played in corridor a lively tune over and over again, collected alms. I froze: matronly fellow-passenger shared travelling-rug with me. Reached Cracow 10.30 p.m. (instead of 7.30).

January 31.—Went to office of *Gazeta Zydowska*: was informed that Dr. Thon had been elected member of Polish Parliament. Furnished with material about pogroms and other anti-Jewish excesses committed in 130 towns and villages in Poland and Galicia in November and December, 1918, and January, 1919. Called at Polish Liquidation Commission: Zuk (head of Press Bureau) said to me: "The German and Italian papers are spreading reports that all is anarchy here. Tell them in Vienna that all is quiet here." In evening had dinner with Dr. Reich and other hostages and Schmorak in restaurant of Hotel Saski. Took leave just before midnight.

February 1.—Caught train at 7 a.m. for Oswiecim: compelled to go there instead of travelling to Vienna direct, owing to Czech-Polish war. At Oswiecim had to wait few hours for train to Kandrzin (in German territory), so went into town, looked up secretary of Jewish community. He told me of attempts at pogroms, warded off on the first

[1] " Eighteen benedictions," the principal prayer in the Jewish liturgy.

occasion by Cracow Jewish Militia, on the second pogromists were injured. Was conducted to Jewish cemetery, saw damage to many tombstones done by gang of roughs. General violation of graves. In Oswiecim station official wanted to subject me to "body search" in a cubicle, but I protested that as I was on an official mission I should be exempt, so he gave me stamped disk, allowing me to go on platform. Left Oswiecim at 4, reached Kandrzin at 9 p.m., left 10.30 for Annaberg.

February 2.—Arrived Annaberg 1 a.m., changed again for Oderberg, arriving 2 a.m. Changed at Oderberg, left 3 a.m., in Arctic frost, arrived in Lundenburg 10 a.m. Long wait in warm station restaurant until 3 p.m., then left for Vienna, arriving 7.30 p.m.—36 hours from Cracow to Vienna, about twice as long as previous journey from Vienna to Cracow.

February 3.—Gave interview to Heinrich Margulies for *Wiener Morgenzeitung*. Called at Jewish National Council, talks with Adolf Boehm, Robert Weltsch, etc.

February 4.—Visit from Dr. Israel Waldmann, who told me he was authorised by President of West Ukrainian Republic (East Galicia) to inform me that in negotiations between Colonel Wade and Ukrainian delegates at Lemberg Wade said he had authority to act on behalf of Entente, requested Ukrainians to retire 20 kilometres from Lemberg, said that mines of Drohobycz, etc., would be occupied by Entente troops; that Jews, if given national rights in Ukraine, would exploit the peasants; and asked for Memorandum on Ukrainian question, but the Jewish aspect should not be touched. Dr. Waldmann authorised me on behalf of East Galician Jewish National Council to protest to British Government against Colonel Wade's action.

Dr. Waldmann brought with him Professor Dnystriansky, former member of Austrian Parliament, member of Ukrainian National Council, and only Lemberg Professor who lectured in Ukrainian. The Professor gave me full exposition of Ukrainian standpoint and demands. Adolf Stand [1] came and gave me letters to post in Switzerland. Then went to Parliament House, large number of police in vestibule to ward off any possible attack upon meeting of German Bohemians taking place. Conducted by journalist Wechsler to German Bohemian representative, Langenhahn, who explained to me demands of German Bohemians.

February 5.—Left Vienna 6.30 a.m.

February 6.—Arrived Innsbruck 9 a.m. Reached Feldkirch 6 p.m., stayed at Hotel Post over night.

February 7.—Left Feldkirch 7 a.m., arrived Buchs 8.30. In station restaurant had talks with Ukrainian and South Slavonian delegates travelling to Peace Conference in Paris. Left Buchs 1.30 p.m., arriving Zurich before 6, met by Dr. Berthold Feiwel. Arrived Berne soon after 11.

February 8.—Met August Zaleski, Polish Chargé d'Affaires, in hotel. He was eager to have my impressions of conditions in Poland and rather disappointed at my account.

February 9.—Attended International Socialist Conference, the first since before First World War. Main topic of discussion was attitude to Bolshevism. Heard speeches by Branting, Kurt Eisner, Ramsay MacDonald, Arthur Henderson, Huysmans, and others.

February 10.—Met H. N. Brailsford, who told me he was going to Poland as member of British Economic Mission: wanted to know about conditions there and asked me for letter of introduction to Jewish leaders in Warsaw. Gave him letter in Hebrew. Also met Dr. Leo Chasanowitch,[2] Berl Locker,[3] and other representatives of Poale Zion attending Conference. Had supper together in Volkshaus and gave them account of my visit to Poland.

February 11.—Visit from Chasanowitch, to whom I gave

---

[1] Member of Austrian Parliament, 1907–14. Died in Vienna, 1919.
[2] Took active part in America in organisation of American Jewish Congress; in his latter years worked for " Ort ". Died 1925.
[3] Now Chairman of Jewish Agency Executive in Jerusalem.

short statement about situation in Poland to wire to Jewish Press Bureau in Stockholm. Told me the Bureau would issue several monographs on current Jewish questions and asked me to collaborate.

Obtained French visa at Consulate and was told I could leave for Paris on the 15th.

Chapter V

THE LEMBERG POGROM

December, 1918

ALL THE people from Lemberg whom I met at Cracow
pictured to me the doleful conditions that prevailed in
their city and urged me to postpone my visit until it could be
carried out without discomfort or danger. The Ukrainians
were bombarding the city daily and many persons had been
killed in the streets; there was no electric light there nor
water supply, and food and coal were at famine prices. Nor
was it always possible to reach Lemberg from Cracow, for
the station just before the disputed city was often so badly
hit that the train could then proceed no further than
Przemysl. The bulletins issued by the Polish Command
generally announced that the situation in Eastern Galicia
was unchanged, which simply meant that the siege of
Lemberg continued unabated. I inquired several times of
the Polish Liquidation Commission—the new Government
authority of Galicia—about the prospects of my expedition,
much as one might, before the Armistice was signed, have
asked about a voyage across the submarine-infested Atlantic.
And when I at last fixed a day there came a message that
the morning train from Lemberg had been hit by the
Ukrainians and several passengers were killed. So I waited
patiently until the situation improved, for I had travelled
from London right across Central Europe in order to visit
the pogrom-stricken city, and I was not going to leave Galicia
without fulfilling my mission. At length the prospect was
declared to be safe. I obtained the necessary military permit, took food supplies for a few days, and bought a railway
ticket.

There were two trains daily that left Cracow for Lemberg, one in the morning and the other in the evening. But as the journey then took twelve hours if there were no hitch, and the morning train would have brought me into a city of dreadful night, I travelled by the evening train. The huge crowd that awaited it on the platform might have made one think that Lemberg was a pleasure resort, but I was told that many of the passengers were bound for intermediate stations. As soon as the long dark mass drew up along the dimly lighted platform there was a wild rush, which became all the more chaotic because it was hard to distinguish the different classes. Neither in the compartments nor in the corridor was there the faintest glimmer of light, although there was no complaint of a shortage of petroleum in Cracow.

After much struggling I found myself in a first-class carriage where, despite the darkness, I espied a corner seat. But on attempting to sit down I sank upon some cold iron object and the wooden framework of the seat, from which the upholstering had been completely removed. My surprise was lessened by my previous experience of railway carriages in Poland, which had been stripped by the disbanded soldiers of everything that could be detached—upholstering, leather window-straps, even the netting of the rack. I sat on my attaché-case for added comfort, and congratulated myself that the windows of our compartment were not broken as in so many other carriages. Although the temperature was several degrees below zero, the train was not heated, but it was so packed with passengers, even in the corridor, that we soon became intolerably warm. A Polish officer who sat in the opposite corner near the window lit a candle which he stuck on the ledge, and after discussing with a voluble gentleman in shaggy fur on my right the prospects of the elections to the National Assembly, he produced half a brown loaf and a chunk of meat, which he ate with the aid of a formidable jack-knife. In the corner just opposite me sat a Red Cross nurse, slim and sallow in a grey uniform, who removed her cap, shook her shorn tresses, and began to smoke cigarettes with feverish vehemence. Between the officer and the nurse sat two portly ladies, who soon fell asleep and snored peacefully, but shortly after midnight they left. The atmosphere was relieved, but only for a short time, as the vacant seats were presently occupied by tired passengers from the corridor. The candle was put out and we all settled ourselves uncomfortably to sleep. When we awoke in the morning, with sore backs, we saw the country covered with snow on all sides.

It was nearly ten o'clock when the train steamed into Lemberg fully two hours late. We all hastened with our luggage to the exit, where soldiers were posted near the ticket collectors to demand the military permits. But so violent was the rush of the crowd that I was able to pass through without showing either railway ticket or permit. No sooner did I get outside the station than my ears were assailed by the dull boom of a cannon. I expected everybody to fly for shelter, but nobody seemed to mind. There were no cabs or taxis to be seen, nor trams nor even tram lines; for the electric power station had been badly damaged by the Ukrainians, the trams were rendered useless, and the tram-lines were buried under mud and snow. But there was a swarm of wooden sleighs, small and primitive, mostly made by their owners, who plied for hire. These sleighs had no accommodation for passengers and were used simply for the conveyance of luggage, but as I had only taken with me a handbag besides my attaché case, a porter without a sleigh was able to carry them.

The long sloping street that led from the station to the city showed traces on every side of the fierce battle that had raged there in the early half of November. Whilst the rest of the world was rejoicing at the ending of the Great War, the Poles and the Ukrainians were beginning their own little war. Lemberg had changed hands several times since Austria had presented her ultimatum to Serbia; but it had remained intact throughout all the four years, for neither

Austrians nor Russians had bombarded the city nor fought within it. But this once prosperous city of a quarter of a million inhabitants was now nearly as badly bruised and battered as many a town in Flanders, and the damage had been done by the fighting of rival troops that but yesterday were united in defending it against the common foe. Not a single building, public or private, had escaped injury, for the machine guns had wrought havoc on every side. The walls looked stricken with smallpox, and the windows were everywhere plastered over with paper, for there was no glass to be obtained. The building of the Military Academy stood like a ragged skeleton, bereft of roof and windows; and gaps and bare patches of various sizes met the eye on every side. My porter told me that he had been in Lemberg from the outbreak of the war, but since the signing of the Armistice it had been worse than ever before. They had all become accustomed now to the bombardment and took no notice of it; if they were killed by a shell they would be saved from death by starvation. Perhaps after the Allies had made peace in Paris, they would try to make peace in Lemberg.

Crowds of people coming from the city asked us if the train had arrived that morning; they had been to the station so often only to learn that the train could get no further than Przemysl. At a street corner I saw a group of shivering women around a water pump, each struggling in turn with the handle, and then taking away an overflowing pail or jug. It was the only way in which water could be got, for the Municipal waterworks, like the electric power station, had been severely damaged, and repair was impossible as long as the fighting continued. A few paces further we came across four or five Ukrainian prisoners, who were being escorted by Polish legionaries; the Ukrainians were a dishevelled band, but the Poles looked equally dejected.

We turned into the Karl Ludwig Street, where a number of young children between the ages of six and twelve were hawking sweets, cigarettes and newspapers. These tattered traders—their faces pinched and blue with cold—were Jewish children, many of them orphans, over whom had swept a few weeks ago the horrors of a barbarous pogrom, but who stood eagerly discussing business with one another, and keeping a wary eye open for customers. *"Lemberger Tagblatt!"*—*"Papirossen* (cigarettes)*!"* piped the infant voices irrepressibly, whilst overhead cracked the roar of cannon. They had seen death so near that invisible guns had no terrors for them. We passed the Hotel Franzuski, the Headquarters of General Rozvadovsky, which, an hour later, was struck by a shell.

I put up in the Hotel Krakowski, which was reputed to be the most up-to-date establishment in Galicia, but its widely advertised attraction of hot and cold water in every room was belied by the stoppage of the water supply. The lift was also condemned to rest, and as I tramped up the wide staircase I had a difficulty in realising that the steps were of white marble, so thickly were they overlaid with dirt. The room to which I was shown also bore traces of neglect, and the table was covered with blobs of candle-grease. The chambermaid brought up a jug of water from the basement, and offered me a towel which had already been used with the excuse that there was no clean one left; but when I declared that I would rather leave the hotel she brought me a clean towel, which she said was her own.

I hired a sleigh to take me to the house of a leading member of the Jewish community to whom I bore a letter of introduction. The floor of the vehicle was littered with evil-smelling straw, and the youthful pockmarked driver wore a military tunic. My new friend proposed a short walk before lunch. We strolled through a part of the city in which the damage was much worse than in the long street leading from the station: the General Post Office and the building of the Galician Diet, once adorned with handsome sculptures, had both been battered into wrecks, without window or roof, and with numberless big gaps in the walls. And wherever we turned we saw broken windows and punctured walls.

"You see those little holes," said my friend. "We call them here 'Wilson's Points'. They have been made with machine guns; the big gaps have been made with hand grenades. We are now engaged in self-determination, and God knows what and when the end will be."

We passed a group of young women with close-cropped hair, who strode along in short skirts and full military equipment, with guns slung across their shoulders, some of them in puttees and others in heavy boots. "Those are some of our Polish Amazons," remarked my friend. "There are about three hundred of them altogether: as brave as men, and some of them more reckless. There are supposed to be thirty thousand Polish troops about here, but there are not more than five thousand at the front. That is why the battle is practically at a standstill."

Presently we came across two or three boys, likewise in full military equipment, who could not have been more than twelve or thirteen years of age. Their guns were almost as big as themselves. They also belonged to the fighting ranks.

As we ascended the stairs to his flat there was a loud crack in the air, which seemed to be quite near. My friend reassured me; but the next moment he pointed to a little hole in the window of an upper landing. "Two weeks ago a bullet came through there and killed a servant girl on the very spot where we are now."

Later in the afternoon the home of my host was besieged by friends who had heard that there was a visitor there from London. "Really from London?" they asked in a voice in which surprise was mingled with gladness. "Then the world hasn't forgotten us altogether. Tell us what life is like now in London and Paris; we get so little news here."

But I told them that I had come to ask, not to answer questions, and so they related the sufferings, the terrors, and the privations through which they had passed, and sighed out the hopes by which they were upborne. And over and over again the conversation was punctuated by the roll of cannon. "That is nothing," one said. "It was worse two months ago."

I was conducted back to my hotel in the evening by two friends, one of whom had a revolver in his hip pocket. It was pitch dark, and footpads—both civilian and military—had been rather busy lately, but we reached our destination without mishap. The gloom of the large entrance hall was faintly illumined by a small oil lamp on the counter of the office, where I bought a slender candle for four crowns (about three shillings and sixpence) to light my room. "Can I have a candlestick too?" I asked. "You will get a wine-bottle upstairs," was the clerk's reply.

The scene presented by the restaurant belonging to the hotel was picturesquely weird. The candles on the tables, mostly fixed in champagne-bottles, revealed a great muster of diners, among whom officers and women predominated. The white epaulettes and red collars of the officers and the variegated toilettes of their lady friends lent a little colour to the scene, but the general effect was sombre and depressing. On a platform in a corner a pianist and two violinists played some merry airs, to which the diners at one of the tables hummed an accompaniment. There was gossiping everywhere, and some flirting too, with the clinking of glasses, as though in a desperate resolve to banish the spectre of misery. Laughing voices rang out from many a table, which was laden with other bottles than those which acted as candlesticks. "Let us drink and be merry, for to-morrow we shall die," seemed to be the legend writ large on every face. The waiter helped me to choose a modest repast, which amounted to over thirty crowns (about twenty-five shillings), and in the intervals between the courses asked me for my advice how he could reach England or America as soon as the frontiers were free.

A buxom dark-eyed girl sat down unbidden at my table, ordered a liqueur, and began to smoke a cigarette. Presently she asked me if I had known the girl who had been carried that day from the hotel to her grave. "People think she poisoned herself because of some love-affair," she said. "It was simply hunger that drove her to it. I saw her dead face. I shall never forget it." She ordered another liqueur and swallowed it at a gulp. The orchestra was playing a lively Viennese waltz, to which she beat time with her nodding head, and when the music ceased the dull boom of the cannon could be heard in the distance.

"Don't forget to take a bottle of mineral water with you," was the waiter's parting counsel. "The pump water is not fit to drink."

There was central heating in the hotel, but I had to grip the radiator in my room in order to be sure of the fact; and as it was too cold to read or write I went to bed early. Before I retired I opened the door of my wardrobe, so that it might serve as a screen at the head of the bed and break the force of any bullet that might stray through the window.

The next day I was conducted through the streets in which the pogrom had taken place. The traces of the great outrage were still evident in abundance. There were cracked and broken windows, jagged gaps in iron shutters that had been forced open with a bayonet, heaps of débris still lying on the floors of some looted shops, which their owners had not the heart to clear away. Some of the windows were pasted over with paper, others were covered with boards. Many shops were still closed; others were beginning to re-open with small stocks. A widow who had been bereft of her husband in the war had lost her entire fortune of 30,000 crowns through the plundering of her business. "But at least I am alive", she added. Next door there was a shop-keeper who had fought through the war and had defended himself in the pogrom, but his wife had died of fright.

Stories of assault, robbery, rape, and massacre assailed my ears from every side as we continued our way through the Jewish quarter, but my fingers were so numbed with the cold that they could not record a tithe of what I heard. Yet everything paled into nothingness when I came into the street where blocks of houses had been wilfully burned to the ground by means of petroleum brought on military lorries; all that remained were portions of brick walls and the damning charred patch on the front of each house, showing where the firebrand had been laid. A synagogue, too, had been utterly demolished, with its priceless treasures of scrolls of the Law, and ritual ornaments of gold and silver, handed down by the exiles from medieval Spain, and two other synagogues had been despoiled, and damaged and robbed even of their charity boxes. A number of dejected yet expectant folk followed in our train, each anxious to tell his tale of sorrow.

We visited one of the Jewish soup-kitchens at the busiest hour: the stairs were crowded with a hungry throng, old and young, men and women, many in mere rags tied with string. Over two thousand persons were fed there daily, with bread, soup and vegetables, and twice a week with meat also. Many of them, two months ago, were healthy burghers, with servants of their own; now they were reduced to beggary, but were treated more kindly than ever beggars were. But there seemed not the least prospect that they would ever receive compensation for the losses they had sustained, although the Polish troops had taken the leading part in the pogrom with the aid of machine-guns and hand-grenades. For the Polish military authorities affected to justify the pogrom as a punitive expedition against the Jews for their having, under the dictates of prudence, declared neutrality in the conflict between Poles and Ukrainians. The Jews had also dared to exercise the right of self-determination, and their presumption was visited with swift and savage punishment.

I lunched in a restaurant which had once enjoyed great popularity, but that was before the pogrom. It had been looted from end to end, every scrap of food, every table and chair, even the salt-cellars and ash-trays had been taken away, and the huge mirror on the wall had been so hacked that little remained after the jagged bits had been cut away. The once jovial proprietor had become a monument of melancholy, and many of the former guests went to the soup-kitchen. "As soon as the war is over—*our* war ", said the proprietor, " I am going to England or Palestine. Who can stop in Poland? I want to live in peace, not in terror ".

Later in the day I was in the Café Warszawa, among a group of friends who narrated their personal experiences of the pogrom. There were a few dim gas-jets, by whose light I took notes. Suddenly I heard a command: " Nobody shall leave the premises! "

A youthful non-commissioned officer with three soldiers had entered and was carrying out what he called a " revision ". The officer said he was in search of deserters and insisted on examining everybody's documents of identity. Similar bands of soldiers had forced their way into this café, and into others too, upon a similar pretence. None of them had ever produced a warrant of authorisation, but all were ready to accept a bribe to withdraw. The proprietor's brother protested against this repeated annoyance of innocent guests. The youthful officer at once declared him arrested for having insulted the Polish Army, and the three loutish legionaries, with fixed bayonets, surrounded their prisoner. The officer completed the examination of the guests, and stared vacantly at the manifold visas on my British passport. But scarcely had he marched off with his prisoner than the proprietor hastened below into the cellar and came back with a bottle of cognac, which he gave to a waiter. The latter rushed out into the darkness, and within two minutes returned with the liberated prisoner smiling.

"Isn't it a comedy? " remarked one of the guests.

" A comedy! " indignantly retorted a tall man with up-turned black moustache, who was described to me as a police official in mufti. " They had no warrant to make a search, and you encourage them by corruption! " " But if they hadn't accepted the cognac, you would have said they had a warrant", replied the proprietor, "and then Heaven knows when I should have seen my brother again".

The next day I called upon the British members of the Allied Mission, who were staying at the Potocki Palace. As they had been sent by the Council of the Peace Conference to mediate between the Poles and Ukrainians, their living as guests of the Poles obviously prejudiced them as arbitrators in the eyes of the Ukrainians, and offered no good augury for the success of their negotiations. There were two stolid sentries at the outer gate and a grey-bearded, imposing-looking officer in the hall. I obtained ready access to the British officers, with one of whom I had already spoken before in Warsaw, and for nearly two hours we discussed the wrongs of the Jews in Poland and the rights they demanded, until the arrival was announced of the Ukrainian delegates, who had come to negotiate an armistice. But meanwhile the cannons continued to boom away unabated.

I stayed in Lemberg three days and a half, and with each succeeding day I became more and more penetrated with the sense of depression that held everybody in thrall. The bitter, biting cold, the dirt and darkness, the famine prices, the lack of amusement—the orchestra at the Krakowski formed the sole entertainment in the city—the isolation from the outside world, the general insecurity, the ceaseless bombardment, all contributed to plunge the inhabitants into the abyss of despair. The liberty of small nations, the right of self-determination! What a mockery these words sounded to the innocent sufferers of Lemberg! "If only Wilson would come here for a short time!" they sighed.

At noon on the fourth day I took a two-horsed " droschke " and was driven through a violent snowstorm to the station. I caught a glimpse once more of battered buildings and broken windows, of saddened faces and bruised souls. The snowflakes scudded through the gaping, grimy windows of the booking-hall, and I sought refuge in the welcome train.

Chapter VI

POLISH JEWRY BETWEEN THE WARS

I

IT WAS nearly fourteen years since my first visit to Poland, and although I had been there in the meantime I looked forward to the renewal of its acquaintance with eagerness because I was anxious to compare its present conditions with my first impressions and to see what measure of progress had taken place. My first visit was occasioned by the outbreak of pogroms and other outrages against the Jews, with which the Poles had celebrated their newly-won independence, and which I went to investigate and describe. The new Republic was then in a state of genesis and chaos, almost literally "without form and void", for the Government in Warsaw had not yet been able to impose its authority over all elements in the capital, let alone over the territory that had just shaken off the Austrian yoke and over the other regions. In Warsaw there was still a German inscription on the walls of the Hotel Bristol, where I stayed; and within there was a military guard day and night on the landing outside the suite of M. Paderewski, who appeared to believe that fate required he should exchange the role of pianist for that of politician and try to produce harmony in the turbulent State. It was a time of kaleidoscopic and cataclysmic changes, when Europe was still trembling after all the carnage and upheaval, when all sorts of schemes for its recovery were feverishly discussed in conferences and Cabinets, and the Jews were wondering whether they were indeed going to enjoy the blessings of peace, equality, and liberty, that had been trumpeted forth as the objects of the Great War.

After an interval of fourteen years it was not too soon to see whether promises and pledges that had been undertaken as international obligations were fulfilled, and whether hopes and dreams that had been indulged in were realised. As I stood in the entrance-hall of the hotel I felt the first faint premonitions of the disappointment and disillusion that I was soon to experience to the full. The place looked dingy and unusually quiet; gone were the bustle and clamour of former years; the restaurant that had been the scene of such tumultuous feastings and political palavers was closed, and there were just a few tables in the foyer for those who still clung to old habits and wished to eat there. The air of depression could almost be felt. It haunted me throughout my stay in the country.

As I sauntered past the great Pilsudski Square, where a catch-penny open-air exhibition, rendered alluring by a raucous radio, had been set up to raise funds for a national air force, I recollected that the imposing, ornate bulk of a Russian church had once dominated the site and that it had been razed to the ground so that the national susceptibilities of the new Republicans should not be ruffled by any reminder of the once dreaded Muscovite despotism. Facing the square was the long terrace of the Café Europeeski, which was crowded in the early evening with an animated throng, of whom ninety per cent. at least were Jews, and who always forgathered there with the regularity of clock-work. They were almost all well dressed, and many of the women presented striking and elegant figures, exhaling ravishing perfumes, and with their cheeks, lips, and finger-nails all tinted the fashionable roseate hue. They did not seem on the surface to share or reflect the prevalent distress, vividly embodied by some hungry-looking creatures who slouched along the pavement; but sitting in the café and talking for hours over a glass of tea or an orangeade was their sole amusement, I was told, and a cheap and harmless way of spending an evening. Both socially and intellectually it was an interesting crowd, for it included various influential and popular personages—Parliamentary deputies and communal leaders, authors and journalists, actors and artists, bankers and lawyers, with a sprinkling of Government officials, military officers wearing all their medals and ribbons, and miscellaneous foreigners. Important visitors from other parts of Poland used the café as their regular rendezvous, so that it was a clearing house of intelligence and a lively news exchange. Here I was able to gather much of the information that I wanted, but I did not by any means limit myself to talks only with the people whom I met there.

Polish Jewry, like Poland itself, had undergone various changes since the plenipotentiaries of the new State had reluctantly appended their signatures to the Minorities Treaty—the first of its kind—the need for which had been so cogently expounded in the historic letter of M. Clémenceau. The object of that Treaty was to secure for the Jews, as for the other racial and national minorities, the enjoyment of just the same civil and political rights as would be exercised by the Poles themselves, and was designed to prevent any legislative enactment or administrative practice that might be prejudicial to Jewish interests. The astutest legal minds, Jewish and non-Jewish, fortified with historical precedents and familiar with the quibbles and trickery whereby for over thirty years Rumania had flouted her obligations under the Treaty of Berlin, had framed the articles of the Minorities Treaty in terms that were confidently believed to ensure perfect equality of treatment for the Jews in Poland. How had they fared under the blessings of that Treaty?

The Jews were represented in the first *Seym* by thirty-five deputies of their own, who were unable to put up a strong fight against anti-Jewish tendencies, which became manifest from the very beginning. Since then, owing to parliamentary reforms effected by the Government with a view to weakening the political power of the racial minorities, Jewish representation in the *Seym* had been reduced to ten.[1] Had the Jewish deputies always been united, they might have been successful in securing redress for the grievances of their people. But unfortunately they were divided from the very outset by differences both acute and complex, partly because of their dissonant standpoints within the Jewish community, and partly because of the varied outlook and mentality generated by the different regions from which they originated. Thus, not only were there conflicts between the Zionists, the "Bundists" (or Socialists), the "Volkists" (or anti-Palestinian nationalists), the Agudists (anti-Zionists, super-orthodox), and the assimilators (who wished to fuse quietly with the Poles, without leaving a Jewish trace behind), but the Zionists themselves were divided as between Congress Poland and Galicia, for those living in the latter territory, being neighbours of the Ukrainians (who were treated by the Government as potential insurrectionists), had contrary views on the question of minorities' policy to those of their fellow-Zionists in Warsaw. Hence the Jewish deputies often expended more energy, eloquence, and bitterness, in attacking one another than in combating the common cause of all their woes. Such was still the state of affairs, even though the economic situation of the Jews had now become more catastrophic and even more tragic than before.

II

Bad as conditions were among the population in general, I was assured by a member of the *Seym* that they were infinitely worse among the Jews. Not only had the Jews the utmost difficulty to make even a scanty living, not only were they taxed to an intolerable degree, but they were bereft of all hope of any betterment, for they suffered from the conviction that their economic plight was the result of the Government's carefully calculated policy. Various Ministers of the Government had ingeniously devised laws, which,

[1] It was later reduced to five in a smaller *Seym*.

A Newsvendor in Warsaw

A Duologue in Warsaw Park

Hassidim in Cracow

though apparently based on purely objective and economic considerations, and free from any relation to religious or racial factors, were nevertheless so framed and so applied as to involve the most galling discrimination against the Jews and to inflict upon them the heaviest burden. It was as though there were a conspiracy, determined though unavowed, to oust the Jew from all positions in the economic life of the country and to reduce him to utter impotence, if not ruin. That was a summary of the position that I heard in the first few moments, and throughout the next few weeks I heard it repeated with mournful monotony like a doleful refrain, with ever new illustrations, in every town that I visited.

There were grievances among all sections of the community—the commercial element, the artisans, the professional people, the students, and those who were concerned particularly with communal and public affairs. The most crying evil among the large business class, who were estimated to have in their hands 80 per cent. of all trade in Poland, was the disproportionate burden of taxation that they had to bear. There was no law imposing higher taxes upon Jews than upon non-Jews, but the fiscal system was so arranged that the urban population, although forming only a fourth of the total population, had to provide over half of the public revenue, and, as the Jews constituted a third of the urban population whilst forming only a tenth of the total population, they had to pay an inordinate share of the State's income, estimated at from twenty to thirty per cent. It was notorious that the tax paid by the Jewish business-man was on the average five times as much as that paid by the Polish tradesman, even though they were neighbours and the Jew might have only a small business as compared with that of the Pole. And, as though to add insult to injury, the tax was exacted from the Jews in the most inconsiderate and ruthless manner, no matter how hard it was to pay. A similar discrimination prevailed in connection with the State monopolies. In 1918, for instance, 90 per cent. of the tobacco trade, wholesale and retail, was in Jewish hands. But after the Polish Government took over the monopoly it reorganised the trade four times, and by the summer of 1931 the number of Jews given licences for the wholesale trade had been reduced to 38 out of a total of 750. The result of the latest reorganisation was that the total number of wholesale firms had been brought down to 360, of which Jews formed only six! There was also a reorganisation in the salt trade, which was likewise a monopoly, the number of Jews engaged in it having been reduced from 62 to 14 per cent.

There were two other grievances of the large commercial class—the Sunday closing law and the scanty credit given to Jews by the State banks. The oppressiveness of the Sunday closing law was felt all the more acutely because, as the Jews rested two days a week (or nearly two and a half days in winter when the Sabbath begins on Friday afternoon) as well as on the numerous Jewish and Christian holy days, they were compelled to be idle over one-third of the year. Repeated representations had been made to the Government to allow a relaxation of the law, and official promises of concessions were made from time to time, but the law continued to be applied with unremitting rigour. There were two Government banks that granted credits, but of the total amount advanced only 5 per cent. was granted to commerce, and of that the Jews received the merest trifle. In 1931 the Bank Polski advanced 700 million zloty in discount credits, but the Jews received less than two million zloty; and whilst the Peasants' Credit Co-operatives were given 10 million zloty of Government money, the Jewish co-operatives were not favoured with a single groschen.

Not only the Jewish tradesmen but the Jewish artisans too, who formed two-thirds of all the artisans of the country, were to be crushed. The weapon for this purpose was the Guild Law passed in 1927, which obliged all masters who wished to take apprentices to pass examinations, and their apprentices to take supplementary courses. This law was perhaps not directly aimed against the Jews, but in practice it barred their way to manual occupations, as it required master artisans to submit to tests not merely in their craft but also in Polish history, literature, and geography, to attend in particular centres, and to pay a fee. Imagine a middle-aged Jewish plumber or carpenter in some remote little town, who had his work cut out just to make a living, poring over the text-books of history and literature and then travelling to a strange city to present himself in an examination-hall like a young student. No wonder that only six per cent. of the Jewish master artisans passed the ordeal. The law also provided for the establishment of Artisans' Chambers to watch over the interests of each branch of industry, but although the Jews formed the majority of artisans in most districts the Chambers were so constituted as to consist of three-fifths Christians and two-fifths Jews. The injustice of this arrangement was most glaring in the large cities, such as Warsaw, Bialystok, and Vilna, where the registered Jewish artisans greatly outnumbered the Poles.[1]

The entry of the young Jew into a manual trade through a technical school was also rendered exceedingly difficult. In the Government technical schools the Jews formed only five per cent. of the students, but half of them had succeeded in getting only into commercial schools, whilst in the Municipal technical schools their number was still less, namely, only two per cent. On the other hand, in the private technical schools, to which admission could be obtained only by payment, the Jews formed over 20 per cent. of the students. There were also 34 Jewish technical schools, with a total register of 3,850 pupils, which received from the Government a subvention of 50,000 zloty. But this did not form more than one per cent. of all the sums devoted by the Government to technical education, despite the fact that the Jews provided, by means of the special supplementary tax to their trade licence, two-thirds of the 7 million zloty which the Government had at its disposal for this purpose. Nor

---

[1] In Warsaw there were 8,414 registered Jewish artisans against 6,278 Poles, in Bialystok there were 5,000 and 1,500 respectively, and in Vilna 2,800 and 1,900 respectively.

was it easy for the Jews to obtain State recognition for their technical schools. There was such a school in Vilna, belonging to the O.R.T.,[1] but although Polish inspectors admitted that the education was good the authorities refused to recognise the school, with the result that the pupils trained there had a difficulty later in finding positions. The obstruction on the part of the authorities was capricious and harassing, almost reminiscent of the old Tsarist days. Whenever the Jews applied for the recognition of a technical school they were requested to submit a plan of the building, the curriculum, and particulars of the staff; after waiting six months they were informed that they must send in a fresh application with a margin for comments; and after a further delay of six months they were told that the building was unsuitable, or some other objection, which could have been made months earlier, was solemnly advanced.

III

The grievances of the Jewish students in regard to the universities were more generally known than those relating to the technical schools, perhaps because the attacks to which they were exposed on the part of their Christian fellow-students did so much to advertise their wrongs; but the nature of their grievances was not so widely appreciated. At all the Universities a *numerus clausus* was enforced against the Jews, although it was not officially admitted. It was imposed most rigorously in the medical faculties, which Jews were most eager to enter, since they could thus qualify for a profession that would afterwards provide them with a livelihood; they were less keen to enter the faculties of arts and philosophy, where civil servants and teachers were trained, since the Government service was closed to them and they could not obtain appointments at Polish schools. In the medical faculties the Jews were limited to a propor-

[1] Russian initials standing for " Society for the promotion of trades and agriculture."

tion of about 10 per cent., and in most cases, so I was assured, those admitted had to make a payment of a few hundred dollars for the privilege, which was not required from any Pole, and which was not supposed to be known to the authorities.

Those who could not secure admission to the Universities were obliged to wander forth to other countries to obtain an academic education. The number of these exiles was about 10,000, dispersed in France, Belgium, Italy, Czecho-Slovakia, and other countries. There was a special society in Warsaw, under Government inspection, to procure travelling facilities for them, to assist them with advice, and above all to secure recognition for their foreign diplomas when they returned home. In Prague alone there were 1,000 Polish Jews studying medicine. In France there were some hundreds, but though they could not practise in that country they could get positions in the French colonies, and thus some of them had even wandered out to Madagascar. So many Jewish students had gone to the University of Tours to learn chemistry as a preliminary to taking medicine at another University, that when there were 200 of them the authorities at the Tours University decided to institute a medical course for their benefit, so as not to lose them. What a contrast to the treatment of Polish Jews in Poland itself and, above all, in Germany!

But when the young medicos returned to their native land their troubles began afresh. The society that looked after their welfare intervened on their behalf, so that they might be able to practise, but before they were admitted to registration (or "nostrification," as it was called) they had to submit to further examination. The process generally occupied two years, in the course of which they had to sit for as many as twenty-two examinations. Some years later the Government refused to endorse the diplomas of students obtained abroad.

I heard of the rather curious case of a Jewish doctor who had qualified abroad, and who, on his return to Poland, did not apply for the recognition of his degree but specialised in Roentgenology and was permitted to practise this in Lutsk, where he was the only specialist. All went well for several years until a Christian doctor, who was a qualified X-ray man, appeared on the scene. Thereupon the local authorities told the Jew that he must quit. He went to Warsaw to appeal against his eviction and secured a prolongation three or four times for six months at a time, until he was at last obliged to qualify as an ordinary doctor by studying medicine anew and submitting to the regulation series of examinations. "Such was the martyrology of the Roentgenologist!" observed my informant.

Jewish students who wanted to become lawyers also found their way obstructed owing to the large numbers already engaged in the profession. Among the 4,000 lawyers in Warsaw there were 1,000 Jews, but this number was rather less than the Jewish ratio of the population. In order to qualify it had always been necessary for the law student to have three years' practice in a clerical capacity in a law court, but very few Jews were appointed to such positions. Besides, owing to the abundance of lawyers, it was intended to suspend the admission of further aspirants, and thus to close another avenue to the Jewish intelligentsia.

IV

Whatever explanation the Government might offer to show that it was not responsible for the obstacles and annoyances that harassed the path of the Jewish student, it could not plead innocence in regard to the exclusion of Jews from the public service. When Galicia belonged to Austria Jews on the railway service formed 8 to 9 per cent., in the postal service 7 to 8 per cent., and in the State schools, as teachers, 4 to 5 per cent. But after Galicia was embodied in Poland, in all these branches they hardly made up one per cent., and even this consisted of survivals of former times. No new Jewish officials were appointed, and no new Jewish teacher could obtain a post in a Polish school. For some years Polish teachers' seminaries refused to admit Jewish students, thus preventing the qualification of Jews for teachers' positions. In the administrative department of the Polish Government there was hardly a single Jew. There were 10,000 Post Office savings-banks in the country, which derived 60 per cent. of their deposits from Jews, but there was not a single Jewish official among them all. It was significant that whereas every elementary school had to have a teacher of religion, in the majority of Jewish schools none was appointed, because the Government would have had to pay.

The Minorities Treaty stipulated that the Jews should receive " an equitable share " of the State funds available for educational, religious and charitable purposes. But, in point of fact, although they formed a tenth of the population, and contributed to the public revenue more than twice their due share, the total amount which they received for all purposes was only 200,000 zloty out of a budget of 3 milliard zloty. All requests that they made for an increase of the allowance to Jewish communities were rejected. On the other hand, steps were taken, by methods of communal re-organisation, to weaken the position and influence of the Jews in the municipalities. This was contrived by adding suburbs to certain towns so as to reduce the Jewish majority. To the question why were the Jews being driven out, the Government representative simply replied: " We cannot allow the Jews who form a state within a state, and form 90 per cent. of the tax-payers, to represent the city." This jerrymandering with the municipalities was serious enough in itself. But the Government went further: it interfered with the internal affairs of the Jewish community. It passed a law depriving those Jews of the franchise in their own community who were known to be lax in religious observance, a law that was open to all sorts of abuses and was diametrically opposed to the sound democratic principle—" no taxation without representation ". It insisted on seeing the budget of the Jewish community, and objected to any item of which it did not approve, although it gave the community the very merest pittance. It demanded the submission of the minutes of the meetings of the communal council, so that it might pry into their discussions. And it practically prescribed who should be the president of the community. For, as the " Agudas Yisroel " [1] was a staunch supporter of the Government, the latter in turn favoured the members of this party in the scramble for office, and even imposed an Agudist president upon a community with an anti-Agudist majority, as I found was the case in Czenstochowa. The Government even dissolved the elected Councils of the Jewish communities of Warsaw, Cracow, and Lemberg, and placed their affairs into the hands of a Jewish Commissioner appointed by itself.

With such an elaborate system for impoverishing, degrading, demoralising, and crushing the Jews, why should the Polish Government have been in favour of physical attacks? It could have achieved its purpose more subtly and securely by enactments and administrative regulations, and thus enjoyed the reputation of being a respectable Government opposed to pogroms.

V

The sorry plight of the Jews was not due merely to the Government's failure to fulfil its obligations under the Minorities Treaty, and to the various measures enacted or devised to undermine their position in every sphere of economic activity. It was also due to a combination of other causes with which the Government had nothing to do, such as the general world depression, the special conditions in Poland, the specific structure of the Jewish population, and the inability of the Jews to organise any adequate defence in their own interest. Let us consider each of these causes in turn.

[1] Organisation of ultra-orthodox congregations, founded in 1912.

The general cheapening of agrarian products had seriously affected the economic life of Poland, for three-fourths of its population lived on agriculture, and their buying capacity had been reduced almost to zero. Moreover, the decline in the purchasing power of other countries, the increased competition of foreign markets, especially of Russia, and the limitations imposed by various countries on imports, resulted in a heavy fall of Polish exports. This had a ruinous effect upon the timber trade, which, owing to Russian competition, had practically ceased. Similarly, owing to reduced importations by England, there had been a great decline in the export of ready-made clothing, which formerly employed thousands of Jewish families in Bialystok, Brzezin, and Ozorkow; and there had likewise been a big drop in the demand for gloves, which formerly occupied hundreds of families in Warsaw and Vilna.

The difficulties due to the special conditions in Poland arose from the fact that the country was composed of three regions, which were once parts of different economic units, and that the creation of a single economic organisation out of these parts was a slow and painful process. The internal situation derived scanty help from abroad, for comparatively little foreign capital flowed into Poland, which was thus unable to exploit its natural resources. Owing to the geographical and political situation of Poland, as well as the nationalist temper, a third of the budget was spent on the army, that is, it was used up without any direct benefit to the development of the country, and in order to provide the budget industry was ruined by heavy taxation. Even in comparatively good times, as in 1925, 90 per cent. of the population earned less than 200 zloty (about £8) per month, and subsequently earnings shrank tremendously.

There was an abnormal proportion of Jews engaged in trade and the business of distribution. Attempts were constantly made to divert them more to productive occupations, but with insufficient success. When goods manufactured in Lodz, Czenstochowa, and other cities, were consumed in large quantities in Turkestan, Siberia, and Persia, a great number of middlemen were wanted, and hence those belonging to this category were severely hit. Even those who were once the heroes of industry in Lodz, Bialystok, and Radom, had become borrowers from the communal loan societies and beneficiaries of the soup kitchens. Poverty was rampant throughout Galicia, and also in Vilna, even before the First World War: afterwards it became infinitely worse. The evil was aggravated in Galicia by the development of a large number of Ukrainian co-operatives, which provided the peasants with everything that they needed for their homes and farms, and which were officially organised by the educated Ukrainians, who were kept out of the civil service. A high official of these co-operatives boasted that the Jews had been driven away from more than a thousand villages.

Unfortunately there was no unified organised action among the Jews for the purpose of their own defence. There was a multiplicity of parties and groups, which were all striving to remedy the situation in their own way, but owing to the limited powers of each and the differences that divided almost all of them their efforts were largely futile. It was estimated in 1927 by the statistician, Jacob Lestschinsky, that there were one million too many Jews in Poland. A careful investigation then made showed that there were 100,000 Jewish families dependent on loans from the communal loan funds (*Kassen*), that is, more than one-fourth of the Jewish urban population applied for loans averaging not more than 100 zloty (about £4), and in the little towns as many as three-fourths of the Jewish population applied for them. The position became much more tragic a few years later, when there were Jewish communities and societies unable to distribute more than 5 to 10 zloty (about 4s. to 8s.) to each applicant. Nevertheless, one-half of the Jews in Warsaw, Lodz, Vilna, and Bialystok, and over two-thirds of those in Vilna, applied for this paltry assistance and were prepared to undergo all the humiliations involved. When kitchens were first opened for the unemployed, their benefits were sought by a large number of people who had always enjoyed the reputation of being well-to-do. Hunger had driven them forth into the streets, just as it had compelled many persons well-known in Jewish literary and artistic circles to apply for kitchen-cards. Nor, sad to relate, were those once given such cards always allowed to enjoy them, for, owing to the overwhelming numbers in need of help, certain kitchen committees decided that those who had cards one month could not have them the next.

"In the little towns people live on potatoes and wonders", reported a social worker. In one town there were only five families who had enough food for some weeks, whilst others always consumed what they earned the same day. In another town the only man who lived without care was a father, who received 38 zloty (about 22s.) a month as a pension for a son who was killed in the war of 1914–18. The committees in charge of the communal loan funds all pointed out that people previously well-off applied for loans of 50 to 75 zloty, although they had contributed such amounts and more when the funds were first opened. The abysmal poverty prevailing was revealed in a letter addressed to the Warsaw office of the Joint Distribution Committee, in which the local chairman wrote: "The 500 zloty (about £20) that we received this week enabled our townlet to revive again. . . . It made one's eyes which had become dim, light up again. We were able to fulfil the wishes of all who asked for money."

But for the loan funds the economic position would have been utterly desperate. These funds operated in 750 centres furnishing loans to 120,000 Jewish families, which might be said to represent 600,000 persons. Founded in 1920, these *Kassen* had a total capital of 10 million zloty, of which the Joint Distribution Committee provided about three-fifths, and they had a turnover of 20 million zloty. The Government recognised their value by contributing the sum of 10,000 dollars a year for a time, and by remitting the stamp duty on the I.O.U.'s, and 165 municipalities gave subventions averaging about 800 zloty. Unfortunately the Jews did not receive any benefit from the Government fund for the unemployed, as the law did not provide for the protection of small artisans and traders. But helpful as the loan funds were, their resources were utterly inadequate to the tremendous and imperious needs; and as aid from abroad had largely diminished in consequence of the depression in America, all sorts of evils inevitably resulted. Beggary was rampant throughout the land, suicide had spread among all classes, and numbers of the youth were driven by despair rather than conviction to the allurements of Communism.

Before the First World War and in the first years after it emigration formed the salvation of those who could leave the country and at any rate eased the pressure for those who remained behind. The natural increase among the Jews before the war was 50,000 a year, and such was the number that went abroad. But in the 'thirties, owing to the frontiers and ports of the once vaunted lands of hospitality being closed to immigrants, only about half that number were able to leave each year in quest of a new home, and hence the powerful and passionate longing to go to Palestine. Never before was the possibility of settlement in the Land of Israel more eagerly coveted: the receipt of an immigration certificate was prized more highly than a successful lottery-ticket, and the eyes and hearts of the Jewish youth were straining after Zion with fretful longing. But the gates of Zion were strictly watched by the Mandatory Power, the number admitted each year formed but a fraction of the myriads who were chafing to enter, and thus the problem of Polish Jewry threatened to become more desperate than ever. Little did they then dream that they were fated to be overwhelmed by a far more terrible catastrophe than all previous calamities that had afflicted them.

Chapter VII

THE WARSAW GHETTO

THE MOST distinguishing characteristic of Warsaw Jewry before the Second World War was its completeness. A community of over 300,000 souls, the largest Jewish agglomeration in the Old World, it had all the complexity, the comprehensiveness, and self-containedness of a little commonwealth. It had all sorts of institutions and organisations, not merely social, philanthropic, religious, educational and intellectual, but also political and economic, for politics and economics played great parts in the lives of the Jews in the Polish capital, and hence they had to have a variety of political parties and also of economic associations, of employers and employees, merchants and manufacturers, trade unions and co-operatives. The existence of this multiplicity of organisations implied a variety of views and tendencies and a frequent conflict of ideas, and also involved a corresponding multifariousness of expression, and consequently there were all kinds of organs of opinion. There were not only daily, weekly, and monthly papers, but also midday and evening journals; there were periodicals that catered specially for those enthusiastic about sport as well as for those interested in literature and drama; there were comic papers and illustrated ones; and they were all, with trifling exceptions, in Yiddish, the others being a daily in Polish and a pedagogical review in Hebrew. An attempt was made to revive a Hebrew daily, but though great zeal was displayed, the funds available were rather sparse, so it failed. The principal dailies, such as the *Haint* and *Moment*, were ably edited, containing the latest news and telegrams from all over the world, despatches from their own correspondents abroad, and special articles on topical questions, whilst the Friday issues provided extra literary fare—contributed by the leading figures in Yiddish journalism—for leisurely consumption during the Sabbath.

It was these journals that helped to furnish one of the striking features of the Warsaw Ghetto, namely, the newspaper stall. It was a primitive wooden stand rather than a kiosk; sometimes it was a little tumble-down cart or a miniature shed; but in every case it made such an attractive display of its wares that one paid little attention to the nature or design of the structure. The news-vendor was often so much absorbed in the contents of his papers that he seemed indifferent to custom, but the female keepers of these kiosks, of whom there were a goodly number, were more alert and seemed to sustain themselves incessantly with mugs of coffee and chunks of brown bread. These little newspaper stalls rather appealed to me as subjects for my camera, but on one occasion the picturesque owner, a sad and scholarly-looking fellow, walked away as soon as he noticed I wanted to photograph him.

"Why are you running away?" I asked him in a friendly tone.

"What!" he replied indignantly, "You want to exploit me and my misery in the papers for your profit? Never!"

His raised voice and angry gestures soon attracted a crowd of passers-by, so I hurried on.

The Ghetto presented a drab and dreary appearance of huge blocks of dwellings, honey-combed with dismal courts and alleys, upon which still dingier blocks of dwellings frowned. The entrance to each "house" was a ponderous gate of timber and iron, and within the gloomy doorway on the wall was a big frame with serried columns of names of all the tenants, but these were so numerous and difficult to decipher that it was easier to find whom you wanted by simply asking one of the groups of gossipers loitering near by. The lower strata of these blocks of houses were filled with endless rows of little shops, most of which seemed to be devoted to the supply of foodstuffs and drinks. There was a veritable multitude of shops selling mineral waters and ice-cream in the summer and tea and coffee in the winter, whilst the other shops specialised in fruit, cakes or sausages. These emporia of edibles were a distinguishing feature of the Jewish quarter, for in the other parts of the city they did not seem so numerous, or at least were not so closely congregated together. And as though they did not provide sufficient for the sustenance of the local population there were pedlars carrying baskets with buns, *beiglach* (crescent-shaped rolls), and other products of the pastrycook's art. There were hawkers with other wares too—cheap ties, combs, toys, paper-bags, socks, studs—all offered at ridiculous prices.

At least half of the Jews in the Nalevki and the other streets in the Ghetto wore the traditional orthodox garb— the long black coat, the black peaked cap, and top-boots, in addition to the natural accessories of beard and ear-locks. One would have thought that adherence to this exotic and conspicuous mode of dress would expose those who indulged in it to the jibes and jeers of the Poles, but a fashion that had been in vogue for centuries ceased apparently to attract attention. Besides, it was not this section of the Jewish population that aroused envy or antagonism but rather the progressive element, who, in dress and deportment, were indistinguishable from their Polish neighbours. But the orthodox womenfolk had no corresponding distinctiveness in the matter of attire: on the contrary, they affected the latest style, and it was quite a common phenomenon to see a gaberdined and top-booted husband, with cork-screw earlocks, demurely walking beside a lip-sticked dame in high-heeled patent shoes and silk stockings.

In many of the streets there were rows of *droschkies* with Jewish drivers—some with grizzled beards—perched patiently behind their sorry nags. These cosy carriages, whose open sides seemed to offer an irresistible temptation to enter them, were used not only for the conveyance of passengers, but also for the transport of all sorts of goods— piles of cardboard boxes, bundles of clothing, bedding, and even tables and chairs, with the accompanying "fare" exerting all his energy and ingenuity to prevent the load from slipping off. But in hard times the Jewish jarvey had often to wait many an hour before anybody rich enough invoked his services, even though the charge for a good distance was only a zloty (eight pence); and it was there-fore natural that he, like those engaged in trades or business, should ponder on the possibility of migrating to some other land. Once I hailed a Jewish driver and bade him take me to the Zionist Palestine Office, where intending emigrants to Palestine were examined and received their passports. Presently I noticed that he was driving in the wrong direc-tion, whereupon I nudged him in the back and asked him in Yiddish where he was going. "Forgive me", he said, "I was a little *vercholemt* (day-dreaming)".

"What were you dreaming about?" I asked.

"I was wondering whether it would be possible for me to get into *Eretz Israel*", he replied as he corrected his course.

"And what would you do there?" I continued.

"I would take my horse and droschky with me, of course," he answered in a tone of confidence that discouraged all further argument.

It was impossible to walk more than a dozen yards in some of the thoroughfares without being accosted for alms. The beggars were of different kinds: some were obviously hardened mendicants, who greeted you with a mixture of a smile and a whine, who never took "no" for an answer, and followed you until you gave them something. Others were timid, and had obviously been forced to this means of livelihood fairly recently. There were both male and female beggars, old and young, generally stationed in the same place, and occasionally hunting in groups, yet seldom venturing beyond the recognised boundaries of the Ghetto. But of all the beggars that I saw the one that made the most moving appeal to me did not stir an inch nor utter a syllable. He was a middle-aged man, in shabby genteel clothes, who stood mute and motionless against a wall, with a look of distress and utter despair on his famished cheeks that must have gone to the hearts of all passers-by who might have troubled to take notice of him. But what impressed me more painfully than any beggars were the numbers of abnormal creatures that I came across—the lame, dwarfs, and idiots, offspring of poverty and disease. I saw more feeble-minded people roaming about than in any other city, and it seemed nobody's business to look after them. Here and there an idiot who proved himself a nuisance was ordered away by a policeman. A woman who was obviously in a state of mental disorder frequently came to a restaurant that I visited. She was an angular and emaciated person of about fifty who dressed like a girl of twenty, and she no sooner sat down at a table than she began talking to herself so audibly that many persons turned round. But as she was a regular customer there, those who had seen her once did not trouble to turn round a second time when they heard her uttering her gibberish.

Far more distressing than the sight of these mental defectives was the spectacle presented by the slums in the Krochmalna and Ostrowski streets. Nowhere had I seen such dirt and misery, nowhere had I met with such a display of abject resignation. "Abandon hope, all ye who enter here!" might have been written in huge letters over every doorway. Your nostrils were at once assailed with the evil odours of the garbage in the gutters. The people were unwashed and unkempt, with little more than rags on their famished bodies: they were not clothed decently enough even to venture forth as beggars, yet the bare-footed children ran about happily enough as though theirs were a normal form of existence. There were dozens of petty little shops, selling mineral waters, decaying fruit, cakes, and similar wares, but the total capital of each shopkeeper was hardly more than a few zloty. The scene in the courts which one

H 113

entered through a gloomy alley was even more gloomy and depressing.

There were huge dwellings four to five stories high, sombre as prisons, with patches of the walls crumbling away. They each housed a few hundred families, far more than those whose names were written on the long columns of tickets in the grimy entrance. Tattered bedding hung over the window-sills, so that it was advisable to give the walls a wide berth, lest some verminous visitant alighted upon you. On a level with the ground and reaching lower still were the windows of the cellar-dwellings, dark insanitary hovels, which diffused an awful stench. On the steps of each dwelling were children of all ages, dirty yet cheerful, the older girls mothering the younger ones, whilst boys were romping about with a ball. One little girl told me that eleven people lived in the cellar that she was minding: her father was in hospital with cancer. From another cellar a woman, dishevelled and distraught, whined to me that her stove had been damaged over a week, her landlord would not put it right, and she was unable to cook: her baby lay listless on a ragged couch covered with flies. Through the open window of another cellar I saw a little child, with pallid cheeks, lying sick and forlorn on a bed. And everywhere there were swarms of children, growing so plentifully in this pestiferous quarter, within smelling distance of the huge shed in the middle of the court, which served as a depository for all the dust and garbage of all the surrounding dwellings, and which was cleared once a week and sometimes not even then.

A man who was selling cold drinks in the court told me that he had been evicted from his room, as he could not pay the rent, and he now slept on the staircase. He was a cadaverous individual, with a stubbly beard and blood-shot eyes. He had rigged up a wooden stand, on which his stock-in-trade consisted of a couple of large jugs with lumps of dirty ice, water from the pump near by, and a handful of cherries. He seemed to do a little business and was determined to fight on.

In some of the hovels on the street level there were bakeries, a smithy, an eating-house, and even a cow-shed, with a solitary and melancholy cow. Crowds of porters were lolling about in the alleys, husky fellows who seemed not to be particular how they kept body and soul together. It was a relief to get away again into a more salubrious atmosphere.

One of the saddest features of the poverty of the Warsaw Ghetto consisted of the number of young children and infants who were abandoned in the streets by their mothers. The deserted babies were mostly those of unmarried mothers, who left a note behind giving the name of the child, which was generally a sufficient indication of its Jewish origin. In cases where no note was left a special com-mission decided whether the child was Jewish on the basis of its appearance and the place of discovery, as some Jewish male babies were kept in concealment by their mothers and were not circumcised. The house for Jewish foundlings which was maintained by the Municipality, had nearly 250 children. The infants were kept there until their fifth year, when they were transferred to the Jewish Orphanage, an institution with 800 children, who were looked after until their sixteenth year. But very often a childless woman, in order to prevent the divorce which an orthodox husband might demand after ten years of sterility, would come to the Foundling Home and " order " a baby for a particular date months ahead. Such adoptive mothers came mostly from provincial towns, where the purpose of their trip to the capital could be explained quite plausibly as the prelude to a happy event. The husband sometimes believed that the child was his, or at least pretended to believe, and if the child was a boy he was doubly pleased, for he had a *kaddish*.[1] Occasionally the foundlings were very fortunate in the parents who chose them, but the antecedents of all who wished to adopt one were carefully investigated before their wish was gratified.

[1] The name of the prayer in memory of the dead, applied to the son who said it out of reverence for a parent.

The burden that lay upon the Council of the Jewish Community was probably greater than in any other Jewish centre in Europe, for the needs were great and growing, and the sources of income were steadily shrinking under the economic scourge. The cares of the Council included not only religious institutions such as the synagogues, but also schools, elementary and technical, cemeteries, and various branches of social welfare. Interest in its affairs was perennially keen, and the election of a new Council was always attended by considerable excitement and agitation, the various parties energetically competing for the support of the voters. The Council consisted of fifty members, of whom the majority were a coalition made up of 22 members of the Agudas Israel and eight "Folkists" and Democrats, whilst the minority of 20 consisted of Zionists of different shades. The meetings were often the scene of turbulence, for feeling between the parties ran high, but on the night of my visit the debate, though animated, was fairly decorous.

When I arrived at the entrance of the building which contained the Council Chamber, numerous offices, and a most interesting museum, I was surrounded by a swarm of persons who wanted a "*Gast-Karte*" (visitor's ticket), for admission to the council meeting was only by ticket and the number issued was limited. Three officials at the main door exercised strict control. After passing them and ascending a broad staircase to the first floor, I was challenged again by two officials seated outside the door of the Council Chamber, and then a little red-bearded man with a black skull-cap appeared and ushered me in. It was a very large and lofty room, with a platform at one end, on which sat the chairman with assessors at a table, whilst facing him were the members of the Council, and behind the latter sat the public. To the right of the chairman stood a young man, dark and clean-shaven, before a high desk, holding forth with fiery eloquence; and on his left were a number of pressmen at a table, writing and yawning. The members of the Council sat at little tables covered with green paper, some taking notes, the others just listening. Most of them were bearded, and there were a few venerable types, but there were also many men in the early thirties. On the extreme right of the chairman was a table at which the president and the members of the Executive were seated. More than half of all those present wore hats, and others skull-caps. The public, who were separated from the councillors by a wooden barrier, were mostly young and middle-aged men, who followed the proceedings intently and often applauded with their hands and voices.

The subject of discussion was the budget, which had been introduced by the President, an Agudist, two weeks before, and which had aroused much passion owing to proposals for the reduction of the salaries of officials and teachers and for the appointment of a batch of new Rabbis.

The councillor who was speaking when I entered was a member of the Poale Zion (Zionist Socialist party). He protested furiously against the reduction in salaries and the appointment of new Rabbis, as well as against the abolition of grants for the festivals and of subsidies to teachers for tram expenses. He attributed the economic troubles and anti-Semitism itself to the capitalist régime, and declared that all evils would cease with the advent of a new social order. He demanded that the rich should pay more, not that people with a lower income than was taxed before should now be subjected to the communal tax. He spoke with ardour and gesticulation, and banged the desk so hard at the end of each sentence that his final words could not be understood. After speaking nearly half an hour, he was warned by the chairman that he had only another five minutes. The chairman rang his bell, but the tempestuous orator went on for another quarter-of-an-hour, during which he exchanged many passages with members of all parties—Agudists, Zionists, and the president himself.

He was followed by quite a different type, a Rabbi with a black overgrown beard, showing a fraction of pale face, with large spectacles on a small nose. He wore a long black coat, black cap and top boots, and was armed with a sheaf of notes. He spoke in a loud resonant voice, energetically defending the budget proposals, and explaining that the reductions of salaries were to be preferred to the reduction of staff. So bad was the situation that the executive had been considering the closing of certain schools (whereupon there were cries from the Zionists: " Is that how you would spread the Torah?"). He retorted that they were all for the Torah: upon that was based the whole of their philosophy: that was the path of historic truth, not the path described by the previous Socialist speaker. He grew hot as he advanced in his argument, mopped his brow, and wiped his spectacles, and at length he was followed by a burly, genial fellow, who was a contrast to both of the preceding speakers. He was a popular shop-keeper of about sixty, with a strong sense of humour, and he roused the applause of the public when he exclaimed that the best thing that they could with the budget was to burn it. " *Verbrennen!* " he shouted, holding a copy of the printed budget aloft, whilst the public laughed and clapped. He told a few stories and jokes which had only the remotest bearing on the subject, but he helped to keep the assembly in a cheerful mood and was rewarded with an ovation when he stepped down from the platform, and the meeting was over.

The debate had lasted three hours, but many more hours of verbal strife and even weeks of deliberation, negotiation, and recrimination had to elapse before the budget was finally passed.

* * * * *

The trials of the Jews under Polish rule seemed of very little account in comparison with the stupendous tragedy that overwhelmed them when Poland was invaded by the Germans in the autumn of 1939, for they were singled out for the most horrible and inhuman treatment. They were the victims of a colossal crime unprecedented in the history of mankind. They were condemned to suffer all forms of oppression and barbarism, which culminated in their extermination in gigantic crematoria in concentration camps, and which reduced their numbers to about one twenty-fifth. Soon after the invasion the Jews in all the large cities were crowded together and immured in Ghettos surrounded by high concrete walls, from where, after months of terrorism, slave-labour, and starvation, they were deported in thousands daily to death-camps.

But not all Jews allowed themselves to be led like lambs to the slaughter. In several cities bands of spirited young Jews, realising that they were doomed in any case, resolved to fight for their lives and contrived to get weapons with which they destroyed very many of their torturers. The most spectacular resistance was that organised in the Warsaw Ghetto, where the Jews waged their first battle against the Nazis in January, 1943, and a thousand of them were mown down by tanks. But the most imposing demonstration of Jewish heroism was made in the battle of the Warsaw Ghetto that began in the middle of the following April and continued for six weeks. It was a desperate struggle against overwhelming odds, in which half-starved and poorly armed men and women fought like fiends against six thousand ferocious Nazi storm-troopers equipped with cannons, flame-throwers, armoured cars, and even aeroplanes dropping incendiary bombs. The outcome was inevitable. Thousands were killed on both sides; thousands of Jews escaped to the nearest forests to join the Polish partisans; but the Nazis triumphed, and 20,000 Jews were driven off to the gas-chambers. It was a fight that will for ever form a glorious epic in the annals of Jewish martyrdom. The memory of the heroes is honoured and perpetuated by an imposing symbolic monument erected on the site of their last stand. The Jewish community of Warsaw has been reduced to a shrivelled skeleton of its former self. Before the days of Hitler it numbered over 300,000 souls; now it contains only about four thousand.

Chapter VIII

PROVINCIAL JEWRIES OF POLAND

I.—CRACOW

OUTWARDLY CRACOW did not seem to have changed at all since I had been there fourteen years before. It looked as old, picturesque, and romantic as ever, and I was glad to renew my fading memories of the mouldering walls of its ancient buildings, to stroll once again in its pleasant leafy promenades, and to hear the curious trumpet from the clock-tower on the animated and spacious Rynek.

At the corner of the Slawkowska Street there is a striking reminder of the Ghetto that once began there—a huge chain fixed to the wall, which in former ages was drawn right across in order to keep out any potential troublers of Israel. But the new generation knew how to defend itself, and Jew-baiting had lost its former popularity. The religious Jews still clung to their quaint mediaeval garb, which could easily be discerned at a distance—the long black gaberdine, top-boots, and flat plush hat; and as you approached you noticed that some of them had the bottom of their trousers tucked into their black socks, and that black ringlets (*Peoth*) adorned their cheeks. These ringlets were worn in two different styles: the disciples of the revered Gerer Rabbi,[1] whose name was one to conjure with among the Hassidim, trained theirs to droop behind the ears, whilst the pietists

[1] Title borne by the most venerated Hassidic Rabbi in Poland, derived from Gora (Ger) Kalvarija, near Warsaw, where the founder of this Rabbinical dynasty, R. Isaac Meyer ben Israel, flourished in the middle of the 19th century. The latter's grandson, R. Arye Loeb b. Abraham Mordecai, who flourished between the two wars, had over 100,000 followers.

who did not belong to any particular conventicle displayed them alongside the lobe.

A friend conducted me first to the "Remo" synagogue, so called because it was built in the middle of the sixteenth century by the father of the celebrated Rabbinical commentator, Moses Isserles, but as it was undergoing repairs it was closed to visitors. Adjoining it, however, I saw the old cemetery, where lay interred the remains of that mediaeval luminary, as well as those of his father, his brother-in-law, and one or two other members of his family, their tombstones standing close to each other in a railed enclosure. The grave of Rabbi Moses Isserles was the scene of a vast pilgrimage that took place every "*Lag Ba' Omer*,"[1] tens of thousands of devotees thronging from all the neighbouring towns and leaving behind documentary evidence of their visit, for they stuck little folded petitions into the crevices of the sculptured filigree of the tombstone. At the foot and all over on the ground there were accumulated layers of such pellets, white, yellowed, or encrusted with dirt—a multitude of mute witnesses to the widespread faith in the Rabbi's virtue as a mediator with the Almighty. In front of the tombstone were two old men praying and shaking their bodies vigorously, apparently not content with their written petitions.

Close by was a much older synagogue, in fact the oldest in Cracow. It dated from the fourteenth century, and its outer walls were literally black with age. Its foundations were far below the street level, for as it was situated near a rather low church, and the law would not allow a Jewish place of worship to rise to the height of a Christian one, the builders were obliged to begin far down, and so the entrance was reached by descending a flight of stone steps. The beadle made me pay for a ticket of admission, for the shrine was regarded as an antiquity. The interior, with its stone floor and lofty Gothic ceiling, supported by stone pillars,

[1] A minor festival in May, commemorating the cessation of an epidemic among the pupils of a great Palestinian Rabbi, Akiba ben Joseph (50—135 C.E.).

was rather sombre and depressing, and on the walls could be seen a sort of frieze. On the *Almemar* (cantor's dais) there was a large wrought-iron candelabra, and affixed to one of the walls there was another iron candelabra adorned with a figure of a man's head, an "image" which, so the beadle explained, the Rabbis, despite the Second Commandment, suffered to remain because it was unique.

In front of the Ark there hung a heavy brocade curtain, to which a legend attached. It was made of a piece of fabric that was said to have belonged to a Jewish bride who wished to get married on a Friday. According to the story, a Rabbi in the middle ages forbade weddings on a Friday, on the ground that the festivities might be prolonged and thus entail a breach of the Sabbath; but a certain young couple defied prohibition, and the nuptial celebrations lasted until the Sabbath, when the house and all the merrymakers were swallowed up by the earth as an act of retribution. To this day there is an enclosed plot of land in the Casimir quarter, on which grass and weeds grew wild, and which is reputed to be the site of that awesome disaster.

The perpetual light in front of the Ark was not red as in most synagogues, but white, because a red light was used in Catholic churches. At the foot of the steps to the Ark was a small lectern for the use of the cantor on week-days, for service was held there all the year round, even in the depth of winter, although the building was not heated, and there was never a shortage of worshippers. There was no gallery for women, but the latter were accommodated in a section that was divided off by a wall with small low windows covered with a flimsy curtain. I jokingly remarked to the beadle that the curtains were not adequate enough, and that the men might catch a glimpse of the ladies and *vice-versa*, to which he replied: "Well, you must not grudge them a look".

He showed me as curiosities of the shrine two old manuscript prayer-books, written entirely on parchment, which had grown yellow and even black with the centuries: one contained all the poetical supplications of the festivals, and both were illustrated with primitive illuminations. They were probably about five hundred years old.

After leaving the synagogue we went through a narrow small street and heard the sing-song of Talmudic disputation. We soon reached the open window of a humble ground-floor seminary, where a group of young students, with black hats and ear-locks, were listening to the argumentative sing-song of a broad-backed Rabbi in a black skull-cap. One or two students were asleep, another was stretching his arms with boredom, others were listless, and only those immediately under the preceptor's eye showed any attention.

From a neighbouring house came another sing-song in childish treble: here it was not the Talmud but the Torah that was being studied. And not many yards away I came to quite a different type of educational institution. It was a large Hebrew *Gymnasium*, built in 1930, which enjoyed the "public rights" of a Polish high school, and where secular subjects, except Polish history, geography, and literature, were taught in Hebrew. The students were streaming out, wearing a blue-white stripe on their caps and their shoulders, and displaying thin strips of silver thread to denote their class.

II.—LWOW

As I entered a taxicab outside the railway station at seven in the morning to drive to my hotel, I could not help recalling and contrasting the very different circumstances in which I had last visited what was then called the city of Lemberg. It was early in January, 1919, when I travelled all night from Cracow in an overcrowded train, deeming myself fortunate to have found a corner place, even though the upholstering had gone from the seat and I had to use my attaché case to replace it. But this time I had travelled comfortably in a sleeping car, and arrived on a fine summer's morning. There were trams and taxicabs in plenty, and everywhere flags were flying, for on the previous day there had been an international motor race. I went to the same hotel as before and found that it had been improved beyond recognition. Then it was dirty and dilapidated, with no light at night except that of candles in beer-bottles. Now it was resplendent with electric illuminations, in which the brass buttons on the page-boys' jackets twinkled with unusual lustre.

The Karl Ludwig Ulica had been changed to Legionska, as one of the results of the war, but the Jews who were promenading along it seemed to be just the same, with the same long black coats and black plush hats, from which depended corkscrew curls. Accompanied by a friend, I first went to the Jewish quarter, to see whether the synagogue and houses that had been burned down in the terrible pogrom of November 1918, had been rebuilt. I found that the site had been left waste owing to the lack of money—a mute witness to the racial hatred and destructive passions aroused by the war. Jewish shops were everywhere in abundance, for Jews formed a third of the population, but they all complained of bad trade.

In the Jewish open-air market there were hundreds of stall-keepers or hawkers, selling all sorts of things—decaying fruits, vegetables, rice, caps, ties, boots, remnants of stuff, and second-hand bicycles. There seemed to be far more sellers than buyers, and nobody's stock could have been worth more than a few shillings. In one street there were several artisans—some cobblers, a bookbinder, and a watchmaker—plying their trade on the pavement, for the day was warm; and close by was a vendor of Hebrew books and of fringes for *taleithim* (praying shawls), which a venerable greybeard was fingering with a critical eye. I took a snapshot of one of the cobblers, who sold me the right to photograph him at work for the price of a bottle of beer; and presently I found myself surrounded by a motley crew of beggars and cripples and dwarfs of both sexes, all wretchedly clad, mostly in rags, and some literally in sackcloth. Nowhere had I seen so many misbegotten specimens of humanity within so small an area.

Tradition still held powerful sway in this region, embodied in the sweeping gaberdines, shiny and threadbare, worn by the middle-aged and greybeards, who trudged along in heavy top-boots beneath the broiling sun, occasionally revealing the fringes of their four-cornered garment. And in strange contrast to these exemplars of religious piety were the porters, sturdy, unkempt louts, with a coil of rope around their neck—the sign of their trade—standing at corners or near a hand-cart, waiting patiently for any job.

As we walked along the busy thoroughfare, and I stopped to point my camera at a salesman of shoes, the latter asked me whether the picture was intended for America. "Perhaps," I replied, whereupon he said: "I wish you could pack me in and take me there. That is, indeed, a fortunate country."

My companion told me that a large number of the Jews of Lwow still received remittances from America: otherwise they could not live. A man with a marriageable daughter who had relations in America stood a much better chance of finding a son-in-law.

In a dingy square there was a large number of motor-buses with scores of Jews swarming around them. Before the First World War the Jews from the outlying townlets—Zolkiev, Tartakow, and others—used to come into the city by cart or slow train, now they travelled by the popular motor-bus for a small fare in order to buy a basketful of wares, which they took back for sale. All these motor-buses, I learned, belonged to Jews; they were rather small, somewhat like a diligence, and were all provided with a Jewish driver. Every passenger seemed to be surrounded by half-a-dozen friends, and the hubbub and excitement that reigned could hardly have been more tumultuous if those vehicles had been bound for some distant country instead of a village in the vicinity. The trade depression was causing them keen anxiety, for the Ukrainians were now proving dangerous rivals to the Jews in many branches of business, especially in the rural districts. For as the Jews were loyal citizens of Poland, the Ukrainians, in their annoyance, were doing their utmost to drive them to the wall. They had established an extensive and successful co-operative organisation, particularly for the export of dairy produce; and the young Ukrainians (many of them educated in Prague), who were unable to find an outlet in Government service, were devoting their abilities to commerce.

In the evening I was taken to a Jewish café, which seemed to be the resort of all classes and sections of the community, seated at different tables and distributed in different parts. There were business people at one table, lawyers at another, Zionists at a third (distinguished by a little flag with the "shield of David"), chess-players at the next, and speculators further on. In a separate room we came across a party of card-players, who, owing to the heat, were sitting in their shirt-sleeves, whilst others were poring over newspapers. Another door led to a chamber with subdued and variegated lights dimly disclosing a bar and reflected in the polished surface of the parquetry, on which the hired "hostesses" in jet-black were dancing with the gilded youths, one of whom smilingly greeted me with *Shalom* over the gleaming shoulder of his clinging partner.

Seated at a table in front of the café, remote from the various temptations within, my companion, who was joined by some friends, told me of the bleak, blank prospect that faced the Jews of Galicia. Active anti-Semitism was confined mostly to the students, but the Government pursued a subtle and systematic policy which was far more devastating than any attack. It kept Jews out of the civil service, refused to appoint any as teachers in Polish schools, and withheld from them all contracts for military and other supplies, which amounted to vast sums every year. Everywhere there was a passionate desire, on the part of old and young, to emigrate to Palestine, and only recently a party of two hundred had gone out to visit the country and

study the possibilities of settlement. But as the prospects
of emigration, whether to Palestine or any other land, were
limited, many young Jews were perforce lending an ear to
the seductive talk of the Communists. It was a sign of the
growing stark despair, which was felt more acutely in the
circles of the intellectuals.

II.—BIALYSTOK

The town derives its name from the river Bialy, which
flows through it, and from the wooded hill, which in Polish
is " stok ", that overlooks it. These natural features endow
it with a pleasantness of aspect that serves to mitigate the
severe, workaday character of this textile centre. It possesses
nothing of historic interest, but enjoys the fame of having
given birth to Ludwig Zamenhof, the creator of Esperanto.
The swarms of Jews that one met everywhere seemed
unusually multitudinous, until one heard that they formed
more than half the population—50,000 out of a total of
90,000. The Jews were adequately represented on the Town
Council, with 22 out of 40 members, and they were likewise well represented in the Municipal Administration, in
which four of the seven departments had Jewish heads; but
the highest office with which they had to content themselves
was that of the Vice-Mayor, as no Jew would be approved of
as Mayor in a town of Poland.

Most of the shops in the principal thoroughfares,
Pilsudski Street and Sienkiewicz Street, bore unmistakable
Jewish names, but the largest number of Jews were employed
in the textile trade. The factories had been idle several
weeks, as the workers had gone on strike as a protest against
the decision of the employers to reduce wages by half. The
factory owners themselves were fighting for existence, for
there was only enough work to keep them busy half the
year, and the struggle was intensified by the support, in the
form of both money and food, which the strikers received

from various parts of Poland. Striking seemed to be infectious, for the road-menders were also resting. The principal street was "up", the men having downed tools although the work had been created for their particular benefit as unemployed.

There was an up-to-date hotel which rejoiced in the name of Ritz, and from my window on the fourth floor I had an excellent view of the public park, whence the dulcet strains of a café orchestra were wafted aloft. The park was full of people strolling about and the benches were crowded, whilst swarms of happy children were scampering about. Many of the people, I found, when I afterwards entered the park, evidently belonged to the unemployed, who sought distraction in watching the playing of a fountain or listening spellbound to broadcast music from an empty band-stand.

A friend pointed out some of the local characters in the throng, and warned me to pay no heed to a gaunt tragic-looking fellow, who was pacing to and fro with a piece of paper in his hand, gesticulating, and declaiming like an actor, for he was a poor, harmless lunatic. We found an agreeable retreat on the café terrace, which, though prices were modest, was apparently not popular in these days of stress, and there he told me something of the local problems and conditions. He spoke with pride of their Hebrew *Gymnasium*, for it was the only Jewish higher-grade school that possessed the rights of a public school—a matter of considerable importance to pupils intending to enter a university. In the whole of the town there were only about 700 Jewish children who attended Yiddish schools: all others went to either Hebrew or Polish schools. There was an increasing number of young Jews who spoke to one another in Hebrew, for not only was the Jewish national idea advancing, but the only solution of their economic troubles seemed to lie in their settlement in Palestine. A large contingent of *Halutzim*[1] had already been provided by Bialystok, and there were now various groups

1 Pioneers.

Hawkers in Lwow

Craftsmen in Lwow

Jewish Quarter in Bialystok

or *Kibbutzim*—of both young men and girls—undergoing training in various manual occupations, with a view to following in the wake of the earlier pioneers. There were also about a hundred Jews with an average capital of £200 each, who were anxious to be admitted to Palestine as small manufacturers. They were denying themselves the most elementary comforts so as to keep their savings intact.

Later, in the lobby of my hotel, I chanced upon a character who afforded me a little diversion. He was a Rabbi with an ascetic face, who had doffed his heavy hat and wore a skull-cap, and spoke to me alternately in English and French. He told me that he came from a neighbouring town, that he had already spent some months in England and also in America, and that he had been offered a lucrative post across the Atlantic but hesitated to leave Poland because of his son. The boy was a wonderful scholar, a most ingenious mathematician, a master of ten languages—in short, an amazing prodigy, and it would be a pity to take him away from his school until he had completed his studies. And then the Rabbi began to discourse about the number of Hebrew works that he had written, mostly super-commentaries on some mediaeval commentaries on the Pentateuch, giving samples of his exegesis and orginal interpretations, interspersed with polyglot quotations, until he was called away by a deputation from the Synagogue Council.

IV.—CZENSTOCHOWA

It is a drab industrial city, bisected by a long wide road along which thousands of pilgrims piously trudged every year to the famous monastery on the hill, to gaze at the pictures of the Madonna with legendary wonder-working powers. But it was a normal period of the year when I was there, and the benches on the long road were occupied by scores of Jews discussing the events of the day and the prospects of the future. The Jews formed a fourth of the total population of 120,000, and most of the shops on both sides of the thoroughfare bore Jewish names. But business was slack, unemployment was widespread, and anybody who had ten zloty a week to live on was considered lucky.

For the last year or two the Jewish community had been rent in twain by the question of the Presidency. A Miz-rachi[1] had held the office since the end of the War until the last election of the Council of the community, when the members returned were four Zionists, two Agudists,[2] four Artisans, and two Democrats. The Artisans joined with the Zionists in continued support of a Zionist President, but the Polish authorities refused their assent, and demanded that the office should go to an Agudist. The attitude adopted by the authorities was part of their policy of in-creasing interference in the internal affairs of the Jewish community, which was illustrated by the new Communal law, of which paragraph 20 prescribed that only religious Jews were entitled to take part in communal elections. They insisted on scrutinising the budgets of the Jewish com-munities and objected to any items of which they did not approve, and even required submission of the minutes of communal meetings, yet the financial support which they were constitutionally bound to give by the minority clause of the Treaty establishing Poland's independence was not forthcoming.

The only hope of the youth lay in Palestine, and many were anxious to acquire a practical training that would qualify them for settlement there. A group of fifty, about equally divided between the sexes, were undergoing such a training at a *Kibbutz* (labour group) about three miles out of the town, and thither I was driven one afternoon in a rickety droschky along a bumpy road. It was orginally an agricultural farm established by the Jewish Colonisation Association many years ago for the training of young Jews,

[1] Member of the Zionist Orthodox party.
[2] Member of the " Agudas Israel ", a non-Zionist super-orthodox organ-isation.

but after the First World War it was taken over by the Jewish community of Czenstochowa. The latter unfortunately incurred a loss on the venture, and it was thereupon transferred to a Jewish farmer, who had been running it for the last few years.

The young men and women who were employed there were mostly between the ages of eighteen and twenty-five. They received two zloty (about a shilling and fourpence) per day for their labour, and they fully deserved it, for in summer they worked from three until nine in the morning and then again from three in the afternoon until eight in the evening. But their remuneration did not include food, which they had to find for themselves. All the men slept in one dormitory, which was by no means large enough for their number. Dinner had just been eaten when I visited the place, and the table was in disorder, with a swarm of flies picnicking on the remnants of food. Some girls were working in the kitchen, bare-footed, with their skirts above their knees.

In a field there were youths and girls picking potatoes and onions, assisted by several Polish girls, and the superior intelligence of the Jewish workers was striking. The field had no regular paths, and everywhere were sand and dust. Suddenly a storm began to threaten, and we were advised to hurry back to town before there was a downpour. The driver whipped his nag, and off we went.

On the way we passed a bearded healthy-cheeked Jew who was leading a cow to the farm.

"How much for the cow?" asked my companion. "Will you take twenty zloty?"

"No," he replied, with a shake of the head. "Nothing less than eighty." Cattle were cheap there.

My companion dilated on the arduous labour of the youngsters whom we had just left. They were willing to undergo any sacrifice in order that they might be able to go to Palestine, where so many of their friends were already settled. It was that thought which buoyed them up in their days of toil and their nights of discomfort. There was also a *Kibbutz* in town, consisting of 50 young Jews who were learning handicrafts in factories, where they received only one and a half zloty (about a shilling) per day.

The revival of enthusiasm for the Zionist cause had led to the acquisition of a new hall, which was still adorned with the blue and white strips of paper that were put up to celebrate its inauguration. On the walls were portraits of Herzl and other Zionist leaders, and likewise a portrait of the Polish President flanked by the Polish eagle. I met there a number of students, whose varied activities and ambitions seemed a reflex of the motley destinies of Israel.

One was studying law at the Cracow University, where there were altogether 1,000 Jewish students in the law faculty; he would have liked to study medicine, but there was a *numerus clausus* in that faculty. Another student, speaking French fluently, had been studying medicine for the last three years at the Montpellier University, where there were a few hundred Jewish students in the medical department. He had to study another three years, and when he returned to Poland to practice—since he could not do so in France—he would have to spend another couple of years in passing examinations in order to obtain the requisite certificate. A third youth was studying architecture at Prague, and he intended going to Italy to enlarge his horizon. A fourth had already been taught agriculture at Mikveh Israel in Palestine, and wanted to supplement his training at the Agricultural High School in Algeria, but he had no money and so he was returning to Palestine. A rather handsome young fellow told me that his ambition was to become a sailor and to help to build up a Jewish fleet. He had been fired with the idea by a Jewish student from Rumania, who had had to flee after an attack on a Cuzist[1] in self-defence.

They all came to the station to see me off, eagerly dis-

---

[1] Member of an anti-Semitic organisation named after Professor Cuza, of Jassy University.

cussing their plans and their dreams, with courage in their hearts and hope in their eyes.

* * * *

The Jews in all the cities described in this chapter were victims of the same dreadful atrocities at the hands of the Nazis that overtook their brethren in Warsaw and throughout Poland. Brutal assault, slave-labour, segregation in crowded Ghettos, starvation, disease, ending in deportation to death-camps, except for those who had been murdered before—such was the irresistible fate that befell them, and from which relatively few escaped. Their banishment from Cracow, which preceded their extermination, was decreed on the ground that it must be made a German city. In Lwow about 40,000 Jews were massacred by the Germans, and since the annexation of Eastern Galicia by the Russians there is an impenetrable barrier between the Jewish remnant in the city and the Jews in the western world. In Bialystok the Jews followed the example of their Warsaw brethren four months later, and after a desperate battle lasting two weeks, in which the Ghetto was set on fire, 40,000 of them fell. In Czenstochowa, which is near the German frontier, many were massacred in the first week of the war; and after the Jews had endured the same outrages as elsewhere most of them were carried off to their doom.

Chapter IX

VILNA—A CITADEL OF TRADITION

I.—CULTURE AND CALAMITIES

THERE is hardly any Jewish community in Eastern
Europe that possesses such a wealth of historic and cultural interest and evokes such feelings of pity as that of
Vilna. Its relations with the outer world were punctuated
repeatedly by calamities—massacres and expulsions, confis-
cations and depredations; whilst within, despite—and
perhaps because of—the chronic oppression, there pulsated
a vigorous spiritual life, which reached its most potent
development in the nineteenth century. Famous already in
the Jewish world as the home of that Talmudical sage,
Rabbi Elijah, the Vilna *Gaon*,[1] long before Napoleon
marched into the city at the head of his Grand Army,
Vilna acquired fresh lustre in the succeeding decades
through the galaxy of humanists who spread enlightenment
through the production of a remarkable wealth of Hebrew
works in prose and verse. Here it was that the greatest
Hebrew poet since the Middle Ages, Judah Leib Gordon,
conceived his dramatic poems so pregnant with passion and
revolt, and that Abraham Mapu infused a breath of romance
into the sober and scholarly domain of Hebrew letters. The
city was charged with the memories of these pioneers of
the Hebrew renaissance and of their kindred spirits, whose
genius still hovered over what I found to be a decaying
and starving community.

Externally Vilna is a charming city, with its old-world
appearance, and its squares and promenades lined with

---

[1] A Hebrew title, meaning " Eminence ", applied to a distinguished
Rabbinical authority.

plane-trees, though its narrow pavements and cobbled roads make walking occasionally an ordeal. So well endowed is it by nature with picturesque surroundings, with hills and woods overlooking the placid river Vilja, on which pleasure-steamers and boats plied in summer and Maccabean rowers disported their colours and their prowess, that denizens of the Ghetto styled it "the Jewish Switzerland", though it cannot compare with the rich and manifold beauty of Helvetia. Its natural amenities, however, combined with its historic associations to afford the people some consolation in their appalling misery. Cut off politically and economically from Russia, its once flourishing factories and industries soon declined and many of them were closed, whilst the Jews who had once enjoyed all comforts were stricken with the acutest distress. In a total population of 200,000, just before the Second World War, there were 80,000 Jews, of whom four-fifths were poor. The streets swarmed with beggars of all ages, men, women, and children, clad in mere rags, with pale sunken cheeks and cadaverous bodies, many of the children half-naked. They begged for no other reason than to keep themselves alive, so that they might be able to continue begging, for they could not hope ever to emerge from their state of destitution. During the ten minutes that I once sat in a café I was approached six times, not for money but just for a piece of bread, by old men and women, by the middle-aged, and by children whose famished looks made a spoken appeal quite unnecessary.

Few cities in Eastern Europe have undergone such a frequent change of masters within so short a time. In October, 1915, the Russians fled from the invading armies of the Germans, who stayed there for over three years, until January, 1919. The Germans were succeeded by the Poles, who were able to remain only for a week, for they were driven out by the Bolsheviks, who established a government over White Russia and Lithuania and continued in power until the following April. Then the Poles came back and entrenched themselves for fifteen months, until July, 1920, when the Bolsheviks returned and held sway for another month. Thereupon the Lithuanians, who had been hoping to recover Vilna as their capital, swooped down upon the city, but were only able to enjoy its possession for six weeks, for suddenly they were dislodged by General Zeligowski, who carried out a *coup d'etat* with his Polish troops. The General, apparently defying the orders of the Polish Government, but secretly acting in accord with Marshal Pilsudski, established a new State of "Middle Lithuania" and set up a provisional government, which continued until March, 1922, when Vilna was formally annexed to Poland. Thus, between 1915 and 1922 the city had experienced the varying blessings of nine different forms of government. Was it to be wondered at that the Jews showed morally and physically the effects of all these political upheavals?

II.—THE SYNAGOGUE COURTYARD

But the heart of the Ghetto remained unchanged not only by the cataclysm of the First World War and the succession of catastrophes that followed it, but by all the vicissitudes of the last hundred and fifty years. The *Schulhof*, that remarkable secluded courtyard surrounded by the synagogues and houses of prayer of all sorts and sizes, was exactly the same when I saw it as when its stones were trodden by the venerable Gaon Elijah during the latter half of the eighteenth century. It is an L-shaped area, entered from one end through a huge iron gate, and flanked on every side by places of religious worship and pious study. How many different synagogues and *Klausen* there were it would be difficult to calculate, for the whole congeries of buildings, extending beyond the courtyard through a covered passage to what is called the *Durchhof*, was literally honeycombed with shrines and chambers, large and small, devoted to every manifestation of the spiritual life. Each

Klaus (a word derived from the mediaeval Latin "clusa" or cloister) was named after some particular trade or craft, whose practitioners were wont to foregather there, such as tailors, joiners, gravediggers, bakers, beadles, tinsmiths, and so forth—a guild system of religious association which had obvious economic advantages. The oldest of these *Klausen* claimed an antiquity that went back to 1440. Poor though all the members were, they nevertheless tried to scrape together sufficient to maintain a few teachers in each *Klaus*, to give them instruction in Mishnah, or the Midrash, or the *Shulchan Aruch*,[1] or some other branch of religious lore. The material poverty of the community was thus more than counterbalanced by its wealth of spiritual activity. The venerable greybeards who pored over Talmudic tomes in those chambers of studious research loved to dwell on the visit of that famous prince in Israel, Sir Moses Montefiore, of which they had heard in their childhood, and to relate how he called on the blind old Rabbi Isaiah (affectionately called "Yeshayele"), who knew the whole of the Talmud by heart, in order to receive his blessing.

The most sacred of all the shrines was the synagogue on the site where the Gaon Elijah was born and lived, erected three years after he had ended his earthly pilgrimage, in the first year of the nineteenth century. Outwardly its only distinguishing characteristic was a gabled porch, but within it was rich with individual features and pious associations. On the southern wall there was a wooden tablet with an inscription in memory of the illustrious sage, extolling his wisdom, his Rabbinical scholarship, his worldly knowledge, and his spiritual grandeur; and below the tablet was a large chest so as to prevent any person from sitting in that holy place. On another wall, within a large frame, were a number of clock-faces, with hands pointing to the times at which different prayers were said on week-days and

---

[1] Authoritative religious code-book compiled by Rabbi Joseph Caro (1488–1575).

Sabbaths; and near by were sixteen charity-boxes arranged in four rows, each labelled with its special purpose, so that the benevolent could choose between supporting the poor, providing bridal dowries, repairing the synagogue, keeping the scrolls of the Torah in good condition, and other laudable objects. On a third wall there was a printed calendar in Hebrew, indicating the major and minor fasts and all the festivals, with a special prayer appropriate to each occasion. There was a large table covered with lead, on which candles for *Jahrzeit* (death anniversary), without candlesticks, burned to the end; and at another table there were men studying the Talmud and writing letters. Ten pious scholars, who had separated themselves from their wives and families in order to achieve perfect concentration, were always engaged here in the study of sacred lore, to the greater glory of the immortal Gaon, and whenever there was a vacancy it was immediately filled. My visit was something of a distraction to these devotees, who wished to know whence I came, how their brethren fared in other lands, and, above all, how they could get to the Land of Israel.

One of them, thinner and more saint-like than the rest, led me up a small staircase to an attic, where, at a plain deal table, with a couple of candles, the Gaon was reputed to have studied and reflected in solitude.

"How can this be," I asked, "if this synagogue was not built until three years after the Gaon had passed away?"

"People here believe it", he replied with calm assurance, "and you must not analyse their faith too closely. In the World War it was always full, mostly with women who prayed for the safe return of their husbands who had to join the army. They would bring their children too, and together they would pray before the Ark in the synagogue, invoking the merit of the Gaon for the benefit of husbands and fathers on the battlefield, in the trenches, the Most High knows where. Oh, what weeping and wailing there was in those days! Worst of all was the year 1917, when

famine and plague raged throughout the district and people
were too weak even to cry. They could just moan and wait
for the end. They died off like flies. So numerous were
the dead that we had to queue up outside the coffin-makers
for coffins, and the corpses were put on the pavement to
be picked up by the lorry-driver who went from street to
street, and even when they were brought to the cemetery
they had to wait for days before they were buried. After a
time like that, how can we now complain? At least we live
and we can learn."

And he cheerfully returned to the faded folio of the
Talmud, which possessed for him eternal freshness, and
became immersed in a legal disputation of the Rabbis of
ancient Babylon. It was the surest anodyne against the
woes of this world.

III.—THE COMMUNAL LIBRARY

Opposite the synagogue of the Gaon Elijah, on the first
floor of a building, was the Jewish communal library. It
was known as the Strashun Library, because it was founded
by Mattathias Strashun, who bequeathed to the community
a collection of 7,000 volumes of Talmudic and general
Hebrew literature and also a house for their accommodation. Strashun, who died in 1885, was a childless scholar,
who had inherited a good many books from his father and
increased the collection by judicious purchases that he
made during his travels in various foreign countries. He
acquired many works and manuscripts of interest and
value, and some of the books contained notes in his own
handwriting. Thanks to the substantial additions made
after his death, the Library ultimately comprised 20,000
volumes, including a few thousand " Judaica " in Russian,
German, French, and other languages, and about two
hundred manuscripts. The place was empty when I was
there, owing to a strike of the Jewish communal officials, and
I was therefore able to browse about the shelves at leisure.

" Before the World War ", the librarian told me, " there

were usually a thousand readers a week here, and even now we almost get that number, especially on the Sabbath. The library has always been a centre of literary activity, and the busiest time was in the days of the Revolution under the Tsar, in 1905 and 1906. Here we saw leaders of all parties and writers of all schools—Medem the Bundist, Nachman Syrkin the Zionist, Abramowitsch—the Yiddish novelist "Mendele"—Neiger and Zerubabel. At other tables were Rabbis and *Maggidim*[1] in skullcaps, all absorbed in learned works, and some seeking for answers to difficult questions of ritual observance."

The visitors' book contained the names of famous Yiddish writers, such as "Mendele Mocher Seforim", "Sholem Aleichem", and Sholem Asch, but far more interesting were some of the books and manuscripts that I saw, a few of them dating from the fifteenth century. The oldest printed books were an original copy of the *Aruch* of R. Nathan of Rome (1477) and a work of R. Immanuel of Rome, the friend of Dante (1492). Among the manuscripts were a Spanish commentary on the Pentateuch in Hebrew cursive script, written in 1415; the minutes of a Jewish communal council of the Province of Lithuania, *Pinkas di-Medinath Lita*, comprising Brisk, Pinsk, Grodno, and Vilna, for the period of 1673–1761; a minute book of the "Society of Grave-Diggers" for over a hundred years, with the names of the persons buried, rules of interment, and prayers; and a little book in the hand of the Vilna Goan, consisting of notes on "The Law of the Priests."

Beneath the Library there was a little room, on the door of which in bold letters appeared the sign of a Hebrew scribe. The door opened as I descended, and out came a hungry-looking man, with sunken, stubbly cheeks, and a dirty collar. I asked him to show me the scroll of the Torah upon which he was engaged.

"I have not had an order for a *Sepher*[2] for the last ten years," he mournfully replied. "There seems to be no

---

[1] Preachers.   [2] Scroll of the Pentateuch.

demand now for the Torah. I write only *Mezuzoth*[1] and *Tephillin*.[2]

As we left him, my companion, an assistant at the Strashun Library, explained to me that the strike of the officials of the Vilna Jewish Community had already lasted six weeks and involved thirty-five employees, who, together with their dependants, made up a total of 120 persons. The strike had been caused by the demand of the officials that no new appointment should be made by the Communal Council without their approval, a revolutionary innovation that the Council indignantly rejected. The President of the community had already been assailed with rotten eggs in the course of the controversy, to the irreparable injury of his suit, and the Vice-President had been threatened with even more serious damage to his person. The hopes of both sides were centred upon the Prefect of the city, who had offered his friendly services to effect a conciliation.

IV.—THE OLD SYNAGOGUE

Adjoining the library, and facing the main portion of the *Schulhof*, was the "Old Synagogue", the oldest in Vilna, built in 1573. It was a large and lofty structure, entered by descending a few steps through a huge iron door, which was opened by the stalwart, greybearded beadle with some enormous keys. On the wall near the entrance there was a Hebrew inscription gratefully recording the fact that the shrine was built by a society of tailors. Legend hath it that when Napoleon came to the city in 1812 he stood on the threshhold of this synagogue, and admired the grandeur of its proportions, the four massive columns supporting the vast stone-floored interior, and the elaborate *Almemar* (cantor's dais), which had a cupola of later construction. The seats were all numbered with Hebrew letters, and a thousand worshippers could pray with ease. There

[1] Little parchment scrolls for door posts.   [2] Phylacteries.

was no gallery for women, but the latter were accommodated in a section with two floors divided off from the main
building by a wall with deep embrasured windows, though
the ground floor portion was used by the men in winter,
as it had stoves, which could not be installed in the
synagogue proper. In front of the Ark, which was very old,
there formerly stood a large handsome seven-branched
candlestick of brass, but on the eve of the German invasion
of the city in 1915 it was sent off to Moscow in order to
save it from destruction, though only to be doomed to fall,
as it were, "out of the frying-pan into the fire".

Perhaps the most curious feature of this venerable fane
was a stone slab placed upright immediately to the left of
the Ark. It was fixed there for the purpose of preventing
anybody from sitting on the seat that was once occupied
by the head of the Beth Din of Vilna, Rabbi Samuel ben
Avigdor, who died in 1791. The story goes that Rabbi
Samuel, at the early age of eighteen, received his appointment as head of the ecclesiastical court through the
influence of his wealthy father-in-law, but he had to suffer
much opposition on the part of the leaders of the congregation. He was supported in the struggle by his father-
in-law and other relatives, but after they had passed away
he could hold out no longer and resigned. Thereupon his
seat was removed and a stone was put in its place as a
warning to future generations to refrain from appointing a
successor.[1] The title was accordingly abolished, and all
subsequent Rabbis were given only the designation of
"Moreh Tsedek" (Teacher of Righteousness). Hence
neither of the spiritual heads at the time of my visit, Rabbi
Rubenstein and Rabbi Grodzinski, had a seat close to the
Ark, but, as every seat was the individual property of a
member, they occupied seats some places away.

The history of the community was rich in the names of
Rabbis, scholars, and authors, who had prayed in this

[1]This is a simplification of a rather long and involved story, which is
fully told in the author's History of the Jews in Vilna.

ancient shrine and acquired immortality in the world of
Hebrew literature through the products of their learning
and wisdom, many of which were super-commentaries on
Talmudical or Biblical commentaries, with florid and
symbolical titles. The Gaon had worshipped there on two
memorable occasions, when he occupied a seat near the Ark.
The first was when, at the age of seven, he delivered an
erudite Talmudical sermon, which aroused the wonderment
of all the assembled sages and laid the foundations of his
fame. The second occasion was during the siege of Vilna
by the troops of Catherine the Second, when, as a greybeard
of seventy-two, he opened the Ark, and, amid the wailing
of the whole congregation—men, women and children—
who had taken refuge there, he led them in the sevenfold
recital of Psalm XX ("The Lord will answer thee in the
day of distress") as a means of saving the sacred building
from injury. His supplication was answered, for a cannon-
ball that was fired from a neighbouring castle-mount fell
harmlessly upon the roof of the house of prayer, where it
can be seen unto this day. The congregation trembled, but
the Gaon calmed them with the assurance that the evil had
been averted. And so it was, for a leader of the Polish
insurrectionists opened the gates of the city to the
Russians, and the siege was over. And in celebration of
that miracle, which occurred on the fifteenth day of Ab,
that day was always observed by the recital of the "Hymn
of Unity" and the giving of charity by those who had anything to give.

On emerging again into the courtard I was attracted by
some clocks fixed on the buttresses of the passage that led
to the *Durchhof* or inner court, and found on approaching
that they were clock-faces serving an important religious
purpose, for they were adorned with the Hebrew admonition, "*Remember the Sabbath day to keep it holy*", and
they indicated the times when the Sabbath began, when
the shops had to be closed, when the candles had to be lit,
and when the Sabbath was ushered out. Beneath the clocks

were framed notice-boards containing various kinds of announcements, mostly of a religious or semi-religious character, whilst on the neighbouring walls and on the doors of the numerous bethels all round there were also little Hebrew posters, conveying messages of import, mainly in regard to matters of ritual, to the denizens of this quarter. During the First World War the courtyard was the principal news exchange. Here the multitudinous communiqués of the German military command were displayed, and here one always learned of the latest deaths, for necrologies in terms of eulogy were immediately posted up for the information of the public.

The sing-song of the boys in the *Cheder* (religious school) above the passage greeted my ears as I strolled into the inner court and was shown the spot where once stood the Gaon's *Succah* (tabernacle). The site was occupied by a workmen's *Klaus*, near which was one of the Hassidim, whilst on the other side was the *Klaus* of the painters, which had a wall covered entirely with scenes of Jewish interest depicted by a single artist.

One could linger in these courts for hours, diving every few moments into a different house of study or chamber of prayer, and listening to endless quaint stories of the ways and wisdom of the unworldly pietists who once worshipped and flourished there before being summoned to the greater life, to which their earthly pilgrimage was merely a prelude. I peeped into the most ancient *Klaus* of all, dating from the middle of the fifteenth century, to see its arched and vaulted ceiling and the curious copper door of the Ark; and then, some distance away, mounting a flight of stone steps that led to a small shrine where once Judah Leib Gordon (1830–1892) pursued his Talmudic studies, I stood in silent homage to the memory of that impassioned poet.

V.—HEBREW VERSUS YIDDISH

When Napoleon came to Vilna he was so impressed by

its dominating Jewish characteristics that he is reported to have exclaimed: "Surely this is the Jerusalem of Lithuania". The epithet was certainly fitting in so far as Vilna has been prolific in the creation of a Hebrew culture that has exercised far-reaching sway. In the service it has thus rendered to Jewry an important part has been played by the printing and publishing firm whose name has spread to the remotest parts of the globe where the traditional ritual of Israel is still preserved. Often in my childhood, as I fingered the title-page of prayer-book or Pentateuch, I wondered who was Widow Romm or the Brothers Romm, whose name seemed such a guarantee of scholarly accuracy and textual fidelity. Now that I was in Vilna and able to visit the famous house, there was no longer any representative alive of the Romm family, which had started its Hebrew printing activity in the year of the French Revolution, though the name still loomed large over the entrance to the establishment.

I was welcomed by the manager, who conducted me through the various parts of the building and described the manifold works that had been produced for nearly a century and a half. Not only prayer-books for all sorts of occasions, but editions of the Talmud, the *Shulchan Aruch*, and all other standard and secondary works of Jewish religious lore had been published. As we walked through one of the departments I saw several sheets of the Talmud being printed, and the manager told me that at short notice they could easily print off six hundred sets of that encyclopaedic work. But from where, in these godless days, was such an order likely to be received? Economic depression had certainly been followed by religious economy, if not religious apathy. Most of the rooms were deserted, the machines were silent, and an air of melancholy reigned throughout.

"Once upon a time", remarked the manager, "we employed two hundred people, now it is only twenty-five, and even so not always full-time. Give us work! We have

K   145

all the machines and men waiting. We still send books to all parts of the world—Australia, South Africa, and South America, but there is a steady decline in orders."

He showed me an elaborate calendar that had been printed, months before the New Year, with detailed instructions regarding prayers for feasts and fasts, and minute regulations about the ritual observances, intended for display in orthodox synagogues throughout the globe. We then left the main building and passed into the courtyard, where I saw a huge iron door, bolted and barred. It looked like the entrance to a hangar, or at least an immense garage. With clanging keys he unbolted and unlocked the iron door, revealing a wooden door that had also to be unlocked, and then we entered a large depot, where there were stored, in an orderly and classified manner, on rows of shelves, matrices of all the Hebrew works that had so far been issued, in boxes bearing their respective titles. It was a wonderful treasury of the makings of Hebrew literature, religious and secular, but the manager bewailed the fact that he so seldom had occasion to disturb its peace.

In strange contrast to the dusk that seemed to be settling over the realm of Hebrew in the " Jerusalem of Lithuania " was the lurid light that was made to play upon the world of Yiddish, for it was in this city that there was founded in 1925 the Yiddish Scientific Institute (commonly known from the initials of its Yiddish name as " Yivo "). Not until I visited its commodious premises, in a building far removed from the Ghetto, did I realise the scope and systematic character of its labours, for its purpose was to collect and classify all sorts of publications—books, pamphlets, and periodicals—that had appeared in Yiddish and to promote research. There were large collections illustrating all the main aspects of Jewish life and thought, ranged under four principal divisions: history, sociology, philology and pedagogics, and culture, the last comprising several sub-divisions, such as art, drama, music, and folk-lore. The Institute filed newspapers from all over the world and kept a card-index of all their important contents, especially signed articles. It had a most interesting collection of portraits of Yiddish and Hebrew actors, and of play-bills and dramatic notices, and likewise a veritable treasury of Jewish music. There was a room full of literary curiosities and articles displayed in show-cases, such as Yiddish revolutionary pamphlets of the pre-war period in the guise of the Passover *Haggadah*, booklets on the history of Socialism in different countries, and photographs of Jewish politicians who had attained any fame. For the benefit of the outside reader there was a large lending library, and in the research room I saw serious students exploring the different fields of Yiddish lore.

The Institute was growing so fast, and it was apparently also so prosperous, that it was found necessary to construct a special home to accommodate it. The director insisted on my accompanying him to the new building, an imposing structure of three stories, situated in a fine part of the city. It had extensive cellarage for archives and old newspapers, with up-to-date mechanical contrivances for protection against fire and water. There was a little house near by, within the grounds of the Institute, containing guest rooms for distinguished scholars, and there was also provision for the addition of another storey to the main edifice. The cost of the land and building, I was told, was 25,000 dollars, raised largely in America. I could not help marvelling that in this city, where poverty was more rampant than in any other part of Poland, so much money should be spent on purely scientific research in the products of a language born of the travails of exile.[1]

VI.—CAVE-DWELLERS

How poor some Jews in Vilna were, I had yet to learn when I was taken to see some cellar dwellings. The homes that I had already seen on ground-floors and upper floors

[1] The Yiddish Scientific Institute was removed to New York in 1940.

were wretched enough, but those that I visited underground
were indeed revolting. They were all situated in a *Hof* or
court, which was approached from the street by a shabby,
cobble-paved passage, and surrounded on all sides by tall
dilapidated houses swarming with poverty-stricken humanity. Cautiously I clambered down a rickety wooden
staircase, twelve steps all askew, and found myself in a
large, cool and lofty cellar. There was a table covered with
white paper, and some hangings ill concealed a ramshackle
bed. A pretty young girl told me that eight people used to
live there before, but now only herself and two sisters. Both
of her parents were dead, and the landlord generously
remitted the rent. She seemed pathetically resigned to her
lot.

From a neighbouring courtyard we descended another
steep and darker staircase, leading to a dank, gloomy, cave-
like cellar, which had a small inaccessible window, encrusted
with dirt. We were greeted by an undersized, hungry-
looking fellow, a tailor, who pointed to a sewing-machine
as his means of livelihood and told us that he had been
out of work for months. He lived there with his wife, three
children—a girl of eight and two younger boys—and three
lodgers. The wife and children slept in a bed, the tailor
on a couch, and the lodgers on different parts of the floor.
One of the lodgers was an artist, sitting disconsolate on a
wooden box. He rose, struck a match, and held it high
overhead to reveal one of his painting on the wall—a boat
struggling in a stormy sea. "What's the good of art," he
wailed, "when even a tailor can't find work?"

Our third visit was down a crooked staircase, at the foot
of which was a glass door covered with a skimpy curtain.
A foul smell assailed my nostrils and bade me halt. I could
just get a glimpse of a small room, bare and tidy, when a
woman with haggard cheeks turned upon us a pair of angry
eyes. "You want to see the Vilna dwellings? Beautiful,
aren't they?" she shrieked. Her voice and her looks were
those of one half-demented.

VII.—WHERE PEACE REIGNS

" Would you like to see where the Jews of Vilna are really at peace? " asked my friend.

He took me, in a *droschke* driven by a Jewish jarvey, to the old cemetery beyond the River Vilja, about a couple of miles from the city, where no body had been laid to rest for over a hundred years. It stretched over a very large area, looking for the most part like a deserted field, with grass growing wild, for the number of tombstones was comparatively small. There were only a few conventionally upright, most of them being mere shapeless stones or boulders, though there were some in the form of little Gothic structures with Hebrew inscriptions, on which the names had been painted over in yellow to facilitate identification. The beadle, a woebegone creature with grizzled beard, wearing a long overcoat with a gap in the rear, conducted us from one tombstone to another, occasionally disputing with my learned companion about the personality of the illustrious scholar resting below and his theological works.

Most famous of all was the tomb of the Gaon, who lay in company with a few other pietiests, including his mother, on a spot covered by a modest mausoleum, which was entered by an iron-barred door. Over the grave were two large concrete slabs, separated from one another by a small space, and on that of the Gaon was a little heap of mouldy notes and petitions, in Yiddish and in Hebrew, entreating the saint to intercede on behalf of suffering suppliants. The names of the Gaon and of his honoured companions were inscribed on the wall opposite their respective plots, and as I began to decipher them I heard a low, plaintive voice. Turning round I discerned in the dim light a young bearded man, cadaverous and pale-faced, standing in prayer, with a book in his hand, his lips emitting now and again a sound like a moan, reminding me of a scene in Ansky's play, *The Dibbuk.*

"He is very pious and poor", the beadle whispered to me, "and often comes here to say psalms. Please give him a zloty."

I slipped a coin into the frail palm. "The Almighty has answered my supplications", said the man of prayer. "May He prosper you on your way!"

The tombstones were not enclosed within the mausoleum, but could be seen at the back of it, standing upright, in close juxtaposition, with long eulogistic epitaphs, and closely protected by a thick growth of shrubs and bushes.

A little distance away was the grave of the *Ger Tsedek*, the "righteous proselyte", Count Valentin Potocki, the Polish nobleman who adopted Judaism, and, after being tortured, was burned at the stake in 1749. From the soil that covered his ashes there grew a vigorous tree almost in the form of a man, with outstretched branches resembling hands and feet, which drew vast pilgrimages of Jews: but the resentment that his conversion had aroused among the Catholic populace continued ever after and found expression in the hacking away of the "hands" and "feet". In order to protect the grave the Jewish authorities had an iron shed built over it, which was painted green with a Hebrew inscription. The shed was kept securely locked, and around it was made an enclosure of big blocks of stone, joined by heavy iron rails: but the Polish soldiery quartered in the neighbourhood repeatedly damaged the rails and stone blocks, which the poor, trembling beadle had been utterly unable to prevent.

Thence we were driven to another part of the city, to see the modern cemetery, which was opened over a hundred years ago. It extended over a vast area and was intersected with fine long avenues lined with trees. A multitude of tombstones faced one on every side, closely huddled together, with epitaphs in Hebrew, Yiddish, and Russian, and adorned in some cases with framed photographs. The inscriptions were not all of a conventional character, for the tombstone of a famous *Marshallik* (jester) bore the legend: "Stop and look! You are still a guest; I am at home."

In the centre of the cemetery was a large mortuary, with separate sections for men and women, whither the dead were brought for the last rites, for here all were buried on the same day as they died. On the opposite side of the avenue was an elevated platform, reached by a flight of steps, from where the funeral oration was delivered. The speaker stood before an iron lectern flanked on either side by lamps in large glass shades, which were necessary in case of burial after night-fall.

Here could be seen the graves of the poet Gordon, of the writers Lebensohn and Kalman Schulman, and of all the other luminaries who irradiated the firmament of Hebrew culture in the nineteenth century. Here, too, could be seen the graves of the victims of various riots and outrages. Nineteen members of the Bund who were killed in the revolutionary rising of 1905 were laid to rest together, their sepulchre marked by a stone column, from where a memorial address was delivered every anniversary. The Jews who were killed by the Polish troops in 1919 also lay together, some of the graves being marked pathetically "Unknown". And over the tomb of the Yiddish writer, Weiter, who was shot in that outburst of lawlessness, was a striking piece of sculpture—an eagle with broken pinion.

From a distance I heard a stentorian voice offering up the prayer for the dead, and thrilling the air with heart-breaking grief in every note. Scarcely had the sound died away, when from an opposite quarter there arose again the same moving piercing chant, but rendered with even more poignant anguish of spirit, as though seeking to give utterance to the infinite tragedy of the Jewish people. "They are poor *Chazanim*",[1] explained my friend, "trying to earn twenty groschen a time from people visiting the graves of their relatives."

As we passed out through the huge gates we were

[1] Cantors.

surrounded by a number of women, gaunt, blanched, almost fleshless—some with babies at their breast, whining bitterly for alms. Blessings poured upon my head in return for every mite I gave, and after I had been allowed to return to my carriage and was driven away I wondered how soon it would be before all those suffering souls would likewise be gathered unto their lasting peace.

* * * * *

The Jews of Vilna were doomed to the same appalling calamity that engulfed all other Jews in Eastern Europe who fell into the claws of the Nazis. Before the German invasion in June, 1941, they experienced three changes of Government. In September, 1939, the city was seized by the Russians; in the following month it was handed over to the Lithuanians; and in June, 1940, it was retaken by the Russians. A year later Hitler's hordes arrived, the Russians fled, and the fate of the Jews was sealed.

By the end of 1942 over 30,000 Jews had been carried off, and deportations and exterminations continued throughout 1943, and until the city was liberated by the Russians. Hundreds of Jews, forming three partisan groups, joined in the fighting against the Germans, and one group named "The Avengers", took part in the revolt of the Vilna Ghetto, led by a talented Yiddish poet, Abraham Sutzkever. Despite the terrible risks and the barbarous sufferings to which they were exposed, the Jews in Vilna engaged in underground cultural activities, including the establishment of a symphony orchestra and the publication of a newspaper. When the city was freed by the Russians in August, 1944, it was found that, of a previous total Jewish population of about 65,000, "no more than 40 survivors came out of their fox-holes."[1] Vilna now belongs to the Soviet Union, and the traditional Jewish life and culture of which it had so long been a citadel are no more.

[1] American Jewish Year Book 1945–46, p. 409.

Chapter X

A KARAITE COLONY

ON THE HIGHWAY that ran from Vilna to the old Lithuanian frontier there lies the charming little town of Troki, which has an interesting history dating back six hundred years, and which possessed an attraction for the studious traveller as the home of a colony of Karaites. This Jewish sect, which first came into existence in Bagdad in the eighth century as a protest against the Talmudical developments of Judaism and based itself on the literalism of the Bible, spread at one time from Persia to Spain. It was most numerously represented in the South of Russia, and it was from the Crimea that the Grand Duke Witold of Lithuania, after his successful war against the Tatars early in the fourteenth century, took a few hundred Karaites captive and brought them to Troki. There he settled them as colonists, giving them tracts of land which they tilled, and which their descendants continued to cultivate down to modern times. In most other parts of Europe and the Near East where the Karaites once lived, they have disappeared, having either reverted to the parental fold or become submerged among the surrounding Christian or Moslem population. But of the few small communities that survived the vicissitudes of time, Troki was distinguished both by reason of the galaxy of scholars it produced in the middle ages and by the scene of picturesque indolence that it still presented in the thirties of the twentieth century. Its most famous son was Isaac ben Abraham Troki, a sixteenth century theologian, whose Hebrew work, "The Strengthening of Faith," was translated into many tongues and was quoted with praise by Voltaire in his attacks upon Christianity.

The placidity of Troki was probably due to the fact that despite the march of mechanical progress even in this part of Eastern Europe it was not yet linked up with any large centre by a railway. The nearest city was Vilna, whence a small motor bus made several journeys a day, covering the distance along a rough and dusty road in an hour. The trip was more adventurous than enjoyable, for you found yourself in a shabby conveyance full of sweating folk burdened with all sorts of baskets and packages, and bulging bundles of linen stowed under your seat to the discomfort of your legs, whilst frequent joltings of the car occasionally threw you into the arms of your opposite neighbour. But the hardships of the road were soon forgotten when, after you had crossed a wooden bridge, you were driven into the main street of the sleepy townlet and began to survey the idyllic charms of this island retreat. For Troki was surrounded by a circular lake, on which there were pleasure boats and fishing keels, and though the reigning peace seemed incapable of disturbance, it was ensured by the water-police, athletic young fellows clad in white and blue uniforms, with round white hats like those of American sailors. From a bend in the road one could see the crumbling ruin of a castle that belonged to Gedymin, the Grand Duke of Lithuania who played so notable a part in the affairs of his country in the fourteenth century.

The entire population scarcely exceeded 500 families, of which a hundred were Jewish and a hundred Karaite, whilst the rest consisted of Russians, Poles and Tatars. The Karaites were mainly vegetable gardeners, who conveyed their produce every morning to the market in Vilna, and who might be met on the country road in the afternoon returning in their long rumbling carts. The Jews were artisans and shopkeepers, but they also supplied the fishermen, who had a co-operative society, which paid the Government 10,000 zloty a year for the right to exploit the bountiful lake. Relations between the Jews and the Karaites were peaceful, if not exactly cordial. Seventy years ago under

Nicholas I, the Karaites insisted upon the expulsion of the Jews, but after the lapse of a couple of years the latter were allowed to return and were left in peace.

Most of the Karaites lived in small, one-storey houses of timber in the principal street. In appearance they differed strikingly from the Jews, for even though they were mainly dark they had the Tatar physiognomy, whilst some of them, especially the girls, presented a fair type. The road was called Kowenski Ulica because it led to Kowno, and the name was retained despite the prolonged rupture of relations with the Lithuanian capital. Troki was, indeed, only four miles from the frontier, which was officially closed, but this did not prevent occasional smuggling both of goods and people.

The Karaite synagogue, which was also situated in the principal street, was a small structure of simple design which had replaced an earlier building. It was approached by a path leading from an iron gate, on either side of which were brick columns, on which was inscribed in Hebrew lettering and Arabic numerals the date of construction—1894. Its cupola was originally surmounted by a " Shield of David ", but the removal of this symbol was insisted upon by the religious head of the Karaites as smacking too much of orthodox Judaism. The offending symbol, however, still remained on the iron gate, from which it could hardly be removed without causing a conspicuous blemish.

My guide was the beadle of the local Jewish synagogue who was on friendly terms with his colleague of the Karaite conventicle, and he fetched him from his home to open the building for my inspection. The interior was in general like that of an orthodox synagogue, with a gallery for women, except that there was no raised platform for the precentor, the latter having only a small reading-desk on the floor. There was a Turkish carpet covering the gangway that led to the Ark of the Law at the upper end, but I was not allowed to walk more than a few feet, unless I was prepared to take my boots off, for the ground was considered sacred.

Nevertheless I was able to get a good view of the shrine. It was spotlessly clean and had been recently painted. The interior of the cupola was pale blue, and a still paler blue tinged the walls.

The Ark of the Law was draped with a red plush curtain: above it, and on one side, were the initial words of the Ten Commandments in gilt lettering, whilst on the other side were twin tablets with the complete text of the Commandments, all in Hebrew. But the Ark contained only one scroll of the Law. At the outbreak of the First World War, I was told, all the other Hebrew scrolls, together with many parchment manuscripts, were sent to Moscow for safe-keeping, and there they have remained ever since, unless they have been victims of an anti-religious holocaust. The solitary scroll was taken out of its depository every Sabbath and opened up on the precentor's desk, but the worshippers who were called to its presence were unable to decipher the unpunctuated script and read their portion from a printed Pentateuch. The Karaite prayer-book, printed in Vilna in 1863, differed radically from the orthodox Hebrew ritual; and the *tallis* or praying-shawl was likewise different from that worn in the ordinary synagogue, as it was more like a scarf and had, instead of fringes, a blue thread emerging from a cluster of white threads.

In one important principle the Karaites had departed from the teaching of their founder, for they had light, even electric-light, on the Sabbath. They defended this on the ground that the Biblical prohibition, "Ye shall kindle no light in your dwelling-places," did not apply to their house of prayer, for this was not a dwelling-place.

The Karaites had a large cemetery, which was situated about a mile away. It was reputed to be five hundred years old, though it contained no tombstones that could boast of such antiquity. Most of the tombstones that I saw were of the nineteenth century; many were of black marble, with epitaphs of gilt lettering in Hebrew or in Russian, and there were also several family vaults with black marble columns.

A special sanctity seemed to cling to the place, for pious Karaites in Vilna always expressed a particular wish to be buried in its soil rather than in that of the great city.

Before leaving Troki I visited the Jewish synagogue, which was in another part of the town. It presented a striking contrast to the Karaite place of worship both in its lack of neatness and also in the obvious hard wear to which it was subjected by the devout members of the local community. There was a schoolroom adjoining, where I found a master of the "Agudas Israel" shade of orthodoxy teaching a mixed class of boys and girls.

On my return to Vilna I immediately drove to the Karaite synagogue to learn something about the sectarians in that city. Here I was more fortunate in my informant, for the precentor himself, a middle-aged man, with slight black beard and moustache, and high cheek-bones, courteously conducted me around. He lived in a house at the rear of the synagogue and immediately donned his official garb, a black tight-fitting robe, with a dark-blue sash, and a round black hat.

The shrine itself, situated in a fine residential quarter, was a handsome new building of white stone, which had been erected in 1923. It was semi-Moorish in design, and was crowned by a cupola, which was surmounted by an iron circle containing the initial words of the Ten Commandments in two columns. The interior was in general like that of the synagogue at Troki, but rather more ornate. There were rich carpets of Oriental design in front of the Ark, whilst on either side of it, in an alcove, lay a bright red silk covering, beneath which, so the precentor explained, was simply a Hebrew Pentateuch. Facing the Ark stood the precentor's reading-desk, and on either side of this was a comfortable arm-chair, one for the precentor himself and the other, somewhat more sumptuous, for the *Haham* (Rabbi). Aloft was a gallery for the women, where they could easily hear but could not easily be seen.

The precentor told me that the synagogue was supported

partly by the members of the Karaite community and partly by the Government. There were only forty Karaite families altogether in Vilna, and there were also small groups of the sect at Halicz and Lutzk. They maintained that they were not Jews by race but Tatars. Their Hebrew prayer-book, which I examined, contained many prayers in the Tatar dialect, but they spoke Polish amongst themselves. Their religious head was invited to all important official functions held by the Government and the local authorities, and I was told (though not by the precentor) that he was not at all particular about the meats that he ate. This indifference even to Biblical prohibitions seemed to have resulted from declining contact with the traditional form of the Law of Moses, for the Scroll was for the most part kept safe in the Ark.

I remarked to the precentor that the number of Karaites had now dwindled to such an extent that it appeared to be only a matter of time before they would become as few as the Samaritans and perhaps have a similar struggle for existence. Thereupon he said that there were 300,000 Cossacks on the Volga who were also faithful to the Karaite doctrine. But inquiries that I afterwards made in other circles convinced me that this figure was a fantastic exaggeration, whilst the Soviet policy regarding religion seemed to indicate that whatever Karaite Cossacks there might have been in former times had probably had their Karaism drilled out of them by the rigorous ministrations of the Government.

The Nazis, however, recognised no distinction between orthodox Jews and Karaites: they exterminated them both alike.

Chapter XI

DISILLUSION IN KOVNO

I

No stranger in quest of admission to the guarded portals of an Imperial palace was subjected to such searching scrutiny or repeated challenge as a traveller proceeding to the city of Kovno. The journey from Dantzic took only eight hours, but it involved confrontation with the officials of four different Governments and a six-fold examination of one's credentials. Your passport was first inspected by the Dantzic police as you departed from the once Free City with all its picturesque monuments, then by the Polish police as you entered the Treaty-made "Corridor", and again as you left it, next by the German police as you came into East Prussia, and anon as you passed out of it, and sixthly and lastly by the Lithuanian police as your train snorted its way across the frontier of the Republic. After running this gauntlet of fussy functionaries, whereby you enriched your knowledge of national uniforms and racial characteristics, you found yourself not in any modern paradise, which might have justified these manifold safeguards, but in a land of mud and mediaeval civilisation. The transition from German to Lithuanian soil was like stepping backward a couple of hundred years, though the first recognisable words that I saw as we steamed through Virballis propelled my mind back as far as two thousand years, as they were the Hebrew inscription on the building of a Jewish athletic club styled "Maccabæan" and adorned with the "Shield of David". The roads that we passed were in a state of advanced neglect, consisting for the most part of vast undulating layers of black mire, whilst the buildings presented a depressing spectacle of poverty and dilapidation, so that long before reaching my destination I was attuned to the sober colours and squalid scenes of Kaunas, as the capital was called under the Lithuanian régime.

A crowd of droshky-drivers, clad in long, heavy coats, fur hats and top-boots, yelled an incoherent welcome as, emerging from the frowsy railway-station, I stepped into the cobble-paved square. Fortunately, a friend was there to act as guide if not as philosopher, and soon we were rattling in a shabby, ramshackle vehicle along the rough, muddy road, which was full of ruts and puddles, bordered on either side by deep wide gutters. We drove through the main thoroughfare, which was named "Liberty Avenue" in honour of the country's redemption from the Muscovite yoke—a somewhat rural street, with petty shops, without a single striking building, and with all the historic distinction still attaching to a one-horse tram that had apparently not been cleaned since the beginning of the 1914–18 War.

There were only two hotels in Kovno that could be visited with a certain measure of safety by the traveller anxious to avoid the perils and pitfalls of the insect kingdom—or is it republic? They were both situated in "Liberty Avenue", not many yards from one another, and together they could hardly accommodate more than three dozen guests, so that the metropolis of Lithuania had hardly qualified as yet to welcome an international conference.[1] The hotel in which I stayed, and which was said to be the less luxurious of the two, bore a name of glorious association, "Hotel de Versailles," but even the coachman of the famous palace of Louis XIV would have disdained to lodge within its plebeian walls. Its redeeming characteristic was an all-pervasive odour of carbolic soap, an eloquent testimony to the zeal of the management for hygienic principles; whilst the most curious feature in its internal amenities consisted in the heating by means of a stove fixed in the wall between every

[1] This was in 1927. A large modern hotel was built later.

The Synagogue Courtyard in Vilna

Street in Vilna Ghetto

Tomb of the Righteous Proselyte
in Vilna

two adjoining rooms, the little door of the stove opening on
to the corridor, so that a servant could replenish the fires
with the logs lying close by, without disturbing the guests.
The name of my hotel was not the only link between Kovno
and Paris, for I soon learned that the city boasted of an
old house, a tall, melancholy pile, in an upper room of which,
with little casement windows, overlooking the Niemen, the
vanquished Napoleon, on his flight from the snows of Russia,
spent a single night of restless slumber. No greater contrast, however, was conceivable than between the grand
metropolis on the Seine, the *ville de lumière*, and this new-
baked capital, which pathetically sought to ape the brilliance
of Western nights by illuminated sky-signs.

It was only after realising the pettiness of the city, the
poverty of its development, and the inferiority of the institutions that go to make up a vigorous national life, that one
could understand the bitterness of the Lithuanians over the
annexation by the Poles of Vilna, for this would at least
have been a worthy capital. This loss, due to a bold act of
banditry by General Zeligowski, which the Polish Government at first pretended to repudiate, but which it afterwards
insisted upon the League of Nations blessing by formal
ratification, explained many happenings in the inglorious
history of the new Lithuania. For the State was orginally
planned on generous lines both as regards territory and the
political rights of its component nationalities. It was intended to be like the old Grand Duchy of Lithuania, including both the region of Vilna and White Russia, and it
was conceived as a State consisting of various nationalities,
of which the Jews and the other minorities would enjoy
internal autonomy. But the frustration of the plan regarding the geographical area brought about a drastic revision
of policy concerning the political constitution, and it was
resolved to make the country a uni-national State.

The Radicals, who were first in power after the newly-
won independence, were very favourable to the Jews, who,
through their intellectuals, rendered valuable services in the

organising of the polity. They gave the Jews complete self-government, with a Ministry of Jewish Affairs, which formed an essential department of the Government: its head was a member of the Cabinet, and it had the right to levy a tax upon all the Jews of the country for the up-keep of all the religious, educational, and social institutions of their community. They even made a State appropriation for the Jewish Ministry, and the highest representatives of the Government honoured the assemblies of the Jewish National Council with their presence and their speeches, so that the whole world marvelled at their magnanimity and praised it as the peer of the Balfour Declaration. But when the educated and sophisticated Lithuanians who had been living in America and other parts of the world returned to their native land in quest of jobs, resolved to subordinate all ideals to their own self-interest, they propagated a feeling of ultra-nationalism, which inevitably led to a change of régime. The Radicals were elbowed aside by Chauvinists and Clerical reactionaries, the generosity towards the Jews was displaced by hostility, and the Ministry of Jewish Affairs, with all its emoluments, prerogatives, and elaborate administration, was swept out of existence as completely as last year's snow.

But the loss of Vilna also provoked an event that had a paralysing influence upon the whole life of the country, for the Lithuanians, by way of retaliation, broke off diplomatic relations with Poland, which were not resumed for many years. These two adjoining lands, united before the First World War in subjection to the common oppressor, were not on speaking terms—even on the telephone. No communication of any kind between them or their peoples was allowed. No letter could be posted direct from one to the other; no railway journey could be made direct from one country to the other, so that the traveller was driven by the roundabout route through Dantzic or Dwinsk. No trade or traffic was permitted between them on the Niemen either, so that this river, once so busy bearing vessels with timber

from the forests of Russia and Poland to the Baltic, was
for years more idle than the Dead Sea. Long before the
First World War the antipathy between the Polish and the
Lithuanian Jew, the *Polack* and the *Litvack*, had become
an accepted tradition, which was transplanted to the Jewries
which they had helped to form in England, America, and
especially South Africa. Now the feud had been transferred,
with an increase of rancour, to the Gentiles of those neighbouring but unneighbourly States.

II

In few countries had there been so complete and determined a descent from the glorious heights of racial concord
to the murky depths of Anti-Semitism. The concessions
granted to the Jews in accordance with the stipulations of
the Treaty by which the Republic was recognised were
gradually withdrawn, and one oppressive disability after
another was introduced. So generous were the Lithuanians
at the time when the Jewish Ministry existed, that they
even allowed the Jewish members of the *Seym* (Parliament)
to speak in Yiddish, a language which many of them could
understand themselves. It was the only instance in which
Yiddish had ever been used for parliamentary orations.
This unusual act of grace was probably due to the fact that
the leaders of the country remembered only too well how
their own tongue was suppressed under the rule of the
Tsar, though it could not be stifled on the lips of the
peasants, so that they were animated by a spirit of genuine
tolerance towards the language of another people; but it
was not long before Yiddish was not only disallowed in the
Seym, but was even forbidden on shop-signs. The Jewish
deputies did not much mind, for they displayed an eloquence in the vernacular which filled their non-Jewish colleagues with envy; but it was a serious matter for the tradespeople to awake in the morning to find the lettering on
their shop-fronts smeared over with pitch, and then to be

threatened with fines if they did not replace the Yiddish
with Lithuanian inscriptions—an injunction from which
doctors and lawyers, significantly enough, were exempt.
But when the attention of the League of Nations was called
to this flagrant breach of Treaty obligations, a peremptory
order was given at Geneva to stop this nuisance, and the
order was meekly though sullenly obeyed.

The attitude of the Government on this language question was all the more incomprehensible as the Lithuanians
themselves had not yet mastered their own tongue. Before
the First World War it was seldom spoken in the towns,
where Russian was the dominant speech; and the philo-
logians were not yet agreed as to the spelling of certain
words, as Lithuanian does not belong to the Slavonic
family, but claims direct lineage from Sanskrit. Even some
of the professors at the local University were still obliged to
lecture in Russian or German, and text-books on many
subjects had yet to be prepared in the national tongue. But
in every Government office Lithuanian was rigorously insisted upon. An old Jew complained to me that whenever
he went to a public office and spoke Russian to the officials,
they upbraided him and demanded that he—a septuagen-
arian—should begin to learn Lithuanian, but that he no
sooner turned his back than he heard them talk to one
another in Russian.

The hostility of the authorities found more effective expression in other directions. They enacted a compulsory
Sunday rest law in the alleged interest of the Christian
Sabbath, but in the real interest of Christian commerce,
for the Jewish tradespeople, who were thus compelled to rest
two days a week, and even a little more, especially in the
winter, when their Sabbath began on Friday afternoon, were
consequently subjected to a tremendous handicap in the
economic struggle. When this law was first proposed, at a
time when trade depression was already sufficiently acute,
the Jewish community made a dignified and solemn protest,
which, paradoxically, took the form of an extra day of rest.

They proclaimed a one-day strike, which was observed with impressive unanimity. All shops, offices and workshops were closed, even the seventy Jewish cabmen of the city deserted their stands, and the whole community filled the synagogues with a passionate outpouring of prayers and psalms to the Almighty to avert the evil decree. But the authorities, so far from relenting after this service of intercession, resented the invocation of the Almighty's aid in what they regarded as a purely mundane affair, prosecuted the venerable Rabbi Kark before a court-martial as the instigator of insubordination, imposed fines upon many shopkeepers, and put the law into effect. Beside this drastic ordinance, which affected the overwhelming mass of the Jewish population and was administered with un-Christian charity, the preference shown by the authorities for the requisitioning of Jewish houses to use as Government offices, for which a mere pittance was given as compensation, was a minor affliction that injured only the people of means. But the Sunday rest law was not the only device for impoverishing the Jews. They were forced out of trade by the Lithuanian co-operative societies, which had not to pay such taxes as private shopkeepers, and which, on the contrary, were assisted from Government funds.

A State which deliberately treated its subjects so harshly had naturally no room for them in its employ, however well qualified they might be. But the Jews would probably not have regarded their exclusion from the civil service as such a calamity if only they had been permitted to remain complete masters in their own community. For the Government, not content with the abolition of the Jewish Ministry, proceeded, in cynical disregard of all its promises and pledges concerning the welfare of its Jewish population, to dissolve all the organised Jewish communities in the country and decreed that they should be replaced by voluntary congregations of a purely religious nature. The Jews were thus deprived not only of their centralised communal system, which was national in character, comprehensive in structure, and possessed of legal status, but they were also despoiled of their fiscal rights, by virtue of which they had hitherto maintained their social, cultural and religious institutions. This last blow was dealt by the Government with calculated cunning and did not fail of its intended effect, for it produced disorder, disintegration, and despair.

"Put not your trust in princes," said the Psalmist of old. "Nor in Peace treaties about minority rights," added the Jew in Kovno.

III

There were 200,000 Jews in Lithuania, dispersed among 180 communities, of which Kovno contained one-fourth of the total. They were all Jewish nationalists. You could not find any Lithuanians of the Jewish faith, nor any Jews with faith in Lithuania. At the birth of the Republic they laboured strenuously for her independence and the enlargement of her frontiers, but the recompense they received in the triumph of Anti-Semitism inevitably resulted in the strengthening of the Jewish national consciousness. United by this common sentiment, they were nevertheless divided into three main parties on the question of the place and method of its practical realisation. The Zionists were the largest in number and the strongest in influence, and played a dominating part in the life of the Jewish community. The Independent Orthodox, for whom the Mizrachi or orthodox Zionists were not religious enough, took the second place. And next came the so-called Autonomists, who were extreme Socialists, opposed to Zionists and Orthodox alike. These Autonomists were the survivals or successors of the obsolete Russian Bund, who clamoured for the national autonomy which the Government had suppressed, proclaimed Yiddish as the Jewish national tongue. and carried on wordy warfare against religious observance. They were organised in a body called "Culture League," of the objects of which the Government evidently disapproved, as the League was dissolved and many of its members were prosecuted.

All three parties maintained their own schools, of which there were about 120 altogether. It was by means of these schools, ranging from kindergarten to *Gymnasium*, that they could best propagate their respective principles and ensure the growth of their particular adherents (though some of them sent their children to a Russian private school, in the hope that the Bolshevik régime would pass away and they would then be able to return to their homes beyond the frontier). In the institutions of the Zionists and the Orthodox Hebrew was the medium of instruction, whilst in one school of the Autonomists everything was taught in Yiddish. The conflict on the language question raged vehemently throughout the country and formed a prominent factor in political controversy, though the Zionists made a concession to popular sentiment by publishing their daily paper, *Die Juedische Stimme*, in Yiddish, and profited by the compromise. The extent, however, to which Hebrew was spoken, not only in the schools but also in the street, at home, in athletic socities, and at public meetings, was most impressive. Its prevalence might perhaps be the natural outcome of the tradition created by Abraham Mapu, the child of the Kovno Ghetto, who was the father of the Hebrew novel: but it possessed much greater significance as a testimony of the seriousness with which the great majority of Lithuanian Jewry considered their destiny to lie in Palestine.

The Jewish schools possessed another distinguishing feature: they were all located in private houses, which were ill adapted for educational purposes. No attempt was made to build a Jewish school, for there was no guarantee that it would be permitted to remain Jewish, nor that in years to come it would be required at all. The handicaps under which both teacher and pupil thus suffered through the unsuitability of the premises were extremely trying; and the task of the community in providing the cost of maintenance, towards which the Government gave merely a paltry grant and the parents could contribute only a slight share, involved the most racking anxiety and necessitated appeals to the generosity of Jews in the more favoured lands of the West. But despite the financial burden, the schools were preserved with zeal and pride as the nurseries of Jewish culture and the power-stations of the Jewish spirit.

IV

Apart from these secular establishments there was also a Talmudical college, whose fame had spread to all communities of Israel that still held in reverence the lore and wisdom of the ancient Rabbis. It was the *Yeshiva* at Slobodka, a surburb of Kovno, to which I paid a visit one grey, wintry morning. I had as my guide a local journalist, who selected for the excursion a droshky with a young Jewish jarvey, with whom we previously arranged the question of fare. Our way lay on the yonder side of the wooden bridge which the Germans, during the First World War, had made across the Vilja, and as soon as the rickety vehicle reached the main road our melancholy nag had to wade through an unending quagmire, which in parts was over a foot deep. Whenever we passed another carriage we were bespattered with mud on coat, hat, and face, and as the traffic was fairly brisk we were subjected to a succession of slimy splashings. There was nothing but mud, black mud everywhere, in streaky puddles, shallow pools, and large, ugly bogs, so that at times our droshky was stuck and I thought that we should be marooned.

"Is it always so muddy here?" I asked.

"In winter always, except when it's frozen," said my companion, "And don't forget that people come here to see the mud as well as the *Yeshiva*. It is also one of the sights of Slobodka."

Slobodka was a straggling, disconsolate-looking village, inhabited entirely by Jews. They lived in timber houses, mostly one storey high, with an exterior coat of dirty grey or green and a homely portico, which they had built for themselves. Most of them were petty tradespeople, with little grocery shops, in whose windows might be seen big plaited loaves, alternating with dairies and smallware stores, whilst in the street one passed long-bearded Jews driving long lumbering carts.

The *Yeshiva* was a big, plain building of brick and timber, which was approached from the street by a modest door leading into a small yard. Even before entering, my ears were assailed by a loud discordant incantation, a raucous medley of shouting and singing, which rose and fell in waves, with brief lulls. Within I saw a lofty, white-washed structure with four stout pillars supporting the roof, from which hung electric lamps, whilst at the further end stood the Holy Ark, with a simple wooden lectern, above which was displayed—rather superfluously—the Hebrew inscription, " Dew and rain," for the seasonal prayer.

Dispersed among the benches, which, intersected by two gangways, were ranged across the chamber, were some hundred students, mostly between the ages of eighteen and twenty-eight, who were all united by absorption in the Talmud, yet diversified by posture, appearance, demeanour, and intonation. Some were sitting and shaking in front of their ponderous folio, which rested on a small reading-desk, the interior of which served as a locker for the owner's praying accessories, whilst others were standing and shaking with even greater energy, and nearly all were singing or shouting snatches of the learned argument, trying to drown their neighbours' voices, and cleaving the air with inverted thumb. All were wearing soft felt hats, some had a fringe of beard intact, and others had their beard clipped. Here and there were little groups vigorously discussing knotty points, whilst two or three, apparently new students, were gazing meditatively at the pregnant page. But there was one young fellow, with hat on the back of his head, pince-nez perched on the tip of his nose, and cigarette dangling from his lips, who seemed resolved to plough his lonely furrow, for he was striding up and down the lower end of the room, with puckered brow and the strange glint in his eye as of one distraught.

"Don't mention that we are Zionists," advised my companion. "They are all anti-Zionists here, members of the *Agudas Israel*. They are opposed to the secular method of rebuilding Palestine, which they say must await the coming of the Messiah. They have their own paper, in which they fiercely attack us. They are fanatical, but I doubt if they are really pious. It is most impressive here in the afternoon, at dusk, when the Rabbi delivers *Musar*,[1] moral exhortation, in which he works powerfully upon the feelings of the younger men and uplifts them to a state of spiritual exaltation."

Presently there entered an elderly man, with a forked grizzled beard, wearing a long fur coat and round fur hat. He leaned over a bench at the bottom of the room and surveyed the scene with searching glance. He was the *Mashgiah* or supervisor, whose arrival was the stimulus to a perceptible crescendo of dialectical incantation. He welcomed my greeting and told me that fifty students had been recently transferred to Palestine, where a *Yeshiva* had been opened for them, and that there were 180 still left. The principal, Rabbi Epstein, had recently returned from America, where he had collected a large sum of money for the transplantation of the entire institution to the Holy Land.[2] Most of the students, he informed me, were provided by the *Yeshiva* with food, clothing, and lodging. Some of them were able to earn a little money by coaching beginners who were the sons of rich parents, and the cleverest of them stood to gain a greater prize by being selected as sons-in-law to wealthy pietists who negotiated with the principal for a Talmudic luminary.

[1] For a fuller account of the moralist movement, see the author's *The Jews of Vilna*, page 209.
[2] The college was established at Hebron, where many students were killed in the Arab riots of 1929.

As we left the college and were driven back to Kovno, we passed a tall, pale-faced student, with reddish beard, striding along in his black gaberdine and carrying a volume of the Talmud. His feet, encased in top boots, sank into the mire of Slobodka, but his eyes, as he peered pensively forward, seemed to rest on the heights of Mount Zion.

V

The land of Israel was the dominating theme in every conversation, and "how long? " was the ever-recurring query. Hundreds of Jews had already bought plots of land in Palestine, thousands were patiently saving up for the day of redemption, and tens of thousands would leave on the morrow if only they saw the way clear.

"We have lived here for centuries," said a Jewish doctor to me, "and Lithuania has contributed an important share to Jewish culture and Rabbinical scholarship. It seemed as if we were entering upon a new epoch of development, but our disillusion has been too painful after all the glowing promises that were made to us, and we cannot resign ourselves to the prospect of a limitless future in this country."

The patriarchal Rabbi Kark, with whom I spent a pleasant hour, recalled the glorious days when he sat as a colleague in the Beth Din (religious court) of that illustrious teacher in Israel, Rabbi Isaac Elchanan—may the memory of the righteous be blessed!—and described the varying phases through which the Jews of Kovno, and of the country in general, had passed during the last forty or fifty years. Did I know that it was largely the Jews of Lithuania, and especially of the town of Schavli, who had helped to build up the vigorous Jewish community in South Africa—a fact that accounted for the strong Jewish consciousness of that community? In the days before the War there was a constant emigration of Jews from the country, if not to South Africa, then to England or America, and the scenes at the railway station when parents took leave of their children. or sisters of their brothers, were distressing.

" Everybody was sad and wept," said the **Rabbi**, "for this breaking up of homes and families seemed such a tragedy. Nobody knew whether those who wandered forth into the distant lands of the *Golus* (exile) would not also wander far from their people and their faith. But now when Jews emigrate, it is mostly to the Land of Israel. Now there are no scenes of sadness and sobbing, only of happiness and rejoicing, for can there be anything more **noble** and sacred than to take part in the rebuilding of Zion? Truly, as it is said in the Psalms: 'They who sow in tears shall reap in joy.'"

But those who were able to migrate numbered only a few thousand in each year, so that the Jews in Lithuania were destined to continue sowing in tears for many a day to come. . . .

They were destined, however, for something inexpressibly worse, for their sufferings between the two wars proved to be of trivial account some years later when hordes of Gestapo barbarians swooped down upon them and drove them into the camps of death. The books from the famous Abraham Mapu Library were publicly burned, and the " ceremony " was witnessed by high German officials, while a German military band played and Storm Troopers danced round the bonfire. The Jews, not only of Kovno but of all Lithuania, were wiped out.

Chapter XII

THE WHITE TERROR IN HUNGARY

THE JEWS in Central Europe had been harassed so long by legal disabilities and bureaucratic chicanery that when the First World War came to an end, and it was generally hoped that the nations on the Continent would all be reconciled to one another and enter upon a new era of brotherly amity, they doubted whether they too would gradually share in the blessings that seemed in store for others. They had been the victims of hostility too long to believe in the possibility of a sudden change, and were therefore not surprised when there were renewed outbursts of violence against them in various regions at the very time when the statesmen of the victorious Powers were engaged in hammering out the Peace in Paris. The worst were the atrocities committed in the Ukraine and White Russia by the troops of Generals Petlura and Denikin, who, in their fight against the Bolshevik Revolution, massacred over 100,000 Jews. There were also excesses on a smaller scale against the Jews in Poland by Poles celebrating their long-awaited independence, and then against those in Hungary by the "Awakening Magyars." The excuse offered for the attacks upon the Jews in Hungary was that some of them had taken part in the short-lived Communist régime of Bela Kun. But the Jewish community was in no way responsible for the actions of the Jewish Communists, who, in fact, were freethinkers and disclaimed any connection with the community.

The news from Budapest that reached London in the early months of 1920 was so alarming that the Zionist Executive requested me to go there and investigate the situation. I was warned that the expedition was dangerous, and when I reached Vienna the warnings increased in solemnity. "For Heaven's sake, don't go!" said many an old Zionist friend, "you will learn here much more about the terrors of Hungary than you can in Budapest. The people there are afraid to speak." But a friend who had recently come, or rather fled, from Budapest, assured me that for me there was no danger. "What! With a British passport! Absolutely safe, only be careful!"

There was a censorship of letters in Hungary, and had I written to anybody there about the object of my journey, I should have helped to frustrate it. So a Viennese friend telegraphed to a cousin in the neighbouring capital that he would arrive on a certain day on important business, and that a room at an hotel should be reserved for him. And in due course I presented myself to our friend in Budapest and claimed the room.

From the moment of my arrival until that of my departure I heard an endless cycle of stories of sorrow—of assault and robbery, of savage mutilations, of sudden raids and amazing disappearances. I seemed to be transported to Tsarist Russia, where any Jew might be spirited away through a false denunciation. But I was soon to learn that the resemblance was fallacious, for in the days of the Muscovite tyranny there was at least a set of rules—even barbarous rules—which directed the exercise of injustice. Here there were no rules: only cupidity, fanaticism, savagery, lawlessness, and an incredible lust for sadistic indulgences.

In the express train that carried me from Vienna to Budapest I carefully studied the British Government's White Paper on the "Alleged Existence of 'White Terror' in Hungary." That White Paper might have been more justly called "Whitewash." My Jewish fellow-passenger, who was travelling on urgent business, and who had often been in Budapest recently, told me more in half-an-hour than the distinguished authors of the Government report had learned in six months. During my brief stay in Budapest I collected such a mass of material about the organised persecution of the Jews that I was astonished that any doubts were still being expressed about its reality. The persecution in Budapest was different from that in the provinces. In the capital you saw no acts of violence by day, and your admiration of the beauties of the city was undisturbed except by the thought that the Budapest Municipality could best celebrate the signing of the Hungarian Peace Treaty by giving the streets and buildings a thorough spring cleaning. It was at night that the crimes were committed, when little groups of "Awakening Magyars," armed with iron staves covered with leather, or officers of the various terrorist groups, sallied forth and bravely attacked an unsuspecting Jew from behind and belaboured him until he was senseless. No wonder that the Allied Missions stationed in Budapest knew so little of the "White Terror." The terrorists, Baron Pronay, Count Ostenburg, and Lieutenant Hejas, were much too wise to carry on their evil work in the full glare of the sun, or to disturb the tranquillity and refinement of the fashionable hotels or aristocratic mansions.

But in the provinces terror was rampant, both day and night, wherever Jews dwelt, for there was no need to study anybody's feelings. Jews were dragged out of their homes, abused, flogged, robbed, tortured, and driven or deported to some other town or to Budapest itself. They were compelled to sign fictitious confessions of penal offences, and if they refused at first they were flogged until they submitted. They were accused of illicit trading, of war-profiteering, of unemployment—of anything that could serve as a pretext: the real accusation was that they were Jews. The tortures that were inflicted upon imprisoned Jews in both the provinces and the capital read like a chapter from the Inquisition. They were flogged naked until they became unconscious; they were then besprinkled with water and asked what was the matter. If the victim was wise enough so say that he had a fall, or something similar, he was allowed to go, though not without a parting warning that if he divulged what had happened to him he would meet with a sorrier fate next time. Some of the worst tortures were practised in the Komarom fortress, where men had to drink blood from their own wounds; others were buried neck-deep in the earth, and others had to hold a mouse in their mouth or to eat the hair pulled off their chin.

The main instigators of the terror were officers who were no longer wanted for the army and who found their livelihood by plundering Jews. These officers belonged to particular detachments of the National Army, but the detachments acted independently of the Supreme Military Command. They probably numbered not more than a few thousand, but they acted with such assurance, energy and effrontery that the Government did not venture to interfere with them. The Government denied there was a White Terror, for it disclaimed responsibility for it. But it was fully aware of the repeated outrages and did nothing to suppress them. It did not utter a single word in condemnation of them, nor make any pretence to punish the malefactors. On the contrary, I was told that various members of the Government gave vent to the most violent abuse of the Jews, and that Admiral Horthy, the Regent of the country, had actually promoted one of the bloodthirsty ringleaders, Captain Pronay, to Major. It was rumoured, and it was probably true, that not all the officers were fond of shedding blood and committing robbery; and, indeed, there were cases where soldiers and peasants had disobeyed the orders of officers to start a pogrom. But, unfortunately, those were the exceptions.

I spent many hours among the fugitives and the deported from neighbouring towns, who were lodged in an internment camp in a Jewish school, under the supervision of the police, until their fate was decided. Those who orginated from Poland or Galicia were transported to their native land. But there were also scores and scores of Jews born in Hungary who were also evacuated from their homes. No mercy was shown to age or sex. Old and young, men and women, they were all huddled away in the middle of the night from towns and villages where they had lived useful and peaceful lives for decades. Many of them had brought sacks for bedding, others miscellaneous household goods. There was a widow with five young children who had lost her husband in the war. There was a young mother who had given birth to her child only eight days before their expulsion. The baby was a puny, wretched mite, unconscious of the cruel world into which it was born, yet a source of comfort to the harassed mother. Many of the children romped about in the schoolyard, all heedless of their parents' sorrows. In one of the schoolrooms I came across a father who was teaching his young son a page of the Talmud, with the persistent aid of a gesticulating friend, and who coolly informed me that he had resumed at the passage where they had left off " at home ". Such was the spirit that no terror could daunt.

But despite the pall of oppression, the leading Jews of Hungary stirred not a finger to defend themselves, or to repel worse disaster that might be lurking. Hungarian Jewry had always prided itself on its ultra-patriotic Magyarism, and it remained true to this policy down to the end. The leaders were afraid that the Hungarian escutcheon might be sullied if they proclaimed their woes to the world, so they were dumb. Nay, they even denied that there were any grievances worth speaking of. " A few hundred Galician Jews—let them go! " said these representatives of Hungarian Jewry. They encouraged the Government to expel the Galician Jews who had taken refuge in Hungary after the outbreak of the First World War; but they little realised that the oil which they poured upon the anti-Semite flame had caused a conflagration that would scorch their own skins. Such was the pride of the Hungarian Jews that a Rabbi once wrote a learned thesis to prove that they were descended from the Hungarian hero, Arpad, and that they had only religion in common with the other Jews of the world. The Chief Rabbi of Szegedin, Dr. Immanuel Loew,

always wore the Magyar national costume and oozed forth
with ultra-patriotic exhortations. And yet he had been in
the Szegedin gaol on the false charge of anti-patriotic senti-
ments. There had, indeed, been a veritable stampede to
the baptismal font, some 30,000 Jews in Budapest alone
having deserted their faith in the preceding nine months.
In some places almost entire communities had gone over to
Christianity. And in the face of all these perils the Liberal
Jews, or " Neologen " (as they were called), still held aloof
from the Orthodox, and both denounced the Zionists as
traitors to the fatherland.

One of the leading Jews in Hungary, Eugene von Polnay
(né Jacob Pollashek), who had been Minister of Food for
two days and afterwards always called himself "Excel-
lency", published a statement in the Hungarian Press,
accusing the Zionists in Transylvania of having a paper
maintained with the money of the Rumanian Press Bureau.
Another "leader", Paul Sandor, one of the few Jews in
the National Assembly, threatened that he would deliver
a speech denouncing Zionism as treason to Hungary; and
still another "leader", Joseph Veszi, the editor of the *Pester
Lloyd*, threatened that he would write a series of articles
against Zionism as an anti-patriotic movement. And all this
at a time when the utmost solidarity was demanded of
Hungarian Jewry. Sandor even declared in Parliament that
Chief Rabbi Loew should be hanged, and the Rabbi of the
Liberal Synagogue in the Tabak Gasse (where Herzl was
born) disclaimed from the pulpit any sympathies with his
fellow-Rabbi who was brooding in prison upon the futility
of his life's work. As long as such insensate Chauvinism
prevailed among the so-called leaders of Hungarian Jewry
(whose own children, by the way, were baptised), it was not
surprising that the terrorists were acting with such audacity
in their anti-Semitic campaign. One or two leaders, when
on a visit to Vienna, resented the intervention of outside
Jews. Those who would not help themselves could hardly
be helped by others.

But in Budapest I met two or three men whose names were not known beyond their own community, and who acted as heroes in the dangerous work of helping the fugitives and those who were wrongfully arrested. They made no speeches and wrote no memoranda, but they were daily performing humanitarian deeds of courage and surpassing merit. I dared not mention their names, and could only offer them a silent and shadowy tribute. But as I was preparing for my first journey to the Land of Israel, I could not help thinking that they were far worthier than I to tread its sacred soil.

* * * * *

The position of the Jews in Hungary has undergone a radical transformation in consequence of the Second World War. Even before the beginning of the war the Horthy Government enacted anti-Jewish laws under pressure from Hitler, and soon after it broke out the sufferings of the Jews became intensified. Some 20,000 were given Swedish protection by being provided with Swedish identity papers, while 7,000 were enabled to escape through Yugoslavia to Italy. About 200,000 are believed to have perished in the Nazi death-camps. Before the Munich Agreement of 1938 Hungary had a Jewish population of 450,000. The present number cannot be determined with certainty, as estimates vary owing to a considerable post-war emigration and also to about 50,000 Jews having been baptised during or just before the war, many of whom still regard themselves as members of the community. The total number of professing Jews is estimated at between 135,000 and 141,000.

Apart from this substantial diminution, the Jewish community differs from its pre-war condition in consequence of Hungary having become a satellite of the Soviet Union. All communal, religious, and cultural activities are under Communist domination, which forbids any relations with international Jewish organisations or with Western Jewry in general. Zionism is proscribed, and emigration to Israel is either obstructed or regulated very rigorously.

Chapter XIII

THE GOLDZIHER LIBRARY

IN THE heart of the Jewish quarter in Budapest, in a house situated only a few minutes walk from the great and imposing synagogue in the Tabak Gasse, there lived and laboured for over forty years one of the most illustrious Oriental scholars of modern times. The street, known by the name of Hollo-utcza, is a long, dreary, narrow thoroughfare, flanked on either side by tall sombre buildings, in which the two most homely features are a modest little bethel and a frowsy kosher restaurant. In a city of picturesque beauty, enhanced by the majesty of the Danube, the Hollo-utcza is a haunt of unrelieved desolation, where nobody could be expected to dwell by choice; but as the Jewish Community owns Number 4, this has always formed the residence of some of its officials. Built in 1869, the lofty four-storied fabric was originally used as an orphanage, a purpose commemorated by the stained-glass "Shield of David" over the huge doorway and again by a similar decoration, with Hebrew date, over the interior door leading to a small dingy courtyard in the back. But ten years later the orphans were removed elsewhere, the building was adapted for private occupation, and the first two tenants were the Rabbi and the Secretary. The Rabbi was Dr. Samuel Kohn, who earned local fame as a preacher and writer; the Secretary was Professor Ignaz Goldziher, who achieved world-wide celebrity as an authority on Oriental lore. But the red marble tablets affixed in their honour on either side of the portal are alike in size and laudatory phrasing.

The secretary of a Jewish community, however able and

conscientious a public servant or however gifted a scholar
he may be, is seldom distinguished by any unique intellectual attainments; but Goldziher held that position for
thirty years, and whilst discharging his duties with
exemplary devotion, developed a mastery in Semitic scholarship that brought grateful tributes from every important seat
of learning in the world. His speciality was the wisdom of
the Arabs, of which all branches were equally under his
command—language and literature, philology and philosophy, history and theology, science and mysticism, tradition
and folklore, jurisprudence and the exegesis of the Koran.
He laid the foundations of his learning during his sojourn
in early manhood in Syria, Palestine, and Egypt. He studied
for a time at the Azhar Mosque in Cairo, and then, returning to Budapest, he pursued his labours with such success
that his writings were hailed and studied as those of an
inspired teacher. Not only Arabic but Hebrew, Turkish, and
Persian lore likewise formed the subject matter of his critical
and literary activity, and his authority in this realm of
knowledge rose to such heights that he was not only
appointed a member of all the learned societies and
academies from New York to Damascus, and from Aberdeen
to the Dutch Indies, but he also received a series of calls to
various universities. He was invited to succeed Robertson
Smith at Cambridge and Noeldeke at Strasbourg, he was
called to the Leipzig University and the Collège de France,
to Heidelberg and Koenigsberg, to Cairo and Upsala. But
to all these luring invitations Goldziher turned a deaf ear.
He preferred to remain in Budapest, to continue working at
his home in the dreary Hollo-utcza.

What was it that fettered him to this sombre dwelling
when such tempting material prizes were dangled before
him? When I first went to visit his home in August 1923,
and, after ascending a dim, circular flight of stone steps,
found myself on the railed gallery that led to the door, and
from which I looked down upon the dirty hand-carts and
the rubbish-heaps in the courtyard below and at the lofty,

grimy wall opposite, which seemed to shut out the light from heaven, I could not help wondering. For forty-two years, I reflected, this world-renowned savant, from early manhood until his death at the age of seventy-two,[1] was content to tread up and down that dim, stone staircase, pace along the narrow, stone gallery that ran round three sides of the building—the fourth being bounded by the gloomy wall—and live in the humble flat that was entered by a door with chequered and bar-protected window-panes. No more drab and depressing surroundings could be conceived, and to be doomed to such neighbourhood for forty-two years! "Such is the *Torah*, and such its reward!"

But when I was admitted by the gentle, greyhaired widow, and taken to the room where he had worked, the riddle was solved. For in this room was the wonderful library, covering the walls from floor to ceiling and overflowing on to extra shelves, which he had thoughtfully and laboriously gathered together from all the regions of the Near East, and wherein he quarried night and day in quest of new truths. It was his passionate attachment to this library, in and for which alone he lived, that made all the glittering offers from other cities, with their promise of superior ease and comfort, appear but phantasms, and its removal seemed to him unthinkable. Here were arranged the well-thumbed tomes in all the Semitic tongues, which he had either bought or which had been presented to him by their authors or by the erudite societies that published them. The works given by their own writers all contained an inscription of homage and often of gratitude, and not a single Orientalist but considered it a duty and honour to send him a first copy. Many of the books were rare, and those that came from Moslem scholars were probably the only copies on the Continent. And Goldziher enriched most of them with his own notes and glosses, written on the fly-leaves and the margin, or on slips of paper, which form a mine of suggestions for those who will delve into them. There were, besides, complete

[1] He died in 1921.

collections of all the periodicals of Europe and America devoted to Oriental lore, many of which continued to come for months after he had passed away. In the centre stood an oak table at which the master had written, or discussed abstruse texts with other scholars, or lectured to students who came from distant lands—from Egypt to America. The little space on the walls not covered by books was occupied by the photographs of friends who produced them —Mommsen and Noeldeke, Wellhausen and Budde, Browne in Persian dress, and Snouck-Hurgronje, who penetrated to Mecca; whilst the eye was also attracted by the Hebrew text, " I have set the Lord before me for ever ", which had been deftly embroidered by the partner of his life as her pious contribution to the chamber's adornment.

Scarcely had Ignaz Goldziher been borne to his grave than the question of the future of the library began to be talked about. Both widow and son deprecated the discussion, for they desired that the contents of the room, which enshrined for them a beloved soul and countless memories, should not be in the least disturbed. But as the months passed by the question began to be urged upon them by interested inquirers. First came a representative of the Hungarian Government, who suggested that it would be a testimony of patriotism if the family would present the library to the State, as though their patriotism were suspect without such an act of self-sacrifice; whilst an alternative proposal that it should be acquired for the State by a group of wealthy Jews in Budapest, fell upon barren soil, because the latter had been soaked only too recently by the blood of the Jewish victims of the "Awakening Magyars." Next came a representative of the Japanese Government, who desired it for the Tokyo University, and then an emissary from the Sorbonne, followed by some prospectors from America.

But the importance of the collection had also not escaped the attention of the Zionist leaders, who saw in it a desirable addition to the Jewish National Library in Jerusalem, and so, after my first cursory inspection, Professor A. Freimann, of the Frankfort City Library, was commissioned to make a more detailed investigation. The result of his report was that I was despatched to acquire the collection of 6,000 volumes and to superintend the transport to Palestine. Before the First World War this would have been a comparatively simple task, but the post-war conditions in Hungary had made it a problem of incalculable difficulty, as permission to export the books had to be obtained from the Government, and it was dubious whether it would be granted. Friends in Budapest with whom I discussed the matter all shook their heads sceptically and predicted that my efforts would be in vain. But thanks to representations that were made to the British Colonial Office and to the subsequent instructions that were sent to the British Minister in the Hungarian capital, the application addressed by the latter on behalf of the Zionist Organisation to the Hungarian Foreign Minister met with a prompt and favourable reply. I was requested to call upon the Director of the National Museum, who told me that as soon as he would receive five copies of the catalogue and a fee based upon the assessed value of the library, the export licence would be issued. To prepare the required copies without delay I had the only catalogue that existed, and which was bound, broken up into six parts, and by employing six typists on the work for two whole days, was able to present the Director with the five catalogues fully a week before he expected them. Meanwhile I had arranged with a shipping agency to deliver the packing-cases in which the books were to be transported.

But the speed with which these preparations were made proved rather disconcerting to old Mrs. Goldziher. Now that the hour was approaching for her to part from the treasures of her husband, she began to show an increasing reluctance. True, the library had been deserted and locked for the last two years, but she had never thought that it would be taken away so suddenly. She begged me to put off the evil day for a couple of months, or at least a couple of weeks, and thought me terribly hard-hearted when I proceeded with the arrangements. Then she wished to be assured about the new home of the books: would they be housed in a building worthy of them and would they be properly used? And when I answered that they would be placed in a new building in the Holy City, whence one could gaze upon the site of the ancient Temple and upon the hills of Judaea, and that scholars and students would flock from all parts of the globe to pore over them, her qualms were stilled.

The following day two officials from the National Museum arrived with the export licence and remained to superintend the packing. Professor Karl Goldziher, the only son of the distinguished Orientalist, first took the books from the shelves and handed them to a couple of workmen, who stowed them into the large wooden cases. The officials now and again examined a volume before it was put away, though they scarce interfered with the progress of the work.

Mrs. Goldziher looked on with a heavy heart and tears glistened in her eyes. "You don't know what these books mean to me, and especially their inscriptions", she said. She handed me a portly volume to inspect. It was a "Dictionary of Technical Terms used in the Sciences of the Musulmans", published in 1862 by the Asiatic Society of Bengal, and containing a dedication by Arminius Vambery to Goldziher on the occasion of his marriage, at which he was one of the sponsors. Another volume that she singled out was "The Episode of the Bab", by Professor E. G. Browne, in which the inscription ran: "As a souvenir of his visit to Cambridge in September 1892, I offer this my first book as a tribute of gratitude for his kindness and admiration for his profound scholarship". And then she lingered over the historic work by Dr. C. Snouck Hurgronje, "Mekka", in two volumes, giving an account of this first European's stay in 1884–5 in Jeddah and Mecca. "All these books are links with the past", she said, "and now they are to be snapped".

After the books were packed into twenty-two cases, which were nailed down and bound with cord, the Hungarian official affixed a red seal to each case and an official from the British Legation followed them and added a British seal. I thought that the work was now over and that the cases could be exported without further ado. But the people at the shipping agency pointed out that a further permit was necessary—one from the *Devisenzentrale*, the foreign currency control office. The obtaining of this document threatened to be a much more formidable undertaking than that of the export licence, but thanks again to the kindly offices of the British Legation the problem was rapidly solved. Only one final formality remained to be discharged —to pay one half per cent. of the estimated value of the library to the Horthy Fund, which was said to be devoted to "charitable objects"—and then the books could go upon their appointed way.

The twenty-two cases were ranged in the library and the adjoining rooms in two rows, between which the frail widow slowly passed, touching each case in turn, as though to retain contact until the last possible moment with the possessions of her husband. They must have seemed to her like coffins, as they were borne out of the dwelling, nor was the sorrow that followed them any less profound than that which accompanies many a real bier. At last they had all been taken away, and she gave a wistful look at the library— bare and desolate. "*Ichabod*—the glory is departed", she said, "and there is nothing more for me to live for".

"The glory is gone from here", I replied, "to the Holy Land, where it will become more glorious still, and where it will confer an untold blessing by bringing Jews and Arabs together in the peaceful pursuit of scholarship, and thus pave the way to a friendly understanding between the two peoples."

The following day the Goldziher library was transported to Trieste, whence it was shipped to Palestine.

Chapter XIV

RUMANIA BETWEEN THE WARS

I

THE JEWISH traveller who arrived in Rumania for the first time was gradually overcome by a sense of disillusion. Having read for years in books and newspapers of the brutal attacks upon helpless pedestrians, of the looting of shops and the desecration of synagogues, his mind was so attuned to evil happenings that he expected, as soon as he stepped out of the train in the railway station of Bucharest, that he would be set upon by anti-Semitic hooligans; and when he saw that he could leave the station without being molested by anybody except some shabby touts outbidding one another in their offers to carry his luggage and conduct him to a good hotel, he had a lurking fear that the place of assault might be somewhere nearer to the heart of the city, and that he might be the victim of an outrage in some sinister by-street. Should he be fortunate enough to be met by a friend, he would at once be reassured, though it might still take him a little time to disburden his mind of a gnawing anxiety. But as the taxicab speedily conveyed him through thoroughfares where life looked much the same as it did in other big cities—but for the salient differences of form, colour, and language, as manifested particularly by the physiognomy and dress of the people and the legends on the shop-fronts—and he reached his hotel without any mishap and without witnessing any riot, he might perhaps feel disposed to revise his previous view of Rumanian policy.

If the traveller confined his investigation of Jewish conditions solely to his own observation, he might spend days and weeks in the Rumanian capital without chancing upon any incident that might confirm the impression of ubiquitous anti-Semitism with which he came into the country. He might pass through the principal streets occupied by Jewish shop-keepers—the Strada Lipscani and Strada Vacarescu—and behold a scene of bustle and animation, in which everybody seemed to be at peace with his neighbour, and where there was a sense of ease and security, if not of orderliness and cleanliness. He might visit the synagogues, even that of the celebrated commentator Malbim, and find that the few faithful worshippers were not interrupted in their devotions by Gentile enemies; or spend an evening at a Yiddish theatre and discover in its simple and half-empty interior that even Jewish lovers of the drama could be indifferent to its appeal. Or he might sit in the Grand Café, facing the imposing General Post Office, which was frequented mainly by Yiddish-speaking business men, who wandered in and out—often without consuming even a cup of coffee—as though it were an exchange and mart, and without being disturbed in their ceaseless chaffering by any more depredatory individual than a hungry pedlar hawking socks and braces.

With the passage of days he would familiarise himself with some of the external features of the capital and its social life, find it reminiscent here and there of Paris or Vienna, and perhaps begin to take a certain pleasure in some of its amenities. He might be attracted to its bookshops and be impressed by the big proportion that French books, especially lemon-covered novels, formed of its varied contents, or gaze at the numerous newspaper kiosks in the fashionable Callea Victoria, with their garish display of illustrated French journals of dubious virtue, and naturally conclude that the reading public must be infused with a leaven of Gallic culture. He might sit in a restaurant and observe that the Rumanians eat just as well and not louder than do Frenchmen or Austrians, and that the cuisine bore

no trace of cannibalism whatever. He might take afternoon
tea in the fashionable pastry-shops of Capsa or Riegler, and
be struck by nothing more than the manner in which a lady
was greeted by a gentleman, for the latter, not content, as
was the average Viennese, with merely saying "*Ich küsse
die Hand*", suited the action to the word and imprinted a
gallant kiss upon the back of the lady's hand, whether it
was still gloved or occupied in scooping cream out of a tart.
He might seek amusement in a picture theatre and realise
that the citizens of Bucharest were moved to laughter by
the antics of Charlie Chaplin—that mirthful leveller of
cultural and linguistic differences—just as readily and freely
as any audience in London or New York. And as he strolled
along the Callea Victoria he would notice that although the
ladies vied with those of Paris in the lavish use of lip-stick,
and that military officers rouged their cheeks and constricted
their waists, there was a general love of good music, as
evidenced by the announcements of concerts by celebrated
artists and the busy trade of the gramophone shops.

Reflecting upon all these things, the Jewish traveller
might be tempted to think that all was well in Rumania
and that the stories he had read of the ill-treatment of
Jews were utterly unfounded. He might be annoyed by
certain things affecting his comfort or peace of mind, such
as the impossibility of getting any cigarettes but those made
of the vile weed of native growth (owing to the narrow-
minded policy of excluding all brands of foreign cultivation), or the difficulty of getting a bath in summer owing
to the inadequate sanitary installations, or the feeling that
he was being victimised in his hotel by the little gang of
" commissionaires " who demanded payment on a generous
scale for the performance of every trivial errand. But these
things were of minor importance beside the question of
justice to his brethren. If he did indeed confine himself in
his study of this question to the evidence of his own eyes
alone, and provided he could not read a Rumanian newspaper, the sense of disillusion which formed his first

experience would, after some days, only become intensified. More than one Christian journalist from Western Europe or America, who thought that he would find the Jewish quarter of Bucharest a scene of riot and bloodshed and was surprised to see that all was quiet, and then had a talk with a Government official, had been apt to believe that Rumania had been maligned.

But the Jewish traveller did not limit himself to observation: he had talks with his fellow-Jews who had been domiciled in the land for years, who told him of their own sad experiences and enabled him to pierce beneath the mirage. And so he learned the bitter truth. It is necessary to emphasise this point, because Rumanian diplomatic representatives in liberal Western countries sought to allay the unfriendly criticism of their own illiberal country by asking the critics to visit Rumania and convince themselves that the Jews had nothing to complain of. I was in Rumania four times between the two Wars, and was not so convinced. I traversed its territories old and new, from Temesvar to Kishineff, from Czernowitz to Oradea Mare, and I heard repeated stories of wrong-doing against the Jew. Fortunately I was never implicated in an anti-Jewish riot, but unfortunately I saw the dreadful effects of such riots.

II

Rumania was a classic land of Jewish oppression. Long before she obtained her independence her Jewish inhabitants had frequently been the victims of outrage and pillage, from which they had no redress, as they were outlaws. She was granted her independence in 1878 on the express condition that she conferred civil rights upon all her subjects without regard to race or religion, but she cunningly evaded her obligation in respect of the Jews by declaring them to be aliens, and continued persecuting them with impunity. Various efforts were made from time to time by the Great Powers to compel her to honour her undertaking, but the ways of diplomacy, before the First World War, were fumbling and futile. When at length the war was over and Rumania, by her accession of new territory, trebled her Jewish population, she could no longer escape the elementary obligations of a civilised country. She was obliged, like other States of Central and Eastern Europe whose frontiers had to be ratified by the Great Powers, to sign a treaty which was designed to bestow all the rights and benefits of citizenship upon her 850,000 Jewish subjects. The clauses this time had been phrased so precisely and circumspectly, they had been examined and analysed so minutely and thoroughly by the astutest legal brains, that it was deemed to be impossible for Rumania this time to wriggle out of her pledge. But the statesmen of the Western world had underestimated the resourcefulness of Rumanian statecraft or rather craftiness, for the latter devised such an interpretation of salient clauses in the Minorities treaty that tens of thousands of Jews were cheated out of their citizenship, whilst even those possessed of civic rights were doomed to see them neutralised by Jewish wrongs.

By the terms of the treaty, all persons habitually domiciled in the country on the date when it was signed, September 4th, 1920, were entitled to citizenship without further ado; but a law was passed which made the acquisition of citizenship subject to proof of ten years' continuous domicile in the same place before December 1st, 1918, and as many Jews, owing to their migratory habits, were unable to show this qualification, they were condemned to being Stateless, with all the handicaps and disabilities attaching to this status. I found that in the Bukowina there were still 20,000 Jews in this anomalous position, and that there were thousands too in Bessarabia and Transylvania. If such a Stateless person wished to emigrate, he was not only denied the endorsement in his passport to enable him to return, but, as the holder of such a document, he forfeited all claims to Rumanian citizenship and ownership of rural property from the moment he left the country. The League of

Nations had the right to take Rumania to task for evading her obligations, but failed to do so. The Jews in the country were restrained from making any appeal to the League by the fear that they might be branded by their Government as traitors (though it was the Government that proved the traitor), whilst all the representations made by Jewish organisations of other countries were countered by ingenious and elaborate quibbling by Rumanian statesmen in an endeavour to prove their good faith.

As for those Jews who were legally citizens, it was at most a second-class citizenship which they were permitted to exercise. They were not allowed to hold positions in the Government or municipal service, though they were made to pay more than their due share of the income-tax revenue by which those services were mainly supported—a burden that pressed with even greater injustice upon those who were Stateless. Income-tax was assessed not solely according to one's declared or estimated income, but also according to the race or nation to which one belonged. In Transylvania and the Bukowina, for instance, the Jews were made to pay at the highest rate, next came the Hungarians, then the Saxons, and lastly—the lowest of all—the Rumanians. There was no law sanctioning this discrimination, for that would have been a flagrant violation of the constitution and of the Minorities Treaty, but it was the common administrative practice. The Ministry of Finance, at Bucharest, in drawing up its budget, assigned definite quotas to different provinces, honouring the latest annexations with a proportionately higher amount than the Regat or Old Rumania, whilst the local officials were left to their own devices in regard to raising or extorting the money. Many a Jewish merchant and tradesman in Czernowitz, Cluj, and Temesvar, complained to me of the petty persecutions to which they were subjected by prying officials, who paid them sudden visits under the pretence of checking their income-tax returns and insinuated, if they did not openly suggest, that their calls could be warded off by a suitable douceur. Backsheesh

A Kovno Match-maker taking Notes

A Rumanian Synagogue after a Pogrom

was the order of the day, practised from the highest to the lowest circles, and the official morality of which it was a typical expression spread cancer-like throughout the new territories.

A prominent Jewish merchant told me that he once received a visit from an income-tax inspector, who declared that he would be willing to send him a lower assessment than he had done the previous year if he would make him a present of a couple of beautiful carpets, which he coveted. The merchant, being loth to part with two carpets, sent only one, trusting that the inspector would be satisfied. Imagine, then, his astonishment when the new demand from the income-tax office was for exactly the same amount as before. Furious with indignation, he hurried to the inspector and asked him whether he had not received the carpet.

" Yes," blandly replied the official, " but our agreement for reducing the assessment was that I should receive two carpets."

" Then I shall make you pay for the one carpet," rejoined the merchant. But it was a vain threat, and he knew it.

Nor was it merely from the public service that Jews were excluded. They were equally barred from positions in the army, though they were obliged to discharge their military duties. They were largely represented in Chambers of Commerce and Stock Exchanges, but by ingenious devices they were kept out of the governing councils. They might provide the bulk or even the whole of the capital of a limited company, but they were required by law to reserve a number of administrative posts for persons of Rumanian race and even to employ a predominantly Christian staff. They could not obtain credit from a Rumanian bank, even though willing to pay the exorbitant rate of interest that was charged. Jewish—like non-Jewish—landowners were expropriated through the Agrarian Reform of 1926, but Jewish peasants, of whom there were large numbers in the Bukowina, Transylvania, and Bessarabia, were denied their share of the expropriated lands in the same proportion as the non-Jewish peasants. The system of economic repression which was ruthlessly pursued against the Jews was exemplified by an order of the Government to the banks to furnish particulars of their Jewish customers, and although the order was suspended out of fear that it might affect negotiations in America for a loan, it nevertheless hung like a sword of Damocles over those Jews who had relations with Rumanian banks. And a further blow aimed at them consisted of a law whereby the Government was to act as the selling agency for wheat to foreign countries, a radical reform that meant the exclusion of thousands of Jews from this branch of commerce in which they had hitherto been engaged, and the substitution for them of Christian officials put in charge of the State granaries and depots in various parts of the country.

III

Of all the forms of anti-Jewish oppression practised in Rumania, the most insidious and destructive was that pursued in connexion with the *numerus clausus* agitation. Ever since December 10th, 1922, the Rumanian students carried on a systematic and violent agitation for restricting the admission of Jews to the Universities to a small percentage. Every Government firmly resisted this demand, which would have involved a gross infringement of the Minorities Treaty, but whatever credit might otherwise be ascribed to this attitude was more than wiped out by the discredit and disgrace resulting from the utter failure to suppress the agitation itself. For this was no ordinary movement, finding vent simply in meetings or propaganda literature, as would be fitting in the case of academic agitators. It was a violent crusade, organised by unscrupulous leaders, and directed not merely against Jewish students but against Jews in general. It took the form of brutal attacks with revolvers and knuckledusters upon Jewish

students, both men and women, in the universities; of
assaults upon Jewish travellers in trains, from which they
were forcibly ejected; of concerted and armed raids upon
Jewish districts. Countless persons were injured or robbed
in these disorders, and two cold-blooded murders stand out
in the sinister record. The first was the murder of the
Prefect of Jassy, Manciu, a Christian, who was shot down
in a court of law by a student, Codreanu, who was being
prosecuted for rioting; and the second was that of a Jewish
student, David Fallik, who was also shot in a court of law
by a Rumanian student, Totu. Both assassins were put on
their trial and both were acquitted, but so far from the
sentences arousing the indignation of the public, they were
approved by the general press, whilst the felons were hailed
as national heroes and overwhelmed with ovations. The
arch-ringleader was a former Professor of the Jassy
University, Cuza, a proved plagiarist, who had carried on
anti-Semitic agitation throughout his long and maleficent
life and poisoned the minds of successive generations of
students.

For many years the Government made little pretence of
attempting to punish those guilty of excesses: a few might
be arrested now and again, but they were soon liberated.
Nor could the Government consistently adopt any punitive
measures, since it was known that it approved and materially supported the misdeeds of the National Christian
Students' Organisation. For not only did the Government
furnish a sum of 15 million lei (nearly £19,000) a year for
the maintenance of students' homes and canteens, but it
gave special grants for students' congresses, which were the
prelude to anti-Jewish riots, and it provided free railway
travel to enable the academic hooligans to get about the
country. Ministers had more than once defended the mis-
conduct of students on the ground that they had carried
into civic life "the spirit of the trenches", and their
speeches were simply an incitement to further outrages. At
times the disturbances in the universities of Bucharest and

Jassy were so grave that soldiers and police had to be drafted into the buildings so as to maintain order during the lectures, and when this measure (owing to the low morale of the armed defenders, mostly peasant conscripts) proved futile, the universities were closed for weeks and even months. Most of the professors, so far from attempting to rebuke or restrain the rioters, fanned their passions by anti-Semitic tirades, and made it impossible for thousands of Jews to be admitted to the universities by ploughing them wholesale in the entrance examinations. The effect was that though there was no *numerus clausus* by law, there was one in fact, which in some cases almost amounted to a *numerus nullus*.

Many were the stories that I heard of young Jews, who, after succeeding in passing the tricky entrance examinations and then braving the jeers and blows of their Christian fellow-students, found themselves forced, with bruised limbs and shattered nerves, to give up the quest of learning at a Rumanian university as too dangerous an adventure. Either they entered business or (if they could find the means) went to some university in a foreign and more hospitable country, whilst some solved the problem—in the despair engendered by ruthless persecution—by committing suicide. Never shall I forget the look of anguish on the face of a father, who told me of the tragic end which his son had put to his life a few weeks before. He was a strapping young fellow of twenty-one, in whom his parents had centred all their hopes, and he had been nagged and goaded to death by the intolerance and brutality of his Christian fellow-students.

By far the worst excesses were those perpetrated at the end of 1930 in Transylvania. The authorities at first tried to deceive the world into believing that only a window or two had been broken, but the evidence of the destruction committed at Oradea Mare, Huedin, and Cluj, was so overwhelming that they decided, upon second thoughts, to express regret and to offer monetary compensation to the victims. I visited Oradea Mare and Cluj three months later, and still found distressing traces of the outrages in abundance.

In Cluj the names and signs over the windows of Jewish shops in the main thoroughfares were defaced or mutilated; large window-panes, which had been smashed, were replaced by smaller ones; and new paint had been daubed over recent repairs. The most savage assaults had been made upon the synagogues, as though in an effort to exterminate the very roots of the Jewish faith. I went to the three principal places of worship—that of the "Neologen" (or Reformers), of the Orthodox, and of the *Hebra Kadisha*—and found that they had all suffered severely. All the windows had been broken, the benches had been hacked and battered to pieces, the chandeliers and electroliers had been demolished, and the Arks of the Law had been despoiled and desecrated—the scrolls of the Torah having been rent into bits, which the students stuck into their buttonholes. In one of the synagogues a dozen men were at prayer when the onslaught was made; they were attacked fiendishly by the students, and one old man had an eye gouged out. The rioting in Cluj lasted only from four to seven o'clock in the afternoon, and was committed by students, who had come from Oradea Mare, whilst their train was waiting in the station, and were protected all the time by the military and police, who even helped them by lending them their bayonets.

The main excesses occurred in Oradea Mare, a pleasant town, with a large Jewish community, which was better known before the First World War as Grosswardein, for it was here that the Congress of 5,000 students assembled. Not only had they received a grant from the Government for their expenses, but they had been provided with free travel on special trains, and they were quartered free in the homes of the townsfolk—mostly Jews—where they ate and drank their fill and conducted themselves like hooligans. The avowed object of the Congress was, from the outset, both anti-Jewish and anti-Magyar; it was intended as a demonstration against the late Lord Rothermere's agitation for a revision of the Treaty of Trianon in favour of Hungary, which was the reason why it was held in a town close to the Hungarian frontier. The Under-Secretary of State for the Interior, M. Tartarescu, had been there a few days before to prepare the way, and was in telephonic communication with the civic authorities all the time that the disorders continued. The Congress opened with speeches on a Sunday, but by Monday noon these had given way to organised assaults upon Jews and their shops, cafés, and synagogues, whilst the final stage consisted of wholesale plundering, which continued uninterruptedly throughout Tuesday night. A large military force, cavalry and infantry, had been drafted into the town, not for the defence of the Jews but for the protection of the students, so that they might carry out their fell purpose unmolested, and many a bayonet was lent to the rioters to wreak havoc. A fire-escape was mobilised under a pretext, and the firemen's tools were likewise requisitioned as instruments for destruction. Women students also took part, carrying stones in their portfolios for the smashing of windows.

The effects of these hostile operations were even more abundant and serious than in Cluj. You could not go a yard along the main business street, which led through the heart of the town to the principal square, without noting that all the Jewish shops had been damaged and defaced. Bits of splintered glass still lay on the pavement, and carpenters were busy with repairs. The interior of the large "Neologen" synagogue looked as if it had been sacked by vandals: not only were the windows broken, the seats demolished, the Menorah lamps pulled out of their sockets, and the Ark stripped of all its sacred contents, but the heavy railing of wrought iron, separating the Ark from the *Almemar* (cantor's dais), had been wrenched out of the concrete floor and smashed into fragments. Two other synagogues that I visited had been equally maltreated, though one of them was already restored. The casualties numbered over twenty persons seriously injured, but they did not arouse one-tenth of the sorrow and indignation that was evoked by the destruction of the forty scrolls of the Torah, one of them a precious manuscript over 1,100 years old.

The Government, which, on the occasion of all previous anti-Jewish disorders, did not even make any pretence of punishing the guilty, found itself constrained at last to bring some to trial. A number were sentenced to various terms of imprisonment, but the hearings in the court at Cluj were disgraced by the slanderous accusations brought by the defenders against Jews and Judaism. Some police officials were dismissed for dereliction of duty, but they appealed on the ground that they had received orders not to touch a hair of the students—and their appeals carried weight. The Prefect of Oradea Mare was relieved of his post, but I saw him walking jauntily in mufti through the town as though he had performed a veritable act of heroism.

The scenes that I witnessed and the stories I had heard in the two cities were distressing enough, but I was much more affected by the fears of the Jews that worse might yet happen. They spoke to me with blanched faces, scared looks, and bated breath. Anti-Semitism among the students had now become such a formidable organised force that the Government could do little or nothing to subdue it— probably because it had no wish to do so. The Government had suppressed the Socialist movement, because it was determined. If the students were permitted to carry on their frightful antics, it must have been because the Government found them a convenient lightning-conductor, designed to divert public attention from its own remissness. The antagonism of the students against the Jews was fed on envy, prejudice and fear: they were the sons of either Government officials or farmers, and they thought that unless they could get rid of all possible Jewish rivals, or at least reduce them to small proportions, they would find it impossible to secure a footing in their future

professions. And so they spent far more time and energy in
filibustering than in studying.

IV

There was still a censorship of newspapers and letters in
the country. All newspapers, before publication, had to be
submitted to the censor, who could suppress news or views
according to his fancy or his fears, a mischievous survival
of War conditions and utterly unconstitutional, but whenever a protest was made in a law-court it was declared to
be in order. The prying into letters was not officially
admitted, but everybody knew that it was practised, and
many were its victims. Not all correspondence, however,
was examined, for that would have required an enormous
and educated staff, but letters—especially those going
abroad—were selected at random, and their writers might
be summoned by the " Siguranza " or political police for an
embarrassing interview. Even books might be suppressed
by the censor, as, for example, a Rumanian translation, in
pamphlet form, of the stenographic report of the
Schwarzbart[1] trial in Paris, on the ground that it might be
a provocation to the Ukrainians: though it was never
known that the censor had suppressed any anti-Semitic
screed on the ground that it might be a provocation against
the Jews.

This interference with the privacy of the post and the
liberty of the press betrayed an uneasy conscience. The
governors of Rumania could not tolerate criticism, they
were afraid of the facts about their maladministration
becoming known abroad, and they accused those who were
guilty of nothing else but telling the truth, of discrediting
their country. They would not or could not see that
those who discredited their country were not those who told
the truth, but those who were responsible for the multiplicity

---

[1] Schwarzbart shot dead General Petlura, who had organised massacres
of Jews in the Ukraine in 1920-21.

of evils contained in that truth. Whilst one was still in Rumania one could hardly appreciate the nervousness of the authorities in regard to foreign opinion; it was only when one was on the point of crossing her frontier and passing into the freer air of a neighbouring land that this sensitiveness stood exposed in all its shivering nakedness. I found that taking leave of Rumania was like launching upon a strange adventure. In the first place, it was forbidden to have any Rumanian money on one on pain of its being confiscated, for the export of Rumanian currency was supposed to affect its stability; and secondly, it was forbidden to have more than ten pounds' worth of other currency, unless one's passport showed that one had more than that amount when one came into the country, or unless one obtained a special permit for the purpose.

Having made several visits before, I thought that I knew all the regulations pertaining to the ordeal of departure, but on the last occasion there awaited me a surprise. It was at Episkopia, the frontier station through which I had to pass in travelling from Oradea Mare to Budapest. Like all the other passengers I went into the customs hall for the examination of my luggage, but whilst everybody else's belongings were inspected rather perfunctorily mine were subjected to a diligent search. The official, with gold-braided uniform and powdered cheeks, espied some bulletins of the Jewish Telegraphic Agency, which I had made no attempt to conceal, in my portmanteau. He asked me what they were, and I explained, adding that the bulletins were printed in London and had reached me through the post in Rumania. He put them on one side for further examination, and I scented trouble. He then examined the contents of my attaché case: it was the same case that I had carried on all my previous visits, and the contents were similar, consisting mainly of official Zionist documents, a large letter-book, a note-book, some newspapers and more bulletins of the Jewish Telegraphic Agency. The sight of so much written matter intensified his suspicions. He had a whispered consultation with a colleague and then declared that I must go with him to the Chief of Police. The bureau of this functionary adjoined the customs hall and as I passed the barrier I saw another official ungallantly feeling the bosom of a woman, presumably to see whether she had any banknotes concealed there.

The Chief of Police was subacidly polite but undisguisedly suspicious. " Will you allow me to examine your documents? " he asked in German, as though I had any alternative but to assent. He distributed some of the typed papers among his three underlings, who immediately began poring over them as if in quest of the betrayal of some great State secrets, but as their knowledge of English was obviously very slight the Chief sent for a railway-clerk who was apparently reputed to be an English scholar. The latter translated some of the passages in the bulletins referring to conditions in Transylvania and to the *numerus clausus* question in Rumania.

An eager discussion ensued among the officials, the Chief of the Police puckering his brows. I saw through the window that all the passengers had now left the customs hall, and I was afraid that the train might leave without me.

" Will I be able to go with this train? " I asked.

The Chief shrugged his shoulders. " It will take some time to examine all these papers, so you will have to go back to Oradea Mare and explain."

"But there is nothing wrong about these papers," I insisted. "They are either copies of my official correspondence relating to Zionist work or bulletins printed in London and circulated all over Europe."

" But they deal with political matters," said the railway-clerk, " and that is forbidden. We still have a state of siege here."

A state of siege twelve years after the First War!

"I must get to Budapest to-day," I urged, "whatever you may do about the papers. You have seen my passport and visiting-card and know who I am."

Again an animated consultation took place, whilst I wondered what I should do if the train, in which all my luggage minus the attaché case had already been deposited, were to steam out without me. The prospect of being stranded in this little frontier town, an object of suspicion to all its inhabitants, was disquieting enough, and the possibility of being sent back to Oradea Mare—perhaps under police escort—was even more alarming. I awaited the result of the conference with impatience.

At last the brows of the Chief of the Police relaxed. "You may go now, but you must leave these papers here. You can claim them through the British Legation." He returned me my case with all the printed papers, whilst retaining those that were typed, together with my letter-book and note-book.

"Will you please give me a receipt for these documents?" I asked.

The Chief and all his satellites glared at me as though I had demanded the State seal, their look of indignation being mingled with scorn.

"The Chief of the Police does not give any receipt," said the railway-clerk, with affronted pride.

Through the window I saw that the conductor was warning the passengers to take their seats. I did not stop to argue, but hastened out in search of my seat in the train, followed along the platform by hundreds of staring eyes.

On the morning after my arrival in Budapest I went to the British Legation to report the incident and to request that immediate steps be taken for the recovery of my property. A telegram was sent to the British Legation at Bucharest, and a despatch was sent to the Foreign Office in London. The news proved a godsend to local press correspondents, who had been languishing for something sensational, and soon it was flashed to the ends of the world.

Eight days later I arrived in London, and after a further fortnight a package containing the confiscated papers was delivered at the Central Office of the Zionist Organisation by a messenger of the Foreign Office. An examination of the package showed that the papers had been carefully examined, but every scrap had been returned: the Rumanian authorities had apparently satisfied themselves that there was nothing noxious in my literary baggage.

My experience was of importance, not on account of its personal aspect (for a frequent traveller expects such adventures now and again), but on account of the light that it threw upon the mentality of the Rumanian authorities. They were desperately anxious lest the outside world should learn the truth about the conditions in their country, but all the devices they adopted to hide the truth had the contrary effect of serving as incentives to root it out. This mentality and this policy have, even under a totally different régime, continued to the present day.

*   *   *   *   *

However harassing and unjust the ill-treatment of the Jews in Rumania was before the war, it was tolerable in comparison with the inhuman persecution to which they were subjected after the country fell under the heel of Hitler. The triumph of Nazism in Germany gave a fresh impetus to Jew-baiting in Rumania, and the Goga Government at the end of 1937 introduced many of the oppressive and humiliating enactments of the Nazi code. But this was merely a prelude to the orgy of atrocities committed by the Rumanians during the war. There were wholesale massacres of Jews in Bucharest, Jassy, Botosani, Timisoara, and other cities. During the four months August–November 1941, it was estimated that the Rumanians were responsible for the murder of 100,000 Russian and Rumanian Jews. The Rumanians also transported over 130,000 Jews from Moldavia, Bessarabia, and Bukowina to their short-lived province of "Transdniestria" in the Ukraine, to which further contingents of victims were added. There the Jews were dumped into primitive concentration camps, where the conditions were so appalling that 250,000 perished.

Extensive outrages were also perpetrated in Bessarabia, where, by the summer of 1942, it was reported that Jews had ceased to exist. Of a total Jewish population in Rumania, of 850,000 before the war, it is calculated that 425,000 met their doom either in death-camps or in some equally barbarous manner.

Since the end of the war there has been a large emigration of Jews from Rumania, the number who left for Israel from its establishment in May 1948 until March 31st, 1951, being nearly 90,000. In 1949 there was also a large-scale deportation to the Soviet Union of Bessarabian and North Bukowinian Jews, who had settled in Bucharest or in the old Rumanian provinces. There are now about 350,000 Jews left in Rumania, whose position, since the country is a Soviet satellite, is in many respects similar to their fellow-Jews in Hungary. All communal, religious, cultural, and economic activities are under Communist domination, which does not tolerate any relations with international Jewish organisations or with Western Jewry in general. Zionism is ruthlessly suppressed, hundreds of Zionists have been imprisoned, the authoritative Jewish " Democratic Committee" wages a vindictive campaign against all forms of Jewish nationalism, and, although there has been an appreciable exodus to Israel, emigration to that country is subject to constant and capricious obstruction.

Chapter XV

A STROLL THROUGH CZERNOWITZ

THE JEWISH community of Czernowitz cannot boast of such antiquity as other communites in Eastern Europe, such as Cracow or Lwow, for even as late as the middle of the eighteenth century the city had only a small number of tolerated Jews, who were subject to capricious expulsion. But it was a stronghold of Jewish traditional life and culture, which has passed through strange vicissitudes since the beginning of this century and now possesses peculiar and pathetic interest for the student of the Jewish Diaspora. It is to the industry and enterprise of the Jew that the city owed a great deal of its early development and urban improvements, and it is perhaps symbolical of the part they played, and of their appreciation of the value of time, that the first town clock was presented by the Jewish community—the wonderful handiwork of the first clockmaker of the Bukowina, a Jew named Abraham Falk, who flourished and fashioned time-pieces a hundred and seventy years ago. A century later they were enjoying a large measure of autonomy, and with their increase in numbers came an expansion of their activity in the commercial and intellectual development of the city. At the opening of the University in 1875 the first speaker at the inaugural ceremony was a Jewish student, Eduard Reiss, who thirty years later was elected and acclaimed as Burgomaster.

Before the Second World War the Jews estimated that they formed a third of the 200,000 inhabitants of the city, but the Rumanian authorities,[1] anxious to minimise their

[1] This was written when Czernowitz belonged to Rumania. Since 1944 the city, as part of the Bukowina, has been incorporated within the territory of the Soviet Union.

importance, put them down at about 42,000. The population constituted a regular *macédoine* of nationalities—Rumanians, Germans, Ruthenians, Poles, Armenians, and others—among whom the Jews seemed to preponderate everywhere. If one took a stroll through the principal street, one would hardly find more than one or two names of non-Jews over the long array of shops on either side. Commerce was largely in Jewish hands, which was probably the reason why the Rumanian authorities tried artificially to transfer the commercial activity of the whole district to Jassy, though the latter was not such a convenient junction as Czernowitz. But this endeavour was only part of the bigger policy—to Rumanise the once pulsating centre of Austrian commerce and culture.

"Before the First World War," said my companion, a Jewish lawyer, as we made our way to the Ring Platz, "we were within the same frontiers as Vienna, and we could get there in an over-night journey. There was a frequent coming and going between here and there, and we felt the intellectual and artistic influence of the metropolis. But now we feel isolated, marooned—geographically and spiritually. Vienna is no longer what it was, it is true, but to get there is some adventure. It means travelling through Hungary or through Poland and Czechoslovakia, with all the harassing annoyances of the twofold customs at every frontier, and that certainly does not encourage travel. But what is our metropolis now? Shall we derive any spiritual stimulus from Bucharest? Balkan cities may intrigue the West European, who may imagine that all sorts of theatrical spectacles are taking place in the streets and dark conspiracies are being hatched in smoky cafés. Bucharest is not as dull as Belgrade, nor as frowsy as Sofia. But can you compare it with Vienna—at least with the Vienna that was once?"

And my companion told me a disheartening story of the policy of Balkanisation or barbarisation, of which the Jews were the principal victims, and the effects of which were

conspicuously manifested in connection with the University. Before 1914 there were seven or eight Jewish professors, but after 1918 there was only one; formerly there
were 500 Jewish students—the majority—but later there
were hardly more than a few score. The old professors (one
of them Leon Kellner, whose *Historical English Grammar*
was once a text-book at English colleges) left on being told
that by a certain time they would have to submit to an
examination in Rumanian. Loyal for the most part to the
spirit of Austria, they could not reconcile themselves to
the prospect of becoming apostles of Rumanian culture;
so they betook themselves to Vienna or to other centres of
learning, leaving their vacant chairs to be filled by the
promotion of secondary school teachers, which lowered the
level of academic teaching at the Universities of Rumania
for years.

The Jewish students left, partly because of the operation
of the *numerus clausus* and partly because of the brutal
violence to which they would have been subjected at the
hands of their Christian fellow-students if they had
attempted to enter the lecture-rooms. They went to Vienna,
Prague, Rome, Liège, even Toulouse—to anywhere where
they could be free from anti-Semitic molestation in the pursuit of their studies. There was no *numerus clausus* law,
but the professors deliberately ploughed the great majority
of the Jewish students who sat for the entrance examinations, and thus secured a drastic limitation of their numbers.
It was in consequence of the public protest of the Jewish
students many years ago to this iniquitous practice that
many of them were arrested and put on trial, and one of
them, David Fallik, was shot dead in court by a Christian
student, Totu, who was tried, acquitted, and applauded as
a national hero.

"The cultural question is a serious one," said my companion, as he led me into a café full of cigarette-smoking
Jews engaged in clamorous chatter. "It is no easy thing to
change the language in which you speak and think. Our

children at school may find it easy, but all the people here still talk German and Yiddish, and we have our papers in these languages. The German theatre has been converted into the Rumanian National Theatre, at which only Rumanian pieces are performed, and in order to ensure a good attendance students are admitted for nothing. There is also a German theatre, but performances are irregular. The famous actor Moissi was chased away by *Haken-kreuzler*,[1] and the Vilna Troupe were unable to play as the police refused to be responsible for order, in other words, they would not keep order for the sake of the Jews."

Presently we were approached by a young Russian Jew, with a high forehead and hollow cheeks, clad in a thread-bare coat. He had escaped—like so many other fellow-Jews —from over the frontier and was anxious to get to Palestine. My companion advised him to apply to the local Zionist office, which would do its best to facilitate the realisation of his ambition.

"We get quite a number of Russian Jews smuggled over," he said. "We are not far from the Russian frontier, you know, and Czernowitz was in Russian hands three times during the War.[2] However discontented we may be here, our brethren under the Bolsheviki consider our lot enviable. From here we send them to Constanza, on the Black Sea, from where the *Halutzim* (young pioneers) from Poland and Russia and this country sail regularly for Jaffa or Haifa."

At a neigbouring table there was a vehement discussion between some men about a burning problem of internal Jewish politics:—whether the leaders of Bukowina Jewry should join the Union of Rumanian Jews, the representative organisation of Old Rumania.

"You see," explained my legal friend, "here we are mostly Jewish nationalists, whilst the leaders of the Union are not nationalists but only interested in securing complete equality of treatment for the Jews in Rumania. We are, of course,

---

[1] Members of an anti-Semitic organisation who wore the swastika.
[2] The First World War.

also concerned about that question—especially the granting of citizenship to the *Staatenlose* (Stateless), of whom we have about 5,000 in the Bukowina. It might, therefore, seem only natural and logical that we should combine to achieve our object. But the thing is not so simple, as we have to negotiate with the leaders of the rival political parties, and whilst our friends in Bucharest are in touch with the leaders of the parties of Old Rumania, we are on friendlier terms with the leaders of the National Peasant party. There are thus wheels within wheels, and not all the wheels are revolving in the same direction, or at the same time, or with the same *tempo*, so the poor *Staatenlose* have to wait year after year until they are allowed to become full-fledged Rumanians."

We escaped from the clouds of smoke into the open air, and in two minutes found ourselves in the large square called " Ring Platz ", along one side of which was a row of shabby cabriolets in the charge of Jewish drivers, who were of all ages but all equally hardy, weather-beaten, and long-suffering. On the Square had been erected a monument to commemorate Rumania's victory over Austria. It was symbolic in design—an ox trampling upon an eagle, with a soldier defending a helpless woman. Its cost was estimated at about £2,000, which, expressed in local currency, and having regard to local prices, was quite a formidable sum, being (at that time) over 2 million lei.

" And from where did most of the money come? From the pockets of us Jews," remarked my cicerone. " Whenever a Jew went to a police bureau for a licence or visa or any sort of official matter—and we have to go pretty often —he was made to subscribe a few hundred lei. He had no alternative. But that is not our only grievance. This monument has been erected on a place where there used to be dozens of stalls and booths belonging to Jewish shop-keepers, who had leases of their sites for ten years. But one fine morning, by order of the Municipality, and without any notice, two dozen workmen came and started pulling the structures down, compelling the Jewish dealers to take their wares away. An application was made to the law-court, which gave an injunction against the Municipality, but the authorities took no notice and trampled on the rights of the Jews as the ox is trampling on the eagle. Still, the story of this monument is not quite so outrageous as that of another monument which is to be put up in honour of Eminescu, Rumania's greatest poet, who died many years ago. He wrote that the Bukowina was once a para-dise, but had been polluted by ' Jewish swine '. And now Jews are called upon to subscribe to a monument for this exemplar of Rumanian culture.

" When these attacks are made on our pockets, it is diffi-cult to defend ourselves," he observed, as we left the Square and wended our way through the Tempel Gasse towards the Great Synagogue, whose lofty cupola could be seen from a distance. " But when an attack was made on our person we found it easier to ward it off. A few years ago one of the leaders of the anti-Semitic students' organisation, Popescu, came here and carried on an attack against Jews in the streets and against Jewish shops. The police remained passive, and the trouble lasted for a couple of days, until our muscular youth organised its forces for the counter-attack, scattered our assailants, and battered the honourable Popescu so thoroughly that by the time he was left alone he reminded one of the verse in the prophet Isaiah : ' From the sole of the foot even unto the head there is no sound-ness in it, but wounds and bruises, and festering sores.' He had to lie in the hospital for a few weeks before he could walk again, and then he left the city and has never shown his face here again."

We arrived at the Great Synagogue, called the Temple, an imposing and magnificent edifice of Moorish design, which was completed in 1877. Its lofty, majestic cupola towering against the sky, surrounded by a number of small and slender turrets rising from every angle of the roof, reminded me remotely of the general contour of the Taj Mahal.

though there was, of course, a world of difference in the composition of the fabric, in the colouring and the environment. From there my friend, discoursing meanwhile on the fame of former Rabbis and on the historic Conference of Yiddish writers, which was held in Czernowitz, in 1908, in order to assert the supremacy of Yiddish over Hebrew as the national language of the Jewish people, conducted me to a huge four-storied structure, over the main entrance of which was the simple yet significant inscription : "*Juedisches Haus.*"

We entered and visited some of the principal institutions housed in the great building. It contained the manifold offices of the Jewish Community, the club rooms of the Bnei Brith Lodge, a large hall for public meetings (in which many a passionate demonstration had taken place), the offices of the Bukowina Zionist Federation, and the homes of other local bodies.

"This is the citadel, the forum, and the headquarters of our community," said my friend. "Within these walls there has been waged many a wordy battle on *Gemeindepolitik*, on *Landespolitik*, and on *Weltpolitik*. We have frequent discussions on *Weltpolitik*. Yes, we are not short of speakers and experts on all sorts of politics."

As we were descending the broad stone staircase he remarked that I ought not to leave the city before seeing Sadagora, the townlet famous for its Wonder Rabbis. "But how to get there? It takes twenty minutes in a fast motor-car, and in a droshky it would take hours."

Providence had smiled on me, for as we reached the street there stood a jaunty car belonging to a medical friend of my cicerone, who, when informed of my desire to visit Sadagora, immediately offered to drive me there himself and to bring me back in time to catch the night train for Bucharest.

Presently we were skimming down a steep, muddy road, furrowed with ruts, which was traversed by a jostling crowd of country carts, and crossed the rickety bridge over the

Pruth, which was guarded by a military patrol owing to the proximity of the Russian frontier. As soon as we had left the city behind us my new companion, who was well versed in local history, began to tell me something about our destination, which was a place of pilgrimage for thousands of pious Jews from Rumania, Poland, and Russia.

Sadagora was a little town with some 5,000 Jews, who formed about four-fifths of the whole population. It owed both its preponderance of Jews and its popularity to the settlement in its midst in 1840 of the famous *Zaddik* (saint) and Wonder Rabbi, Israel Friedmann. The latter, who was much better known as Reb Israel the Ruschiner, from Ruschin, in Podolia, of which he became Rabbi at the age of sixteen, was a great-grandson of Baer of Mesiritsch, the favourite disciple of the illustrious Baal Shem.[1] He had established a regular court at Ruschin and surrounded himself with such pomp and magnificence, never appearing in public except in a carriage drawn by four horses, that he aroused the suspicion of the Russian authorities, who, owing to the murder of two Jewish informers, threw him into prison at Kiev, where he was kept for nearly two years. He thus acquired the reputation of a martyr among the Hassidim, and when he transferred his activity and his court to Sadagora hundreds of faithful followers immediately flocked to settle in the vicinity. He revived the splendour of his previous career, and the wealth that he amassed and the influence that he acquired caused the story to be circulated that he intended building a Temple in Sadagora like the ancient one in Jerusalem. He died in 1850, leaving behind him several Hebrew works containing expositions of his teaching, of which the leading principles were that it was a religious duty to enjoy life and that he, the *Zaddik*, was the medium through whom the prayers of all Israel were brought to the ken of the Almighty. His doctrines

---

[1] The founder of the Hassidic sect, Israel ben Eliezer, of Miedzyboz (Poland), 1700–60, who was credited with the power of working miracles by the name of God and hence was known as the *Baal Shem Tob* (Master of the Good Name).

were propagated with zeal and with profit by his six sons, who, like the Rothschild brothers, and perhaps with a similar material end in view, extended their ministrations to different centres, the two eldest remaining at Sadagora, whilst two went to Rumania, and the other two to Galicia.

Before long the car was racing along the main road of the little town, a dusty, forlorn-looking thoroughfare, attracting many people out of their houses and stopping a few yards from the entrance to the cemetery.

"There is a Jewish Burgomaster in the town," remarked my companion, as he alighted, "and there always has been one for many, many years. But the place is not so important now, as the two heads of the Friedmann dynasty left for Vienna during the War and never came back."

The grizzled keeper of the graveyard, in a dirty gaberdine green with age, muddy top-boots, and greasy skull-cap, approached us. "You want to see the grave of the Rebbe?" he asked. And without awaiting a reply he led the way.

The cemetery was in a depressing state of neglect and disorder. The paths were rough and dirty, and the tombstones were toppling over one another. But the inscriptions on the stones were of peculiar interest as they were adorned with figures representing fruits, flowers, a lion and a unicorn —designs that are not seen even in the ancient cemetery of Prague.

We followed the keeper to a humble shed, which had been built over the graves of six departed Wonder Rabbis. Over each grave was what looked like an open coffin made of plain white boards, bearing at the foot the name in Hebrew of each saintly inmate, and in each receptacle was a dusty heap of little curled-up notes in Hebrew or Yiddish, containing prayers for intercession before the Almighty, which had been placed there by scores of believers in distress. Over the grave of Reb Israel the Ruschiner was the largest pile of petitions—a testimony to his reputed supremacy. Here the keeper stood, with a mien of professional reverence perfected by prolonged habit, expecting me also to deposit a little supplication; and then, seeing that I remained motionless, he raised his voice, offered up the prayer *El Mole Rahamim*,[1] with a vigorous shaking of his body, for the repose of the Wonder Rabbi's soul, and added in Yiddish: "May the Almighty help us all now and at all times." He looked to me for an immediate realisation of his own personal need for help, and I slipped some coins into his grimy palm. Yet, in that darkling atmosphere, I could not help being strangely impressed by this spectacle of credulity.

We hastened away, for the sun was setting; the car went careering along the road that had been trodden by so many thousands of pilgrims; and by the time we approached the bridge again the heavens were illumined with a host of twinkling lights.

[1] " Lord, full of mercy."

Chapter XVI

THE PLIGHT OF SALONIKA

I

A MONG all the cities in Eastern Europe that were scourged or scarred by the First World War, few underwent such a radical transformation as Salonika, although it was spared both a siege from without and a battle within. The change that occurred, partly in its physical appearance and still more in its ethnical composition, was due to two fateful events—the fire of 1917 and the flight of the Greeks from Turkey a few years later. The effects of these two calamities were profound and far-reaching. The sweeping nature of the metamorphosis was brought home to me at once on the night of my arrival—a night of torrential rain—when a friend who met me in the dimly-lit station for the purpose of conducting me to an hotel took me to what seemed to be a private house. Yet I was assured that it was an hotel and the best in the city.

After being in the house a few moments and realising that it had never been built as an hotel, and after noting the deficiencies in my room, which lacked the conventional comforts, and learning that there was only one bath in the establishment, and that even that could not be used owing to the shortage of water, I wondered what the second best hotel could be like.

"Have you nothing better in this city?" I asked in astonishment.

"We had," replied my friend "We had very fine hotels, as fine as anywhere else, until the great fire came and swept them away. It consumed many other things too—

synagogues, schools, theatres, restaurants, and houses without number. But the most important thing that it destroyed was the Jewishness of Salonika. It is a terrible story."

At Almosnino's, a neighbouring Jewish restaurant, which was the favourite rendezvous of the Allied officers during the First War, especially on account of its toothsome dainties, and which became as popular with Greek as with Jew, my friend recalled some of the horrors of the great catastrophe, and described some of its tragic consequences. The fire was the result of an accident, but few prolonged bombardments of any city caused even a tithe of the devastation which it wrought. The history of Salonika Jewry records a fire in the sixteenth century, when some 8,000 houses and 18 synagogues were demolished. But this was a minor disaster beside the fire of 1917, which destroyed 20,000 houses, thirty synagogues, and eight schools, besides all kinds of other buildings and institutions, and rendered homeless over 50,000 Jews and 20,000 Christians. So vast a conflagration inevitably gave rise to sinister rumours respecting its origin, and the theory was advanced, though without adequate reason, that it was the work of the Allied Armies. The only ground for such grave rumours was that General Sarrail, who was in control of the city, finding it impossible to extinguish the flames, owing to the scarcity of water and the narrowness of the streets, gave the order to blow up large blocks of houses, though nobody could say that the destruction would have been less had this drastic precaution not been taken.

The material loss was incalculable, baffling the most ingenious attempts to frame an estimate. For it was not merely buildings that perished, but all the accumulated wealth within them, stores of variegated treasures—scrolls of the Torah, mediaeval manuscripts, entire libraries, synagogue ornaments in gold and silver of cunning design, wondrous vestments of embroidered silk in richest hue—all the sacred freight brought by the Marranos from the Spain of Ferdinand and Isabella, by fugitives from intolerant cities in Italy and Germany, or preserved by the misguided followers of the pseudo-Messiah Sabbatai Zevi, the Donmeh, and cherished for centuries in what was the most hospitable homestead of Jewry throughout the East. And what enhanced the loss a hundredfold was the destruction of so many historic links with the past, each synagogue having formed the stronghold of some particular community, from Seville or Granada, Toledo or Aragon, Apulia or Sicily, to which its members had clung with pious devotion and with a pride in their several rites and traditions. Nor was it merely the shrines and their contents that had been ravaged, but it was as though all the culture, the romance, and the sentiment that had lived in and around them had also been engulfed in the common havoc, so that Jewry, which once had flourished here materially and spiritually so vigorously that even some of its prayer-books had boldly altered the prophet's words into: *"For from Salonika shall go forth the Law"*, had been rendered homeless and hopeless.

II

The next day, when a flaming sun had dried up all traces of the night's downpour, I was taken to the scene of desolation. We went by a tram, in which there were Spaniolish advertisements in Hebrew letters—proof that the custom of the Jewish public was still thought worthy of quest. The car clanged its way along the quay-side, which, before the War, had swarmed with tumultuous traffic, but which was now only moderately busy, the ships in the gulf being both few and small. Fronting the sea for the length of a mile, and a little distance away from it, lay the charred ruins of the once famous Ghetto, a sombre succession of collapsed walls, battered buildings, mounds of bricks, heaps of rubbish and rubble, alternating with level gaps where the fire had raged with exceptional fury. It was a woeful spectacle, such as could otherwise have been caused only by a month's incessant shelling, and yet the people had grown so accustomed to it that they scarcely noticed it. Conspicuous among the débris stood a big school building of the Alliance Israélite, which, though damaged, provided an asylum for hundreds of Greek refugees. Rebuilding in many parts of the stricken quarter had been going on rapidly, but it was believed that a number of years would still be required before all traces of the catastrophe were utterly removed.

My friend took me to the editorial office of his Spaniolish journal to relate the sequence of misfortunes that had befallen the Jewish community since its eviction from its ancient home. His office, comprising both editorial sanctum and printing works, divided off by a skimpy screen, consisted of a single room on the first floor of a frowsy wooden building. The long corridor, from which it opened, served as the encampment of two-score refugees, who had squatted there compactly—men, women and children—on sacks and blankets, and slept as soundly as on beds of down. They had little portable braziers, on which they cooked their meals, the pungent odours arising from their frizzling pans being only a minor affliction compared to the risk of a possible blaze. The sight of the crowded refugees, all crouched round their temporary hearth, and fanning the flames in the midst of all their wretched bedding, made me realise how quickly fires could break out in the East, and how difficult they were to extinguish.

"You want to know what the Government has done for the victims of the fire?" said my friend. "The Christians were given grants and lodgings; the Jews nothing at all. In fact, the Jews were absolutely forbidden to rebuild their homes. The Government decided to replan the entire city in Greek interests, and so it expropriated the entire area laid waste, confiscated one-third of it, and made a pretence of purchasing the other two-thirds by fixing an unreasonable valuation and compensating the former owners by non-negotiable *bons* payable on indefinite dates. The result was that thousands of Jews were reduced to beggary. Moreover, although important sites were reserved for churches, not a single plot of land was allotted for a synagogue to replace the thirty that were destroyed. These are only what you may call sins of omission, grave as they are. Now come the sins of commission.

"After the proclamation of the Republic, the Revolutionary Committee decided that in the elections for the Constituent Assembly the Jews of Salonika should form a distinct electoral college. The reason given was that we were suspected of being monarchists, and it was feared that if the Jews were allowed to vote with the general population we would influence the result in favour of the Monarchy. The Council of the Jewish Community protested against the institution of a separate college, stating that they would not take part in the elections unless either this measure were withdrawn or a declaration was made that the college had been decreed in accordance with the international treaty conferring upon the Jews of Greece minority rights. The college was maintained, and the Government refused to accord us the rights of minorities. The result was that we boycotted the elections. Out of 7,000 electors only fifty-two took part, and the four deputies returned are not our most worthy representatives.

"Then came another phase—a movement to ruin us economically. After the defeat of the Greeks in Asia Minor nearly half-a-million were compelled to quit Turkish territory and flee to Greece. Most of them came to Salonika, so that the population of the city was almost trebled. Before the War, in a total population of 190,000, the 80,000 Jews had formed the largest national group, being more numerous than either the Turks or the Greeks. But now, in a population of 500,000, the Jews have become a small minority. The economic conflict soon began. An agitation was started against Sunday trading. The Municipal Council, on which for so many years we had a majority, was now dominated by the Greeks, and the representatives of the refugees on the Council invited the Government to enact a Sunday closing law for all the inhabitants of the city. Parliament acted with unseemly haste, for within two months the law was passed. Think what this meant: for hundreds of years Jews in Salonika had been allowed to trade on Sundays, and as they rested on Saturday the whole city had to rest on that day too: for all the commerce was in Jewish hands; they were the shippers, the bankers, the brokers, the lawyers, and even the porters and the dock labourers, so that the Turks and Greeks had perforce to rest on the seventh day. Now the Jews were forbidden to trade on Sunday, and thus they were exposed to unfair economic competition or tempted to break the Sabbath. We protested against the law as a violation of the Treaty of Sèvres, which promised us the rights of a national minority, and at last, as a concession, we were allowed to keep open two hours in the morning. But how vigilant the police are to see that no shop is opened a minute before ten or closed a minute after twelve! Many Jews have already been fined for breaches of the regulations."

This concession, in response to renewed agitation by the refugees, was shortly afterwards revoked; but President Pangalos, upon becoming Dictator, decreed that the concession should be restored and even extended to three hours.

III

The bitterness of the cup that the Jews of this city had to drink could be appreciated only by those who could conjure up a vision of their romantic past. For Salonika Jewry could boast of a history of two thousand years, reaching back to the days when Paul came to preach his gospel to the people of Thessalonica, though the community only rose to fame at the end of the fifteenth century, with the influx of the hosts of fugitives from Spain and other lands of Christian ill-will. Not only had they spoken the language of Castile for the last four hundred years—using it at home, in busi-

ness, in the synagogue, and in literature, but generations
of Gentiles living in their midst had learnt it from them
and used it frequently in intercourse with them. But even
more remarkable was the fact that hundreds had retained
their Spanish nationality century after century, always
having their children's births registered with the local
Spanish authority; while a number of Jewish families from
Italy had similarly preserved their Italian nationality. The
Turks had never insisted that the Jews of Salonika should
speak Turkish, for the latter dominated the city with their
numbers, their influence, and their overflowing energy.
But the Greeks demanded that they should learn and speak
Greek, and keep their business books in that language.
How could they, who had seen their neighbours adopt their
speech, reconcile themselves to adopting that of another
people? And even though the language they were expected
to abandon was that of their ancestors' persecutors,
time and tradition had made it their own and rendered its
sacrifice a vain demand. For the young the acquisition of
a new tongue was no insuperable task, but for the elders
there was not only the inherent difficulty of the problem
but also the unwillingness to overcome it, due to the brooding sense of wrong under which so many of them laboured,
and to a feeling of uncertainty regarding the future.

How musical a language Spaniolish or Ladino is, I first
experienced at a public meeting that was held one Saturday
morning in celebration of the seventy-fifth birthday of the
president of the Independent Order Bnei Brith. This order
—one of the notable contributions of America to Jewish
solidarity—was a potent force in the Near East, and the
meeting in honour of Mr. Adolf Kraus[1] filled the principal Cinema Hall with hundreds of eager listeners, who
flocked thither with un-Eastern punctuality. The oration
delivered by the local president was an impressive eulogy,

[1] Adolf Kraus, born at Blowitz (Bohemia) in 1850, emigrated to the United
States in 1865, became editor of the *Chicago Times* in 1885, was President of
the Independent Order of the Bnei Brith from 1905 to 1925, and died in
1928.

couched in eloquent terms, and spoken with no little distinction. But what impressed me just as deeply was the fact that a mass meeting was held at eleven o'clock on a Sabbath morning. It was a characteristic manifestation of Jewish national life, such as I had already seen in the larger Jewish community of Warsaw. For the Sabbath was kept not merely as a holy day but as the national day of rest, and as divine service was held at a very early hour it was not unusual for public gatherings, especially of a ceremonial character, to take place in the forenoon. Many were the regrets expressed that there was no Jewish building where the celebration could be held, owing to the desolation caused by the fire, which had almost consumed the splendid home of the local Lodge.

The prevalent discontent had already found an outlet in emigration. The Donmeh, who for centuries had formed a distinctive and picturesque community of their own, number ing some ten thousand, had left the city soon after it came into the hands of the Greeks, as they were regarded as Turkish Moslems, and found refuge in Adrianople, Constantinople, and Smyrna. But the Peace, which meant no peace to the Jews of Salonika, caused a fresh exodus. A few hundred had sailed for Egypt; a few thousand formed a new colony in Paris; every month saw a dozen families or more embark for Palestine; and now and again some bolder spirits set out on the great voyage to America. At first the Palestine emigration bureau was besieged daily by people clamouring for permits, and even after the rush abated there was hardly a ship that left for Alexandria or Jaffa but bore away a band of happy emigrants.

Perhaps the most interesting group who had transplanted their homes and their energies to the Land of Israel were the fishermen. They were the only organised body of Jewish fishermen in the world, descendants of the exiles from mediaeval Spain, who had handed down their craft from father to son and were even associated together in a synagogue of their own. They were tall of stature and

robust of frame, and for centuries they had been the only
fishermen in the Gulf. But their dominion was brought to
an end with the conquest of the city by the Greeks, when
thousands of the Christian refugees who came swarming
back from Turkey and Asia Minor settled in every nook
and cove along the shore and began to compete with them
for the limited catch. The Jewish fishermen who worked
only with a rod were ousted first and had to seek a livelihood as porters and drivers. But those who went out to
sea with nets were able to survive the contest much longer,
until they too found it increasingly difficult to hold their
own. An appeal was thereupon addressed by the Council
of the Jewish community to the Zionist Organisation to
help in transferring these fishermen to Palestine. Two of
their leaders were delegated to investigate the fishing possibilities along the coast from Jaffa to Acre; and after they
had found a promising stretch between Athlit and Acre,
some sixteen families were transported, with all their boats
and fishing tackle; and there they are now busily and
happily plying their craft off the safer shore of their own
land.

Although rich in historic and human interest, Salonika
had little to offer either in the way of natural beauties or
architectural attractions. It possessed neither spacious parks
nor leafy promenades, neither palatial buildings nor artistic
monuments. The only edifices that a curious traveller might
deign to contemplate were the former mosques converted
into churches or the ancient Arch of Galerius, which had
lost two of the four pillars of which it originally consisted.
But one could easily find compensation for this paucity of
notable sights in a study of the conditions of the city and
its motley inhabitants. Walking was no pleasant task,
however, as the uneven and irregular pavements soon made
one footsore, while at every hundred yards one was accosted
by peripatetic photographers. The most popular stroll,
away from the dust and din of the city, led past the famous
Villa Allatini—where Abdul Hamid had been kept prisoner

by the once powerful "Committee of Union and Progress";
but its terminus, on the elevated outskirts whence you
could have a fine view of the harbour and of the drab bar-
racks of the refugees, was disappointing in its lack of
foliage or a traveller's elementary comforts.

"Where are the nice parts of Salonika?" I asked my
friend.

"How long are you staying here?" he enquired.

"Another few days," I replied.

"Sorry! You can't see them in that time."

"Why, are they so far off?"

"No. Because they are not yet built!"

By way of consolation he took me to see the carnival
procession, the festival being held here a week later than
in Western Europe. The streets were crowded with onlookers, but the costumes of the revellers, most of whom
were rouged, were rather tawdry, as they belonged mainly
to the working class. But there was one thing that outraged
us—some men and women were wearing the traditional
Jewish garb of Salonika for the purpose of ridicule.

"Before the War," said my friend, "no Greek would
have dared to put on a Jewish costume to mock us, nor
would he even have thought of doing so. We should have
soon known what to do with him. But now we can't say
anything; we are a weak minority."

We passed a Jewish vendor of confetti, whose little boy
was dressed as a Greek and had his face daubed with paint.

"What's the meaning of this?" said my companion to
him in Spaniolish.

"It's the only way in which I can do business," came the
emphatic reply, 'and the youngster cried his wares in the
only few words of Greek that he knew.

"Anti-Semitism is slowly but surely advancing here,"
remarked my friend, as we retraced our steps. "A series of
articles has been appearing in an Athenian paper, the
'Eleutheros Typos', in which all the legends about Jewish
Bolsheviks and the Protocols of the Elders of Zion have

been served up with illustrations. There can be little doubt about an anti-Semitic International. The illustrations to these articles are reproduced from photographs and have English titles, which show that they originally appeared in an American paper."

We found rest at a little table in the garden behind Almosnino's restaurant, with the blue sea stretching before us, and a clear view of Mount Olympus in the distance. At the neighbouring table was a gentleman fingering a string of yellow beads. When I first saw a man carrying a string of beads in the street I thought he was taking it home as a present for a child, but when I passed numbers of men, both young and old, all swinging or fingering their "chapelaine", I scented some local foible. The trinket, I was told, took the place of a cigarette or cigar, and playing with it was thought to have a steadying effect upon the mind. Some men were apparently too shy to indulge in the practice openly, and kept their "chapelaine" in a convenient pocket, into which they could easily slip their hand.

We had finished our coffee, and I noticed that my friend's hand had disappeared into his coat pocket. Soon I heard the faint click of the beads. It was a sign that he was thinking.

"I was wondering how long more I shall be gazing at Mount Olympus; it has been familiar to me from childhood," he said. "So many of my friends have given up the struggle here in the face of the increasing anti-Semitism and gone to live in some other country. But what is the good of going to another country where there may be just the same evils or even worse? I am longing for the day when I can leave for our own country."

"And exchange the view of Mount Olympus for that of Mount Zion?" I added.

"Quite so," he returned. "On that day I shall no longer need my chapelaine."

But for the present he continued to play with his beads.

* * * * *

As in the case of most Jewish communities in Eastern Europe, that of Salonika too suffered terribly in the Second World War. Indeed, its losses were far greater than those of most communities. Of 56,000 Jews who lived there before the German invasion, about 95 per cent—men, women, and children—were deported by the Gestapo to be exterminated in the death-camps of Poland. The famous historic centre of Jewish life has now only about 1,500 Jews, whose thoughts are bent not upon any possibility of its revival or restoration, but upon leaving it for ever to begin life anew in the State of Israel.

Chapter XVII

DESPAIR IN SMYRNA

A PICTURESQUE vision lay before us as the ship dropped anchor a mile from the shore. Beyond the calm, green sea, and beneath a sky of wondrous blue, there stretched a long, dream-like city of greyish-white, relieved here and there by the red and yellow of some painted house-fronts and by occasional tints of darker hue. Its graceful outlines spread gently upwards over a spacious hill, which formed a pale background to some lofty cypresses, crowned on the extreme left by the crumbling ramparts of an ancient tower, and flanked, in the foreground, on the right by a gaily-coloured mosque. It looked, beneath the genial sun, like the chaste and silent abode of eternal peace—this city that has been rent and ravaged by earthquake, fire, and plague more often than any other city in the East.

A flotilla of boats soon came swarming around the ship, and the cries of the befezzed boatmen rose in rival chorus. But before I could descend my passport was scrutinised and stamped by an official wearing an astrakhan hat, broadside on, like that of Mustapha Kemal, and examined again by another official standing at the top of the ship's ladder; whilst after I had been rowed in a dilapidated tub to the shore I had to present my passport once again to a third official on the quay, and then to give it up to a fourth and superior functionary, who, seated at a table in front of his office, handed me a dirty receipt in a Turkish scrawl. I now had, and deserved, the right to roam the city that had given birth to two such diverse celebrities as the greatest of Greek poets, Homer, and the most notorious of false Messiahs, Sabbatai Zevi.

Leaving the quayside for a shabby street, and threading my way through a succession of other streets of similar shabbiness, I presently came to the bazaar, a long narrow thoroughfare, closely bordered with shops and stores of every kind, which were stocked with silks, carpets and divers fabrics, and which alternated with busy little restaurants and cafés. Then I passed through a covered avenue of boot-shops, whose pungent odours mingled with those from the neighbouring bakers and butchers, and upon emerging I found myself in a noisy road, in which newspaper boys were shouting the latest news about the Kurdish revolt and met with a quick sale for their papers.

Suddenly the din and bustle ceased, for I had reached a quarter where all the shops were closed, the windows being covered with dirty grey shutters, bolted and barred. It looked like a city of the dead, for not a soul was to be seen, nor a sound to be heard. But it was only the Jewish quarter, enjoying the peace of the Sabbath. I had a letter of introduction from a Jewish merchant in Athens to a friend, but the address was that of his shop, and as this, like all the others, was closed, I stood perplexed, disappointed at the thought of being baffled in my quest. But a moment later I was approached by a middle-aged Jew in a fez, who greeted me in French. I showed him my letter, but he was unable to tell me where to find the person to whom it was written.

"All Jewish shops in Smyrna, with very rare exceptions, are closed on the Sabbath," he explained. "They are also closed on the Friday, which is a compulsory day of rest, and all those who infringe this regulation are fined. Many Turks complain of this new law and say that it is unnecessary. They declare that Friday is simply a day for prayer and that there is no religious precept that shops must be shut. But whilst the Moslems close only one day, we have to close two, and that does not improve our position."

"Will you show me the town?" I asked. "I have just two hours, until my ship leaves."

229

He smiled, half in pity, half in wonderment. "There is nothing to see—nothing. Whatever there was to see before has gone, destroyed by fire—you know, the great fire."

"I want to see the part that has been destroyed," I said.

"It's dangerous," he replied, "occupied by thieves, by people who have come from other towns, by refugees from villages, who have made their homes among the ruins. Nobody dares go there."

"Let's go as far as we can, if not to the inner streets," I urged.

We soon came to the stricken quarter, the scene of the terrible fire that took place in 1922, when the Turks entered the city. There were streets of ruined and roofless houses and shops, gaunt fragments of walls, jagged parts of window-frames, scorched and battered doors, heaps of bricks and rubbish, vast yawning cavities that once held the foundations of stately mansions, whilst every hundred yards revealed the débris of other streets in an endless perspective of chaos and desolation.

"The whole fire was over in less than a day," explained my companion. "Don't ask me to tell you how it came: it is over. No Turkish houses were burned—only Greek and Armenian, by the thousand. And thousands of Greeks were killed too, and all their things stolen. . . . You see that horse and carriage,"—pointing to a passing vehicle driven by a disreputable-looking Turk—" they once belonged to a Greek, who either had his throat cut or else had to flee."

"And were Jewish houses destroyed too?" I asked.

"A few hundred—houses, shops, and offices. I lost mine."

"And did you get compensation?"

"From whom—how?"

"And has any beginning been made towards restoration?"

"So soon? One must be patient."

"Take me now to the Jewish quarter," I said, "and tell me about it."

We left the scene of devastation and presently came to a long, quiet street, remarkable for its cleanness, in which all the houses and shops were covered with shutters. We passed the principal synagogue, a tall building of semi-Byzantine character, access to which was barred by locked gates, whilst on the opposite side was a school with a Hebrew inscription. A few yards further we reached the premises of the Bnei Brith Lodge, which is installed in what was once a private house, and we entered. There was a convenient suite of rooms—for reading, smoking, billiards—all simply furnished, and also a library consisting mostly of French books, with some photographs on the walls. We were joined by another member of the Lodge, also in a fez, and a servant brought in three tiny cups of black coffee, accompanied by the inevitable glasses of water.

I was told that the Lodge had a hundred and fifty members, and maintained close relations with the more important Lodge in Constantinople. There were still 30,000 Jews in Smyrna,[1] after a migration of nearly 8,000 to Greece, Constantinople, Palestine, and to various parts of the East and West. There used to be a total population of half-a-million in Smyrna: now it had only half that or less. Economic conditions for the Jewish community had become very hard owing to the two obligatory days of rest, and hence some Jews were being slowly compelled to open on the Sabbath.

" Are there any Jews on the municipal council? " I asked.

" No," was the reply. " The Turks don't want us—neither on the municipal council, nor on the Bourse, nor in any branch of public activity. So we hold aloof, we keep quiet, we efface ourselves, though when the Turks want our money for charity or anything else they find us."

" Have you any Jewish paper? "

" No. We had before the fire, but the office was destroyed, and we had no money or courage to start another. Why should we? We want to be quiet. We attend to our affairs honestly, diligently, and at night we stay at home. We

---

[1] Since my visit to the city the Jewish population has declined to 6,000, at least 6,000 having emigrated to Israel between 1948 and 1950, besides considerable departures to Palestine before 1948.

don't want to mix with the others, or to give any excuse for making trouble."

"Have you any Zionist society here?"

"How can you ask? It doesn't exist: it cannot. *C'est interdit.* Did not Palestine belong to Turkey before the war? But with what happiness and yearning we read of all that is taking place in the Holy Land, and how we rejoice that such progress is being made."

We went out into the street again. There were several men and women seated in front of their houses, looking sad and silent—the men in fez and long fur-lined gaberdine, the women mostly in European dress—staring at me as at a being from another world.

Presently we passed a couple of policemen stationed at the entrance of a courtyard that led to a plain but solid building. "That's a prison," remarked my companion. "There are only Turks there—not a single Jew."

We approached a large, open space, covered with shaggy patches of grass, extending over a slope. "That used to be a Jewish cemetery for four hundred years," explained my guide. "But a few years ago the Turks thought that it would be more suitable for a park. So they decided that it must be cleared of Jewish bodies, and they compelled the representatives of the Jewish community to sign a declaration agreeing to their removal. The corpses were all disinterred and transferred to another place. So even the dead were made to realise that a new regime had been introduced. . . . Just notice the 'park'."

"And did you receive compensation, or were you given the new place free?"

"Neither one nor the other. We had to submit. I wonder whether the outside world knows what is going on here. The capitulations have been abolished, thanks to the Allied Powers, and the city has suffered ever since. Commerce is steadily declining—look at the idle port—for the Turks have no appreciation of its value or importance. They have made Ankara their capital, though they have the great and beautiful city of Constantinople. What other proof do you want of their stupidity? "

Suddenly I observed some stores with Spaniolish notices in Hebrew lettering in the windows. "Are those Jewish shops?" I asked.

"No. They belong to Turks who have Jewish customers. That is why they are open."

For some time we walked in silence, hastening our steps as we made for the quay.

"Do you think the Allies, or at least England, will interest herself in our fate? " asked my companion.

"I'm afraid not. England has her own worries."

"Yes, but England is interested in Mosul," he rejoined.

We had to interrupt the political argument, in order that I might recover my passport. As we approached the quay-side I remarked that the waves had become very choppy. "That is nothing," he said, "I would brave the most stormy sea if I could only escape from here."

I stepped into the boat, and he turned upon me a look of unutterable resignation and envy as he wished me "Shalom!" (Peace!).

Chapter XVIII

ISTANBUL IN ECLIPSE

THE CITY of Constantinople, officially Turkified as Istanbul, presents a spectacle of majestic grandeur to one who arrives by sea, arousing the admiration even of the most jaded traveller who is already sated with the wondrous sights of the gorgeous East. There stretches before him, as far as the eye can reach, a brilliant panorama of mosques and palaces, of domes, minarets, and towers, with clusters of cupolas and pencil-like turrets dispersed in the vast teeming background, gleaming white beneath a sky of speckless blue, and fronted by a forest of ships and boats, with their criss-cross of masts and rigging, lying back along the margin of the green, animated sea. I gazed, with dim recollection of some half-forgotten romance, upon the broad bosom of the Bosporus, whose swirling waters bore dismal cargoes from the ports of the Black Sea; I was charmed by the sun-bathed vista of the Golden Horn; and I contemplated the beautiful and imposing fabric of Saint Sophia, the crowning glory of the splendid scene, a monument alike of art and antiquity, once the guarded shrine of despotic Sultans and now open to every infidel for a trifling fee.

But meditations upon the vision before me and upon the mingled memories they evoked were rudely dispelled by the cries of rival boatmen, who came swarming in their tumbling boats to the ship's side, causing a deafening babel as they touted and fought for passengers. It was with more anxiety than relief that I found myself, after paying an exorbitant tariff, in a weather-beaten bark with an oarsman and a French-speaking dragoman, who engaged in a violent dispute with one another during the brief passage to the shore—doubtless concerning the exact division of the backsheesh that they reckoned upon swindling out of me after we reached the quay. The young boatman had no easy task to wrangle with his countryman and at the same time avoid collision with other boats, but once I was safely landed and had passed the customs I thwarted their predatory plans, hailed a taxi, and soon was speeding to my hotel. I had expected to be helped over these harassing preliminaries—a veritable pitfall to the unknowing foreigner—by a local resident, to whom a friend in Athens had promised to send a telegram, and I wondered whether the promise had been forgotten or the message had miscarried until, two days later, the local resident called at my hotel and bashfully explained that he had been unavoidably detained, as he was being married at the time.

There is no greater contrast conceivable than that between the view of Istanbul from the sea and the impression that it produces when you are walking in its midst, even in the European quarter, where you are denied any glimpse of its wonderful waterways. It is as though the panorama you have just witnessed were merely a mirage, dissolving at closer view into a frowsy Levantine city, busy, dirty, and squalid, with narrow streets and narrower pavements, and with only one road—and that both steep and serpentine, traversed by clanging tramcars—that has any pretensions to a modern thoroughfare. Indeed, those who first arrive by train must be sorely perplexed to discover any charm to justify the city's reputation for beauty, for all that they can see spells decay and degeneration. The removal of the seat of government to the interior of Anatolia has deprived the whilom metropolis of much of the importance and dignity that it formerly enjoyed; its diminished glamour is vanishing into thin air; and the capital of Constantine and of Abdul Hamid, the centre of an erstwhile mighty Empire, the oft-coveted goal of rival Powers, has, with its silent mosques, its derelict palaces, and its tenantless Yildiz Kiosk, become a mere museum for foreign tourists.

I arrived on a Sunday afternoon, when, forgetting for the moment that I was entering a Moslem city, I expected to find the customary calm of the Continental Sabbath, but I was soon aroused to the realities of the situation, for all shops were open and the streets presented the busy appearance of a working day. But beneath all the animation of the cafés and cinemas and the thronged pavements, enhanced by some crowds of American tourists driven about in labelled motor-cars, there existed, I soon discovered, a feeling of depression, of uncertainty regarding the future.

It was at the house of a Zionist friend, whom I had not seen for a few years, that I learned of the changes that had taken place since the First World War. It was a house in which many languages, Oriental and Occidental, were spoken with equal facility, and in which I met some Jews who had preserved the Spanish nationality of their fugitive ancestors of four hundred years ago.

"Our best time was whilst the Allies were in occupation of Constantinople," said my host. "That was a glorious time for us and for Zionism: the enthusiasm was tremendous, we had big meetings, and everybody gave money. It was generally believed that the Jews here would become Palestinian citizens *in absentia*, and that increased our prestige. Let me give an instance of the influence we had. At that time only the British, the French, and the Italians had police rights in this city. One day we heard that Rumanian soldiers had arrested some Rumanian Jews in the streets as deserters, with the object of having them sent back to Rumania, where, of course, they ran the risk of being shot. We at once appealed to Sir Wyndham Deedes,[1] who was attached to the British Embassy, and he sent three British soldiers with bayonets to the Rumanian Legation, from where they rescued the Jews by force."

"And now?" I asked.

"The feeling of the Government against Zionism is very strong: the movement is forbidden. When the Government

[1] Afterwards Chief Secretary to the Palestine Government (1920-21).

authorities formerly gave a visa for Palestine, they issued only an inland permit, for Turkey, trying to keep up the fiction that Palestine still belonged to them. Now they gave the visa for ' Angleterre,' so as not to mention Palestine.[1] Since the war this city has been a place of of transit for several thousands of Russian Jews coming from Odessa, as well as for large numbers from Anatolia, Kurdistan and Persia, who have gone on to to Palestine."

The conditions of the Jewish community, I found, had undergone a marked decline in consequence of the Government's determined policy of Turkification. Although some Jews had played so important a part in the once famous " Committee of Union and Progress," and there had been Jewish deputies in the Ottoman Parliament before the First War, they were no longer welcome in the political or public life of the State. There were no Jews in the National Assembly, nor did any Jews even offer themselves as candidates. They were excluded from the Chamber of Commerce, and were not allowed to join a produce exchange that had been created by officials ignorant of the methods of working it. And a further step in the process of purification was an announcement that in future only Turkish would be allowed on the telephones, and only Moslems would be employed—a measure involving dismissal and distress for thousands of Jewish girls who had hitherto worked at the telephone exchanges.

The chauvinism of the Government had also dealt a grave blow at the prestige and the stability of the Jewish community. Before the war the Council of the community, together with the Rabbinate, enjoyed official recognition and possessed even judicial authority, which was backed up, if necessary, by the arm of the State. But the community no longer wielded such powers, for, with the abolition of the Caliphate, official recognition was likewise withdrawn from the administrative and ecclesiastical organs of Jewry, with the result that disintegration and debility had set in.

[1] That was while the British Mandate for Palestine still existed.

Formerly the Jewish community could meet its budget by levying taxes, which were paid with the knowledge that the State, if required, would enforce them; but now that the community was left to administer its affairs solely on a voluntary basis, as in English countries, the soul of the Turkish Jew had been found wanting. The payment of the customary dues was increasingly ignored, and the community had to maintain itself on a depleted treasury. No wonder that the former Chief Rabbi of Turkey, Haim Nahum, transferred his spiritual ministrations to Egypt. Unfortunately, Istanbul Jewry was being infected with the disease from which so many communities farther east had long been suffering—a moral anaemia which expressed itself in a growing lack of responsibility and an increasing dependence upon relief from the west. Moreover, the difficulty of maintaining a well-organised community was aggravated by the division of the city, through the broad waterways, into distinct districts, which were effectively sundered from one another, tending to dissipate all sense of solidarity.

I visited one of those districts, the famous Jewish quarter of Haskeui, one afternoon, accompanied by a young Russian Jew. The journey on the steamboat, although the vessel was grimy and antediluvian, was agreeable, for we sailed along the Golden Horn, whose array of splendour is unfailing, and my companion told me of his interesting and troubled past. After the outbreak of the First War he had been driven from Dvinsk to Vitebsk, and thence went to Ekaterinoslav and Sevastopol. But as he was still a boy at the time he returned to Ekaterinoslav for a couple of years to attend a high school, and during that period he experienced the blessings, or rather the curses, of eighteen governments, including Denikin, Wrangel, Machno, Grigorieff, and the Bolsheviks, in oppressive alternation. One whole month was taken up with pogroms, a ghastly saturnalia in which the Cossacks were changed into beasts of prey and ran amok every night. . . . From Ekaterinoslav he went to Tiflis, which, owing to famine, he was allowed, with many others, to leave for Batum, and thence he sailed for Constantinople.

Haskeui is one of the most wretched localities I have ever seen. Its dirty, desolate streets were badly paved with insufficient cobble-stones, whilst the middle of the road was everywhere full of holes and ruts, which became pools and ponds after a rainfall. There were several petty shops and little cafés, in which befezzed Jews sat playing cards and dominoes, but for the most part the entire quarter was occupied by houses. And what houses! They were all of timber, ramshackle, dilapidated, and decrepit with age. Some of them were three or four storeys high, with balconies feebly supported, looking as though they would burn like match-wood or collapse in a storm, and I could not help wondering that they had survived so long. Here and there, indeed, I came across the remains of some destroyed dwellings, such as the lower parts of walls, besides heaps of rubbish, whilst there were many empty spaces that heightened the sense of desolation.

We searched for a synagogue, and after applying to two or three grown-up persons in vain, we were conducted by some little girls to a humble shrine within a school-ground, which was entered by a door over which the year 1858 was inscribed. The school was founded by a benefactor named Kamundi, and near it was a big, long room, which was fitted as a synagogue, with an Ark covered with a plush curtain. There were seats all round, and at the end opposite the Ark was a platform for concerts or speeches. The children told us that they had two days' holiday for Purim, and we saw some boys whirling rattles (three pieces of wood tied with string) to give vent to the traditional execration of Haman.

We soon left the residential area and came to the cemetery, which had neither entrance nor fence. It lay open on all sides, spreading over a far-extending hill, with a multitude of gravestones lying scattered about in chaotic confusion. There were thousands of these stones, all with a brief Hebrew inscription pointing to a date that was somewhat between and one and two hundred years ago. Some of them were used to mark the border of the burial-ground, which continued upwards until we reached a high-way, and then we found that it extended to the other side of the road, which had, indeed, been constructed right through this God's acre. And the further portion was like-wise bestrewn with a veritable sea of tombstones, all lying pell-mell, neglected, scorned, as though symbolic of futile hopes and broken lives—the most distressing and discon-solate cemetery I have ever seen.

We were glad to hasten away from this scene of desolation, and returned to the city by a circuitous road which was shortened by our animated talk. My companion told me of the Jewish colony, Mesillath Hadasha, which had been established before the First War by the Jewish Colonisation Association, and of the many Russian *Halutzim* (pioneers) who had acquired an agricultural training there during the few months that they had to wait for their visas. He had often walked there all the way, a distance of some fifteen miles from Scutari, to spend the Sabbath with the *Halutzim*, sharing in their trials and their hopes. They had all now gone to the Land of Israel, and he too was looking forward to shaking off the dust of this declining city in order to labour with them for his people.

We had reached the highest bend of the road, whence we were able, on looking back, to see the setting sun adorn the Golden Horn with an effulgence of glory, and I beheld a glint of it in the eyes of my companion.

*　　*　　*　　*　　*

During the latter part of the Second World War Istanbul played an important part as a neutral and safe exit through which many Jews from the Balkans as well as from Central and Eastern Europe escaped from Nazi persecution and extermination. After the establishment of Israel the new State was recognised by Turkey and friendly relations were developed between the two countries. Between 1948 and 1950 the Jewish population of Istanbul declined from 53,000 to 32,500 largely owing to emigration to Israel.

Chapter XIX

ITALIAN SKETCHES

I.—THE GHETTO OF VENICE

Not with the curiosity of the conventional tourist did I journey to the city of Venice, nor with his simple emotions did I sail on its silent canals or thread my way through its labyrinth of narrow, bustling alleys. Neither the prospect of gazing upon its manifold beauties nor that of pacing the deserted halls of the Palace of the Doges affected me so deeply as the wish to behold a spot unique in the troubled annals of my people. For it was in Venice that first arose the inspiration to isolate the Jews within a special quarter, barred and guarded, so that the chosen people might not contaminate the chastity of Christendom. It was here that the first Ghetto was founded—the product of persecution, yet the preserver of Judaism. And ere the last vestiges of that once pulsating home of Jewry had been swept away by the broom of Time, I wished to revive the memories of those who had once played a brave and brilliant part in the struggle of Israel against the nations. For it was in this splendid sea-girt city that refugees from the Inquisition of Spain found peace; here the illustrious exile, Don Isaac Abravanel, statesman and Biblical commentator, solved the problem of Venetian relations with the Kingdom of Portugal; and here, for nearly a century, a diligent printing-press supplied a host of harassed communities with books of Hebrew lore.

It was near the old Rialto Bridge (whence the spirit of Shylock, if ever it had tarried there, long has vanished) that I boarded a steamer one morning, and was borne along the Grand Canal, which shimmered with the rays of a smiling sun. Even the mouldering palaces seemed to have lost their frown in the radiance that abounded, and the multi-coloured pillars with gilded tops that rose from the water before them like mute sentinels seemed to have taken on a brighter hue. From one bank to the other the steamer steadily ploughed its way, discharging passengers and receiving others at the primitive piers, until at length, on reaching the junction with the broadest tributary of the Canal, the Cannareggio, the boatman called out in a lachrymose voice: "San Geremia!" and I alighted, for here was the approach to the ancient Ghetto. The first thing that met my eye on the landing stage was a saint-like statue of grey stone on a pedestal, contemplating the scene below with pensive sadness. Could this be a figure of Jeremiah? I thought; and why should the prophet of lamentation be stationed at the threshold of the Ghetto? But as I drew nearer I saw that the statue held a cross in its hands, and on its head was perched an iron crown with five stars fixed in the circumference. They were not really stars but miniatures of the traditional Jewish emblem, the Shield of David, and they were intended to represent thorns. And when I recognised the wearer of the crown of thorns, I wondered whether it had been the irony of some departed prelate that had made him the guardian of the portals of Jewry.

The gate of the Ghetto long had vanished, leaving no trace behind. After passing the church of San Geremia and continuing along the bank for a few hundred yards, I crossed the bridge that spans the Cannareggio and found myself gazing at the tall gloomy houses that formed the boundary of the ancient Ghetto. From most of the windows hung shirts and skirts and other miscellaneous garments of glowing colours, drying in the sun. I asked my way of some men gathered round a stove, on which huge potatoes were boiling, and was directed to a dark, narrow street and told to go ahead. The street was silent; few people were about; only the dulcet voice of some invisible maiden was heard trilling an amorous song. I looked for signs of Jewish life, and had almost begun to despair of finding any when I came to a little restaurant, with some strange-looking viands in the window and a bill with the Hebrew inscription "Kosher". It was a dim, depressing place, with a low ceiling, not as squalid as a little eating-house I had seen in Cracow, but also not as lively. The only human element was a girl who, humanly enough, was examining herself in a glass.

A little further on I was greeted by three dilapidated beggars, of ages ranging from twenty to fifty. "*Arme Juden!*" they cried in German, with open palms. That was my first fraternal welcome in the oldest Ghetto of Europe.

"Do you wish to see *die Schule, la scuola, il tempio?*" they exclaimed in a mixture of German and Italian. "*Ecco il levantino!*"

They pointed to a tall, sombre building, without external grace, which formed an angle with the end of the alley. In the porch stood a uniformed functionary in a top-hat, with a silver breastplate hanging by a chain from his neck, on which appeared the word "*Portiere.*" That glistening decoration reminded me strangely of the yellow badge of mediaeval days.

Passing up the stairs I pushed open a swing-door and found myself in a moderate-sized synagogue, rather dimly lighted. The congregation was very sparse for a Sabbath morning, and the contrast of the white silk *Talith* (praying-shawl) against the dark oak benches made the scantiness of the assembly all the more striking. On a lofty *almemar* at the upper end, from which there gleamed silver hanging lamps and many tall waxen candles, the reader in a rather nasal accent cantillated the Torah at a rapid pace, while at his side stood a young man with olive-brown complexion, wearing a fez, the symbol of their Levantine nativity, which else is reflected in the ritual. But there seemed nothing of the Levant nor of any other part of the Orient in the haughty mien of the well-fed, shaven beadle, who strutted about with a silver breastplate hanging from his neck, inviting different worshippers to ascend to the Law, without any apparent authorisation from a superior official. I wondered what title was inscribed on his breastplate, when, as though divining my curiosity—perhaps suspecting the sincerity of my visit—he strode forward with heavy steps, and I read the legend on the silver plaque: *Nunzio*. At once my memory flitted back to the pages of my school history, and my conception of the papal legate sustained a revolutionary shock. In my surprise I looked up and beheld the ladies' gallery, which seemed at an unattainable distance from earth, and which concealed the daughters of Israel far more effectively than any synagogue gallery I had seen in Western Europe.

The morning was advancing and there were other houses of prayer to visit, so I quietly retired; though even as I passed out there followed two or three congregants, who were hastily leaving the presence of God for the more pressing business of man. The three beggars were patiently awaiting me, and had meanwhile probably settled their respective shares to the largesse which they expected to flow. They escorted me to two or three other synagogues, all situated within a few yards of one another, and all remarkable for their plain exterior, their ornate interior and their sparse congregation. The fewness of the worshippers, however, would not have been so depressing if these same worshippers had been a little more devout and decorous. But there was a very free and easy spirit among them—the restlessness of the Southern blood, it was called in palliation by a Jewish scholar that I met—and they chattered away, heedless of the cantor's roulades, and unhampered by the beadle's reproof, walking across the tesselated marble floor with loud steps and banging their seat-lids as they put away their garment of devotion—and their devotion itself—whilst the service was still in progress. In one of these small shrines of the Italian rite there was a French family group of tourists, whom I had seen earlier in the morning coming out of the Church of St. Mark, and who were now gazing at this Jewish house of prayer with wondering eyes, the paterfamilias whispering snatches from his Baedeker to slake their thirst for knowledge.

The restlessness of the congregation, which here does not find vent in the shaking of the body, was most marked in the German synagogue—*la scuola tedesca*, whither the triumvirate of beggars conducted me with a quasi-national pride. It is situated in the New Ghetto, officially known as the "Ghetto Nuovo," which is separated from the older quarter, the Ghetto Vecchio, by a small bridge spanning a diminutive canal, the Ponte di Ghetto Vecchio. There is nothing new about the New Ghetto except the name: it has the same dreary, dingy look as its counterpart, and contains just as few Jews or even fewer, it is a large irregular quadrangle, with three disused wells in the middle, and bordered by towering grim dwellings, gaunt and shabby, from whose lofty windows hung the inevitable clothes to dry. A short, stone pillar in the centre, used by the boys for leap-frog, bears the date "19 Oct., 1866," and an inscription of gratitude to "Vittorio Emanuele, Re d'Italia." There is nothing distinctive about the architecture of the German shrine except its excessive plainness: it is even possible to visit the New Ghetto and cast a glance around without becoming aware of the sacred building, for it is entered by a simple doorway uniform with that of the private dwellings. But the eye of the keen observer is not likely to miss the small square patch of white high up on the dingy façade, just below the middle one of five windows, on which are inscribed two Hebrew words: *Zecher Lechurban* ("In Memory of the Destruction"). It is not the destruction of the Ghetto nor of Judaism in Venice that is commemorated by that crude tablet, but the destruction of the Temple. Was it mere conformity with the traditional custom of displaying a souvenir of Israel's woe that had prompted that patch of white, or did the architect, with sardonic subtlety, desire to avert attention from the local decadence of

Judaism to the greater and more far-reaching disaster that had overwhelmed the Jewish people, Whatever the motive —and it was probably the former and unsophisticated one— that white patch with its black-lettered Hebrew legend impressed me as the most significant and pregnant phenomenon in the entire area of the Ghetto. The memory of the national glories of old was still preserved.

" *Venge, venge!* " (Come, come!) exclaimed my ragged retinue, rousing me from my musings. They vied with one another in conducting me across to the door of the synagogue, setting up at every few paces a miserable whine of " *Arme Juden!* " and holding out their hands expectantly. Some boys came along and began turning somersaults, as though to show that they could do something to deserve the alms for which the beggars clamoured without any claim. But they were quickly beaten off by my escort, and I meanwhile vanished into the dim doorway of the synagogue up a lofty flight of steps, and so into the house of prayer itself.

Small though it was, it possessed some artistic beauty, but it was difficult to indulge in aesthetic contemplation when one's ears were assailed by the furious gabble of the precentor, who seemed to be bent on catching a particular steamer home, and when one's eyes beheld a handful of lackadaisical worshippers, half of them boys, wrapping up their *taleithim* (praying-shawls) and locking them up with a bang and then exchanging Sabbath greetings with a hearty voice, though the cantor was still in the middle of *Na'aritzcha.* Had they also a strain of Southern blood? Even the warden, a fat-faced man, with a prominent paunch, was in a hurry to leave his spiritual dominion, and, gathering his three young sons around him, he gave a hasty handshake to his friends and bustled out. An hour later I saw him standing in the doorway—which he filled—of his shop in the Piazza di San Marco, with a seductive smile for any possible customer.

On emerging from the synagogue I found my tattered

escort still loyal, upborne by indomitable perseverance.
"*Arme Judem!*" they again set up their doleful chorus, heedless of the Sabbath law that forbids the offering of the
particular kind of charity which they desired. They made
a bee-line for a house on the adjacent side of the square,
which had the appearance of an asylum for aged poor. In
an upper window I caught a glimpse of the sallow, wrinkled
face of an old woman, with a white cotton bonnet, who
was peering through her spectacles at a book. A slim and
youthful matron beckoned me inside and showed me over
the institution, which housed six tottering grey-haired
women who wore an air of contented resignation. The small
infirmary was vacant, the matron remarking in a merry
voice: "*Tutte bene*". And then she conducted me down-
stairs again into the garden, where a new wing was being
built for the accommodation of men.

"Are there many Jews living in this Ghetto?" I asked.
She smiled at my ignorance. "Very few. They have all
gone to the Piazza." And she accompanied her answer
with a wave of the hand in the direction of the famous
square.

Still resolute of purpose and undaunted of hope, the
beggarly trio awaited my exit and set up a more agonising
wail than ever. Fearing that I doubted their Jewish fealty
one of them unbuttoned his waistcoat and displayed his
tsitsith (four-cornered fringed garment), which was badly in
need of a wash. That religious appeal was difficult to turn
aside: so, conforming with the local custom (for the indis-
pensable use of the steamer on the Sabbath to reach the
synagogue involves the handling of money) I gave them a
few soldi each and left them bowing and bestowing
blessings.

On my return journey along the Grand Canal I gazed
once more at the handsome palaces, whose majestic exterior
now so often conceals bare echoing chambers or a suite of
uncomfortable apartments, and I wondered how many of
them had come into the possession of the children of the

Ghetto. For the palace of the illustrious Baron Treves was not a unique phenomenon: there were other Jewish grandees who now lived in the stately homes of their former persecutors. Time brought healing in its wings, I thought, as I recalled those distinguished citizens of Venice, the historian, Samuel Romanin, whose bust was exhibited in the local Pantheon, the politician Maurogonato, who once presided over the Chamber of Deputies, and Daniel Manin, a half-Jew, who led the revolution in Venice in 1848 and was Minister-President of the Venetian Republic. And even more famous in recent times was Luigi Luzzatti, Prime Minister of Italy in 1910.

II.—FLORENTINE JEWRY

Saunter where you will in the city of Florence, scenes of beauty surround you, storied memories wake within you. The spacious squares and imposing monuments, the ornate churches and mouldering towers, the palaces, mansions, and even some of the lowly houses, the straggling streets and ancient bridges, the very walls of the hoary buildings with their patches of fresco and fragments of frieze—all are eloquent of an age when the passion for beauty savoured of religious emotion and the sentiment of civic patriotism drove men to deeds of heroism and despair. What treasures of gold, what wealth of genius, were lavished upon the city's adornment!—making of the ephemeral capital of the Medici an everlasting centre of pilgrimage for worshippers of the beautiful. What generous enthusiasm, as munificent as magnificent, was bestowed upon letters and arts and science, stimulating the spread of the Renaissance throughout the academies of Europe. Visions of painters and poets, of sculptors and scientists, of philosophers and statesmen, rise before you at every turn as you pace the narrow, humming streets; the martyrdom of Savonarola, the imprisonment of Galilei, the exile of Dante, are recalled by the glimpse of a square, a tower, a bridge. The history of the city is engraven on its stones, and the people of the present are ever confronted by the ghosts of the glorious yet chequered past. And intermingled with this shifting shadowy throng the discerning eye may see the ghosts of the Jewish past.

For fugitives from the tentacles of the Spanish Inquisition found friendly refuge under the tolerant sway of the Medici; the Marranos threw off their mask, compelled no longer to worship the God of their fathers in the gloom of underground chambers. In the sunshine of patronage that spread over all who toiled in study or studio, who added to the knowledge and the uplifting of humanity, the descendants of those who witnessed the revelation of Mount Sinai also enjoyed a comforting warmth. Philosophers and physicians, authors and scholars, were summoned from the scattered tents of Jacob by Lorenzo the Magnificent to his court, and the study of the Talmud rose into a polite fashion. Savants of noble lineage took lessons in the mysteries of the Cabbala from Jewish exiles; universities vied with one another in conferring professorships upon the philosopher, Elijah Delmedigo (who took part in a religious disputation in the presence of Lorenzo); and the commercial prosperity of the city, too, was improved by the influx of Spanish immigrants, who opened up new channels of trade with their co-religionists in Brabant and Portugal, in Marseilles and the cities of the East. Papal edicts did not hurt them, for their edge was blunted by their humane protectors. Did the Medici, perchance, recall the debt of their ancestor, Giovanni delle Bande Nere, to the Jewish physician who amputated his leg? So warm, at one period, was the affection of the Florentines for their Jewish fellow-citizens that they even went to war against the Milanese Duke of Visconti, because he had refused to receive a Jewish ambassador. But *autres temps, autres moeurs*. A later generation saw the introduction of the Ghetto, with all its accompanying indignities.

But now neither Ghetto nor vestige of one will you here

discover, for it has long been swept into oblivion. But there is another bond with the past, more artistic, more worthy: mute yet appealing, carrying the mind back to an age immeasurably remote from Ghetto captivity. High up, on the Piazzale Michelangelo, dominating the city, looms the bronze statue of David, the youthful strenuous figure wherein the inspired sculptor symbolised the valorous Florence of his day. The marble original, after holding vigil four hundred years in the square of the Signoria, had an arm broken and was removed, with the limb restored, to the safe shelter of the Academy: but its withdrawal was followed by the erection of the bronze copy, which stands, brave and stalwart, against the sky, a splendid embodiment of the sculptor's art, but likewise an enduring monument to the prowess of the first king of Israel. Could any Jewish patriot desire a more glorious crown to this glorious city? Turning from the imposing statue and gazing down upon the panorama below, tinted with the radiant colours of a garden, you behold towering above a cluster of buildings and foliage a majestic dome, sombre yet stately. It is the dome of the synagogue, proudly set in the heart of the city.

It was from the lofty coign of the Piazzale Michelangelo, the climax of a long afternoon drive wherein I had circled the outskirts of Florence, that I first beheld the famous synagogue. I had cherished the vision of a temple of wondrous beauty, a shrine of peace and piety, worthy of the artistic splendour of its environment, worthier still of the purpose to which it is devoted; and soon my desire to view the structure at closer quarters was attained. The synagogue was, indeed, beautiful: spacious, majestic, massive, with tall slender columns and sculptured arches supporting the surrounding gallery, the walls adorned with a rich expanse of arabesque, the marble floor patterned in pleasant hue, the broad aisles stretching beyond the pillars, the costly pendent chandeliers, the festal array of tall gleaming candles, the shadows lurking about the Ark of the Law, the sunlight streaming through the narrow windows aloft, and

above all the vast vaulted dome—truly a noble habitation
for Israel in exile! A masterpiece of architecture and a
monument to the munificence of a single Jew. The building was perfect; but what of the people? So few were they
even on the Sabbath, and so dispersed about the multitude
of benches, that they formed the one discordant note in
the sacred symphony. . . . Their scantiness accentuated the
wandering echoes of the choristers' voices rebounding from
pillar to pillar, in ill accord with the pealing tones of the
organ; and the rapid recital of the cantor, so far removed
from the worshippers, fell upon the ear like intermittent
snatches of a nasal incantation. And, as in the synagogues
of Venice, there was the same strolling about and exchange
of greetings, the same hurried flight to business while the
cantor was still beseeching the Almighty to grant fulness
of peace unto His people. . . . Verily a temple of beauty,
but scarcely a shrine of peace and piety, though the closing
incident of the morning's service had in it a touch of old-
worldly devotion, for all the boys—the future pillars of the
synagogue—trooped to the Rabbi to receive his blessing.
Who shall say the blessing was not needed?

* * * * *

Later in the day I was in the study of the Rabbi, a scholar
of the modern school, animated by the national sympathies
that transcend the narrow horizon of the ultra-modernist
pastors of western Jewry. We spoke of the situation in
Zionism and then we turned to the condition in Italy, and
I asked the reason of the decadence of Jewry.

"Decadence?" he asked in surprise. "If you mean that
the conditions of Jewry here are distinguished from those of
other countries by decadence, I deny it. You must
remember what the Jewish population of Italy is—merely
fifty thousand, and they are scattered through a hundred
different cities and towns. Dispersion is always a powerful
source of weakness in Jewish life; and there are two other
things you must take into consideration, the perfect political

equality and the poor economic conditions. In every country Judaism loses at the two extremes: the rich become assimilated and absorbed, and the poor have to fight for their living to the detriment of the Sabbath."

"What an imposing sight it would be if your synagogue were filled on the Sabbath," I observed. "I felt this morning it was like a mausoleum."

"And in London, in the synagogues of the rich?" he asked. "But still," he continued, "the conditions here are really improving."

"Are there many cases of intermarriage?" I asked.

"Cases occur, but not to any great extent," he replied. "I could tell you of two rather interesting cases. The nephew of a Rabbi fell in love with the niece of a Catholic priest, and they were married in the synagogue with all the traditional rites. The priest was indignant, but his niece was in love not only with the Jew, but with Judaism. She keeps a strictly *kosher* house, and here comes the irony— she has made her husband much more observant of Jewish ceremonies than he was before marriage.

"The other case is much more peculiar: it spreads over three generations. Some thirty years ago a Jew married a poor Catholic woman in a church, and he died soon after the birth of a daughter. The child was brought up, of course, as a pious Catholic by the struggling mother, and when she grew up she married a fellow-Catholic. The husband was a brute, and the young mother died after giving birth to a son, who was taken care of by the grandmother. The husband soon followed the wife to the grave, and then the grandmother, reflecting upon the sorrows of her life, looked upon them all as a punishment of God for the apostasy of her Jewish husband. So she resolved to have her grandson brought up as a Jew, and this is what is now being done. I know the little boy and he can read Hebrew quite fluently."

In the gloaming there gathered together a small congregation of the pious in a chamber adjoining the beautiful fane,

to usher out the Sabbath with traditional rites. Students of
the Seminary were there, the pathetic figure of a Hebraist,
an emeritus professor of law, and a handful of more humble
laymen. As the service progressed lights were lit, and the
youthful son of the beadle distributed little wisps of myrtle
among the congregants. When the cantor reached the
benediction upon the spices in the quaint ceremonial everybody rubbed the wisps between his hands and drew in the
sweet scent of the myrtle. There was a general rustle of the
stalks, and the atmosphere filled with the pleasant fragrance,
redolent of the spicy groves of the East.

III.—A LIVING ARTIST AND A DEAD POET

Strolling one morning through the rooms of the Uffizi
Gallery, and gazing at the endless panorama of Biblical
scenes upon the walls, I mused on the peculiar fact that
the people whose ancient history was illustrated in such
manifold variety in this famous collection was not represented by a single painter of its own. The paradox, like
most paradoxes, was susceptible of easy solution. Painting
was an art that was looked at askance by most Jews until
quite modern times, for it was regarded as a transgression of
the second Commandment, which forbade the making of
" the likeness of anything that is in the heavens above, or
on the earth beneath, or in the waters under the earth."
And if, perchance, there were some soaring spirits in the
mediaeval Ghetto, who scorned this interpretation and were
moved to seek expression for their vision of the beautiful
on glowing canvas or in chiselled marble, what facilities were
there to favour such promptings? The lack of patrons was
a minor hindrance, but had patrons abounded and had they
all been as wealthy as all Jews are reputed to be, what
painter could have warmed to his task in a haunting fear
that there might be a sudden irruption of the mob into the
Ghetto, or that a decree of exile might burst upon the

community? Hence the People of the Book illustrated its teachings by their lives, whilst their persecutors illustrated it by their art. If only the latter had shown gratitude for the inspiration of the Book in their dealings with the People! Italian art reached its highest efflorescence in the service of the Church of Rome, and Jewish suffering passed through its bitterest moments in the shadow of the selfsame church.

Musing thus, I passed imposing canvases in golden frames depicting the sacrifice of Isaac and the discovery of Moses, the judgment of Solomon and the heroism of Judith, the works of Paolo Veronese, Tintoretto, Bassano, and other names of greater or lesser lustre. But these scenes from the Old Testament, many in themselves, seemed few indeed beside the endless series of pictures, filling room after room in apparently endless succession, which celebrated every incident, in a multitude of conceptions, in the life of Jesus. Not a single painter, from Michaelangelo and Rafael down to the obscurest wielder of the brush, but seemed to have dedicated his ripest genius to a representation of the Madonna and child, a group whose strength of appeal lies in the simple naturalness of the situation. What a powerful tribute the selection of the idea forms to the maternal devotion of the women of Israel, the sentiment that proved so fertile a source of consolation in the troubles of mediaeval times. The tribute, however, was unconsciously given and is scarcely perceived by one in a thousand of the cosmopolitan throng that streams through the gallery every year.

As I entered the room sacred to Botticelli my ears were assailed by a staccato recital, which a tall sharp-featured American lady was delivering from her Baedeker to a group of friends, who were likewise tall and sharp of feature. They stood in effusive admiration of Botticelli's "The Virgin and Child", known as "The Magnificent", which a young artist was copying. The picture, in a heavy round frame and ornate gilding, represents the Virgin gazing fondly, hope-

fully, and reverently, at the child in her arms, who is pointing to a passage in an open book, while two devout maidens,
one on either side, are placing a beautiful crown upon her
head. For several moments I compared the original with
the copy over which the artist was labouring, and then I was
suddenly struck with something peculiar in the artist himself. He was a lean, sallow-cheeked creature, with a shock
of black hair on his head and a small pointed beard, dressed
in a white flannel shirt with a black butterfly-tie. He had
dark dreamy eyes, which, set in his hollow cheeks, gave
him a weird and woebegone air. Instinctively I felt that he
was a Jew, and I wondered why he should have selected a
canvas with such an obviously Christian appeal.

" *Shalom Aleichem!* " (Peace unto you!) I ventured in the
traditional Hebrew greeting.

" *Aleichem Shalom!* " he replied, after a moment's hesita-
tion, resting his palette on his knee.

" I have wandered throughout this gallery," I said, " without seeing a single picture by a Jew. At last I have found
one, but it is only a copy."

" And you wonder at finding me here, not so? " he replied
in German in a low voice, " Well, here I am free, here I
may practise my art and pursue my ideals. I was born in a
different world, a world of intellectual bondage; but I cast
off the fetters, and my mind is free to develop, to dream, to
create."

" Do you come from Poland? " I asked.

" From Galicia. I was born in Zloczow and was dedicated
from childhood to the study of the Torah by my parents,
who were poor pious shopkeepers. Soon after my
Barmitzvah [1] they sent me to a *Yeshiva* [2] in Lemberg, where
I sat and shook myself over the Talmud the whole day
long, in company with a dozen other youths. To while away
the time, when teacher and supervisor were both away, I
took to making pencil sketches of my fellow-students on
the margin of the big heavy folios. I got into trouble as a

[1] Religious majority at the age of thirteen.   [2] Talmudical College.

Interior of the Spanish Synagogue in Venice

Ark of the Law in the " Schola Canton "
(Canton Synagogue) in Venice

reward for my pains, and was put down as an idler and
ne'er-do-well. But meanwhile I began to feel that I had some
artistic ability, and that if only I were favoured by opportunity I might achieve something—something, however
little, that would give me more moral satisfaction than
droning over the barren dialectics of the sages of ancient
Babylon—their memory be blessed! And the visits that I
used to pay secretly to the Art Gallery quickened the artistic
flame within me. I longed to get away from the narrow life
I was leading, and inwardly revolted against the whole code
of traditional laws by which I felt my soul enchained. And
whilst my mind was passing through this revolution I got
married before I was twenty."

He paused for a moment as a studious Frenchman with
pince-nez entered and fixed his gaze upon the famous " Birth
of Venus."

"Don't look surprised," he continued in an undertone.
" Marriage among the orthodox of Galician Jewry is an
affair in which neither bride nor bridegroom is consulted:
it is all settled by the parents, and the children, not having
been able to develop any particular likings of their own,
accept the parental choice. I remained in Lemberg, living—
as the custom is the first year or two—in the house of my
father-in-law, who was a well-to-do shopkeeper and a great
fanatic. The marriage proved a failure: my wife was an
ignorant girl of seventeen, with the temper of a spoiled
child, and my father-in-law had daily outbursts of rage at
my growing heresy. The result was a divorce.

"At last I felt free: I forsook my home and friends and
wandered to Vienna. There I lived eighteen months, painting anything from portraits to shop-signs in order to make
a living, whilst at the same time I attended a school of art.
Among my fellow-students I heard a great deal about Italy
and its mediaeval painters, and how every true lover of
art looks upon a pilgrimage to this country as the highest
ideal. So I too, the poor Talmudical student of Galicia,
whose parents had predicted he would be a great Rabbi

and a light in Israel, was seized by the same longing to
worship in the world's shrine of art. I saved whatever I
could and here I am."

"Copying a Madonna of Botticelli," I observed.

"Well, and if so?" he returned with a shrug of the
shoulders. "To me this picture is simply a great work of
art, free from religious suggestions or historical memories.
What appeals to me in it is its beauty and pathos—the
reverent love of the mother for the child who is showing
the first signs of wisdom. It reminds me of the doting
affection lavished on me by my own mother, who dreamed
that I should become a wonder-working Rabbi, with a fame
spreading far and wide. It reminds me also of the hope in
the heart of every Jewish mother that she may be favoured
to give birth to the Messiah."

He resumed his brush and began to touch the hair of
one of the adoring maidens.

"Is your picture intended for some foreign Gallery?" I
ventured.

He hesitated slightly, then said: "It is for an American
patron, to whom I was introduced by a Jewish lady, a
sculptor who is also studying here."

"And after that?" I continued.

"I shall devote myself to Jewish art. Yes, there is such
a thing as Jewish art. What else are Hermann Struck's
types of Polish Jews, or Leopold Pilichowski's scenes of Jews
at prayer, or Hirszenberg's remarkable picture, *Golus*
(Exile), showing a host of terror-stricken Russian Jews fleeing in search of refuge?"

"But how can you cultivate Jewish art in Florence? You
must at least live in a Jewish environment."

"True," he said pensively. "But did you think I had
taken a vow to spend the rest of my days in Italy? Now
that my talent has developed and I feel able to paint pictures
of my own I shall go to the Land of Israel to paint scenes
of the new life of our people."

"May all your hopes be happily fulfilled!" I said.

The only response was a wistful look in the dreamy eyes of the artist.

On leaving the Uffizi I passed through the imposing portico which leads to the Arno, and pursued my way along the Lung' Arno della Borsa. The road was silent and deserted, except for a couple of dogs who lay curled in peaceful slumber, for the midday sun was burning at its fiercest. The heat came beating down upon me, and I was driven to seek the shade. I turned into the first by-street, a narrow straggling thoroughfare, with a lofty wall on one side and the back of some famous mansion of old on the other. In a recess of the wall there was a barrow with a heap of second-hand books, behind which nodded a man on a little wooden box. The store of literature, as forlorn as its keeper, attracted me, and I turned over the musty volumes, printed in various tongues, which had long survived the function of adorning a library and could scarce serve any longer to enrich the mind. The proprietor seemed annoyed at my curiosity: he wished to continue his sleep, but felt that he dared not do so as long as a stranger was sampling his wares.

Stimulated by his suspecting frown, I resumed my search more vigorously, and after casting aside a number of the leather tomes, mouldy and moth-eaten, I lighted upon a small book of Italian verse with a yellowish cover, which bore the name "Salomone Fiorentino" stamped in gilt letters on a square of red morocco. The title-page showed that it had been printed in Leghorn, in the year 1815, but despite its great age the book was remarkably clean. It was as compact as though it had newly left the press; its pages were innocent of a stain or a marginal comment; its edges still retained somewhat of their pristine whiteness. I wondered whether these were the signs of a jealous care or of complete neglect. The only external proof of age lay in the ribbon bookmark, which was red with a streak of white so far as it nestled between the pages but was turned to a dull yellow in the part that hung outside.

"*Due lire!*" snapped the bookseller with a growl.

" *Una lira*," I promptly replied, having learned to perfection a friend's advice always to offer half of the demanded price.

The man was too drowsy to bargain and evidently wished to be rid of me; so he took my coin and I pocketed his book.

The name of Solomon Fiorentino had only once flashed across my horizon, but I still had a vivid memory of this hapless poet of Florence, who at the end of the eighteenth century suffered imprisonment for his liberal views, and was released only to suffer privation until the Jewish community of Leghorn provided him with a professorship of Italian literature. Of his work and his title to fame I had but a faint notion; whether he had rhymed in Hebrew or Italian was also a matter about which I was not quite clear. But now his complete contribution to the world's literature was securely tucked away in my pocket. What years of suffering and experience, what a soul of courageous hope and reflection, had gone to the making of this book! And its fate was to be thrown on the rubbish-heap of a second-hand bookseller, to be picked up for a few pence.

In the cool of the day I pored over its pages and marked the minor key to which most of the verse was attuned. A cycle of elegies on the death of his wife and a sonnet on the death of a little son bore witness to the grief that the poet had endured, apart from the visitation of political trouble. Was ever sorrow so poignant as his?—he asks in a brief apologetic preface, wherein he explains why he makes public the verses indited to the memory of " a lady who was a gentle companion, a faithful friend, and a most affectionate mother." In polished yet passionate strophes he traces the episodes in her earthly departure, finding consolation in the remembrance of her virtues and in the thought of her soul's eternity. A chastened and even mystic philosophy breathes through most of his writings, establishing a kinship with a poetic namesake of mediaeval Spain, Solomon ibn Gabirol. He had a blank verse disquisition, in two books, on " The

Spirituality and the Immortality of the Soul "; a series of sixty-six rhymed octaves on the perils of youth; and a sonnet on the necessity of matrimony. But mystic though he was, he kept abreast of the political movements of his day, prompted to a sonnet by the political state of Europe in 1792 and to another by the peace between England and France nine years later. And withal he fulfilled the role of a poet laureate, tuning his lyre to mournful strains on the death of the " *augustissima Imperatrice Maria Teresa d'Austria* ", sounding forth a jubilant paean on the coronation of Leopold II, and keeping his muse in prompt and pliant readiness for every occasion of public importance. But though his muse was dedicated largely to personal emotions and political incidents he was not estranged from the synagogue, for he devoted his talent to translating some psalms and prayers into Italian verse.

The struggling artist from Zloczow and the slumbering poet from Monte San Savino—what a strange couple of friends to make in one day, and within the same hour! Children of a scattered people, they both reflected in different degree the tribulations of the Jewish soul.

IV.—A SABBATH IN ROME

I

Long before I stepped out of the crowded train into the shrieking station of the Eternal City, long before I had ever dreamed that I should set foot in the capital of the Caesars, I had conceived an image of the ancient Mistress of the World as she now lay stripped of all her barbaric strength. Vague and amorphous as such an image must in some measure be, capriciously moulded of a store of historic memories and pictorial glimpses of mammoth ruins, it was informed with a sense of brooding majesty that still haunted the site of triumphal spectacles. But the conceit of the brain, when applied to an unseen, far-away city, seldom accords with the throbbing reality. And so it was with a feeling of disillusionment that I found the city sacred to the memory of Caesar and Cicero usurped by all the conventions and innovations of the twentieth century, with a network of electric tramcars, fashionable hotels, popular music halls, noisy cafés, cinemas, and the heavens at night illuminated with all sorts of coloured advertisements.

It was a somewhat similar feeling of disappointment that possessed me when first I made my way to the Ghetto and found the site dominated by a magnificent synagogue. The vision of a gloomy *Judengasse*, with its tall and teeming tenements, with its piety and its pathos, its squalor and its hope, was rudely dispelled; and before me, on a wide open space on the bank of the Tiber, opposite the Tiberine Island, stood an imposing Temple of glaring whiteness, which seemed to emphasize that a new chapter had begun in the history of the Jews of Rome. Strange, indeed, that the Ghetto which had been preserved and maintained by law long after all the other Ghetti of Europe had become mere curiosities for the traveller, has been almost utterly demolished, leaving behind but a few vestiges whose scantiness enhances their interest. As my eyes rested upon the shrine of massive and elaborate masonry, which stood in splendid isolation, boldly rearing its glittering cupola to the skies, and as my ears were assailed by the clanging bells of the tramcars which sped on their course a few yards away, I could scarcely realise that the scene had once been occupied by a compulsory Ghetto, which was annually flooded by the muddy river, and to live in whose unhealthy confines the Jews had to offer an annual petition even so late as 1850. I thought of the *Judengassen* of Mainz and Worms, which still remain practically the same as they were centuries ago, save for the removal of the gates and the peaceful immigration of Gentiles. Here the destroying hand of Time has been more rapid and violent, perhaps because the memories

of persecution were more galling and nothing but a wholesale uprooting could atone for the sins of the past. But the
relics that still survive are sufficiently numerous and concrete
to aid the imagination in building a picture of mediaeval
intolerance.

My attention was directed to them by a young Jew, short
and swarthy, who had been standing in one of the doorways
of the synagogue and who sidled up to me with friendly
enterprise. Greeting me with an effusive *Shalom*, he introduced himself as a Hebrew teacher, who had often acted
as cicerone to historians, and who could therefore at least
be of equal service to me. He conducted me to the little
Church of St. Gregory, close to the ruins of the Theatre of
Marcellus, and pointed to the text in Hebrew and Latin
inscribed on the door. The text was from the book of
Isaiah: *"I have spread out my hands all the day unto a
rebellious people, which walketh in a way that is not good,
after their own thoughts, a people that provoketh me to my
face continually,"* and the perverted application of the
words was emphasised by a fresco of the Crucifixion above
the inscription. Exactly opposite to the door of this little
church had been the double gate which guarded the Ghetto,
and the " rebellious people " who emerged from it each day
to follow their vocations had been faced by a reproach which
must have become dim to their eyes even before the gilded
lettering lost its lustre.

Scarcely allowing me time to note the text my guide
hurried me off to a shabby red-brick building several yards
away, the private abode of a Christian, and pointed to a
small round slab of white marble in the wall, which bore
a Hebrew inscription of four words: *Kodesh Ladonai
Kehillath Rom* (Sanctuary of the Lord, Congregation of
Rome). The small white slab is the only remnant of an
ancient synagogue which is believed to have existed near
the old stone bridge, the Pons Fabricius, which was also
called the " Pons Judaeorum." The Jewish authorities have
made several attempts to buy it, but the owner of the

263

house would not part with the sacred stone, to which he attributed talismanic powers. Then the pedagogue who had elected to show me the path wherein I should walk made a bee-line in the opposite direction, past the synagogue upon which the spirit of the Sabbath was slowly descending, and plunging beneath an arch into a squalid alley which was bordered by dark cave-like dwellings whose poor inhabitants seemed quite at home, and mumbling the word *"Mezuzah,"* he brought me after some labyrinthine turnings to a big doorway and pointed to a narrow incision about six inches long cut diagonally in the sidepost. That slender groove had once been filled with the word of the Law as prescribed in Deuteronomy, for the doorway had led to a Jewish school. But the word of the Law has now gone forth both from the school and also from the doorpost, and the teachers and pupils took up their abode in the Palazzo Cenci, the mansion wherein the hapless Beatrice brooded over her fate, and whence her brutal father spread terror into the hearts of the children of the Ghetto. The Cenci are now but a name, a byword, and the walls of their ill-starred palace re-echo with the chant of the Law of Moses which triumphs over its persecutors.

The shades of night were thickening, so my orthodox guide, muttering *" Shabbat,"* hastened his steps towards the house of prayer. The interior of the synagogue was bright and festive in honour of the welcome to the Sabbath Bride, and the congregation who were present to greet her were indeed of goodly numbers for these days of laxity. Most of them belonged to the poor, working class, whose shabby clothes were in striking contrast with the rich decorations, but whose joyous outpourings of prayer filled the building with something far more precious than the golden patterns on the walls, the snow-white pillars of marble, and the galaxy of seven-branched candlesticks. The feast of light and gaudy colour was almost dazzling: the brightest and loudest of hues seemed to have been chosen for the embellishment of the walls and the dome, and these were enhanced by the profusion and glaring whiteness of the marble. But custom has its way, and the strophes of *Lecha Dodi* were sung as lustily in this ornate temple as they had been in the lowly bethels of the Ghetto when the Pope held domination.

Dazed with the surrounding glitter I closed my eyes and gave myself up to the chorus of praise that swelled and soared aloft, while memories of bygone days came slowly filing past like a procession of wraiths. A group of Jews with the badge of shame upon their breast, mocked by a grinning crowd and driven like sheep to a church to listen to a conversionist sermon; a Rabbi humbly offering a scroll of the Torah in homage to a newly anointed Pope and cowed with a contemptuous refusal; a youth forced to run naked for a prize at a riotous carnival; a public disputation on the true faith between a fanatical monk and a timorous Rabbi; a holocaust of the Talmud in the Campo dei Fiori and a slaughter of its devotees in the arena of the Colosseum: glimpses of heroism and memories of martyrdom came crowding upon me, transfiguring the present with a vision of the past. And the congregation sang with unquestioning faith: " *God will quicken the dead in the abundance of His loving kindness; blessed for evermore be His glorious name.*"

II

The following morning the congregation was rather sparse, and there was an air of emptiness in the spacious sanctuary. But the beadles, in their long red-edged sashes and title-bearing breastplates, stalked up and down the aisles with the mien of authority as though they had to hold in check unruly thousands. The ministers too were present in full muster, the white-bearded *Rabbino Maggiore* (Chief Rabbi) in a robe and hexagonal hat with braid of yellow hue, according to the laws and ordinances of Roman Jewry on ecclesiastical vestments. Their figures and distinguishing colours stood out against the elaborate brass screen behind which the choir and organ were situated, and the general effect of the spectacle was curiously reminiscent of the picturesque pomp of a cathedral. At the lower end of the synagogue were some shabby loungers, men and women, who came in through one door, looked on listlessly, and passed out through the opposite door.

The usual service was diversified by the presence of a *Bar-Mitzvah*,[1] the centre of an excited group of relatives, whose excitement waxed still higher when the youthful hero, taking upon himself the responsibility of his sins, stood before the open Ark of the Law, and the Rabbi, placing his hand upon the boy's head, invoked the blessing of Heaven. The boy kissed the hand of the Rabbi, and the latter kissed the boy on both cheeks and added a chuck under the chin. Then the boy, having duly solemnised the attainment of his religious majority, hurried back with flushed cheeks to receive a kiss from his father, whereupon they and the entire group of relatives quickly packed up their *talethim* and prayer-books and hurried off to celebrate the event in feasting, leaving the rest of the service for those whose sense of religious seriousness was more strongly developed.

Behind me, at the lower end of the synagogue, were seated two women, each with a child in her arms. The younger was dressed in festal finery, and stole a tender glance ever and anon at her babe in its fine long clothes of spotless white. Their appearance in that part of the building seemed to me somewhat strange, seeing that there were three capacious galleries for the especial accommodation of the fair. But the mystery was unravelled when the service was over, for the young mother, accompanied by her beaming husband, carried her babe to the *Almemar* and presented it to the senior cantor, who recited a prayer for its welfare and formally welcomed it into the Congregation of Israel— a custom unknown in the orthodox communities of Northern Europe. Then the proud parents trooped back again with the infant and straightway departed. The other

[1] " Son of the Commandment," a boy on attaining his thirteen birthday.

woman with the child remained, as if expecting something further to happen, though the whole corps of clergy had now retired. Presently more ladies appeared, in rustling silks and nodding plumes, accompanied by well-groomed men, and the beadles, suddenly assuming an obsequious air, ushered them with repeated bows to the front seats. Evidently something of importance was about to be enacted, and a few straggling worshippers of the poor class remained to look on.

In the midst of my conjectures the organ struck up a solemn prelude, a door near the elaborate screen opened, and there emerged a fashionably dressed, middle-aged lady, with a lorgnette and wrist bag, who was conducted to a seat on the *Almemar* by the archbeadle. Next, the minor clergy took up their positions, and presently, as the choir added their voices to the peal of the organ, there entered in slow and stately procession the white-bearded *Rabbino Maggiore,* the senior precentor, and a young girl in short white frock and long white gloves, with a bridal wreath and train covering her luxurious black hair. The Rabbi stopped at the Ark and opened it, the precentor and the girl bowed low before it and then continued walking slowly and solemnly round the reading-desk until they reached the Ark again, when they again bowed low. The precentor proceeded to his seat, and the girl remained before the open Ark.

When the voices of the choir had died away, the Rabbi began in resonant tones to put the maid through a catechism, and it became clear that this was a confirmation service. He asked her her name, the object of her presence, the nature of her faith, the number of the Commandments and of the Creeds and their significance, to all which questions she returned a brisk and audible reply. Then she delivered a long declaration of faith in Italian from a printed document which was handed to her by the senior precentor, and at the end of her recital the Rabbi, spreading his *talith* over her head, invoked the blessing of Heaven and uttered a prayer that she might become like those virtuous women of ancient Israel, Sarah, Rebekah, Rachel and Leah—whereupon the lady on the *Almemar* removed her lorgnette and wiped away a motherly tear.

" *Gentilissima signorina*," then exclaimed the Rabbi as he began a long exhortation in florid phraseology, wherein he impressed upon the maid the meaning of the ceremony, the position of the Jewess and her duties. Much of what he said, doctrinal abstractions in high-flown diction, must have been lost upon the flurried soul, but he also pointed out the value and beauty of the home ceremonies, and his fancy played about the kindling of the Sabbath lights. Throughout the address the maid stood still and attentive before the open Ark, and when at length it was over and the choir gave forth a sonorous hymn she joined her mother, who bestowed upon her a lingering kiss. When the final strains had died away the Rabbi shook mother and daughter by the hand, and then the heroine was besieged by her relatives and friends, who were eloquent with praise, and the marble pillars re-echoed with a peal of kisses. Freed from these affectionate embraces, the maid now tripped boldly down the aisle—a buxom girl of fourteen, with olive-brown cheeks and lustrous eyes—and on reaching the poor-box nailed to the wall she produced a coin from the pretty little purse at her waist and dropped it in, and then walked across to the other side where she dropped another coin into the donation-box for a new synagogue. At the ringing echo of these contributions I imagined what would have been the rage of some Rabbi of the *Agudas Israel* at such desecration of the Sabbath, as he would have deemed it, within the very sanctuary itself; and a few moments later I wondered whether there would have been bounds to his indignation when the lorgnetted mother and her consecrated daughter with a couple of friends drove away in a carriage. From the Rabbi himself I learned that the confirmation of girls took place here only on the Feast of Pentecost as a rule, but an exception had been made in the present case, as the girl was a visitor from Alexandria and her mother, who had handsomely subscribed to the synagogue, had particularly desired the ceremony.

III

As I left the building, the pedagogue who had acted as my guide the previous day offered to show me another curious survival of the mediaeval Ghetto. Five synagogues in one building was the historic phenomenon in which he sought to rouse my interest. I needed no second invitation, but straightway followed him to the quaint nook, within a stone's throw of the temple, where these five shrines were entered by a single doorway. They formed a remarkable memorial of the intolerance of bygone days, when only one building was allowed in the Ghetto for divine worship, and likewise a memorial of the manifold sources or origin of the Jewish colony, for each sub-national group imported its own rites and customs and desired a separate shrine for their observance. On the ground floor were the Sicilian Synagogue, now closed, which had the Italian rite, and the Catalan and Aragonese Synagogue, which had the Spanish rite. The latter was a picturesque fane, containing some fine marble carving and a couple of Arks, in which a few devout worshippers were droning the Psalms. Mounting a staircase we came to the Castilian Synagogue, above the Sicilian, a narrow yet beautiful house of prayer, with a couple of quaintly carved Arks and a lofty dome that contained the women's gallery. Adjoining it was a two-storied modern building, the "Scuola del Tempio", or Temple Synagogue, where the Italian rite was observed; and a dark narrow staircase led us to the "Scuola Nuova," in which a stretch of lattice work above the *Almemar* concealed a cramped and musty gallery.

The silence of the venerable shrine was soon broken by the tramp of feet, and I was interrupted in my inspection of a framed code of twenty rules for the election of the Bridegroom of the Law. The white-bearded Rabbi had come to expound the Scriptures to those who were still zealous for the Law, and the dozen students who gathered round the table included the minor clergy. Seated on a high cane-bottomed chair the Rabbi announced the chapter and verse in the Book of Job which they had reached, and the students diligently turned the leaves of the worm-eaten volumes before them. The exposition of the lamentations of the man of Uz was conducted by the Rabbi in an accent of pathos, and the philological explanations were interspersed with homilies. The students followed carefully, and for the most part in silence, but now and again one would venture a remark which would arouse general discussion and relieve the tedium of the misanthropist's moralisings. As the Rabbi pursued the solemn disquisition, and the mid-day sun beat down upon the holy page, the senior precentor removed his black bowler to mop his brow and remained uncovered; and presently a layman followed the clerical example. But the Rabbi, heedless of these bare heads, pursued the even tenor of his discourse.

As I left the ancient building, sanctified by the prayers of countless generations, I reflected that the reading of the Book of Job is reserved by custom for days of mourning, and I wondered over what the Rabbi and his students could be mourning. Was it over the departed spirit of traditional faith?

V.—THE JEWISH CATACOMBS

The drowsy coachman who was nodding on his seat, amid all the racket of the electric tramcars in the Piazza di Venezia, looked puzzled when I asked him to drive me to the Jewish Catacombs. Did I not mean the catacombs of St. Callixtus, he asked, scratching his head; everybody went to see the catacombs of St. Callixtus. "No, the Jewish catacombs in the Vigna Randanini," I repeated, and the fear of losing a passenger suddenly quickened his memory. So I leaned back in the cosy vehicle, which could not yet be faithfully described as fly-blown, and soon we were skirting round the ruins of the Capitol and the Palatine Mount and driving on the long country road famous in history as the Via Appia. Some returning carriages with garrulous tourists and a couple of rude rustic carts drawn by oxen with tinkling bells were all that we passed on the way. The historic imagination might have peopled the road with figures clad in togas and adorned with laurels, but the sultry afternoon was more conducive to listlessness as the mare pursued its monotonous trot on the dreary road. At length we came to a big assemblage of empty carriages drawn up on either side of, and opposite to, a wide doorway in a lofty, far-extending wall, through which a line of visitors were passing. " The Catacombs of St. Callixtus ", observed my coachman, who then exchanged some words with a fellow-driver. Another few hundred yards and we reached a small, insignificant-looking wooden door in the lofty wall on the other side. It was the entrance to the Jewish catacombs.

There were no waiting carriages or stream of visitors. The door was locked, and nobody was visible. The driver pulled a chain hanging down beside the door, whilst I endeavoured to decipher the faded inscription above it, which was in a curious mixture of English and Hebrew, embellished with the design of a seven-branched candlestick. I was able to make out that the place had been discovered in 1859, and all doubt as to its identity was dispelled by the simple legend: " Entrance to *Jewisk* Sepulchres." Suddenly a grey-haired woman looked down from the top of the wall and held parley with us as though we had come to storm a citadel. She had not expected visitors to-day, and we must wait until somebody brought the key. She disappeared from view and my coachman remounted his perch, desirous of resuming the doze that I had interrupted in the Piazza di Venezia. I was just beginning to wonder how often the stillness of this strange habitation was broken by the curious traveller when a bronzed and grizzled man, who seemed to have dropped from the skies, plodded his way towards us with a bunch of jangling keys. In another minute the door was opened, and after ascending a small flight of stone steps I found myself in a garden of palms, where a cool stream trickled from a rock-fountain and timid canaries twittered from their cage on the wall. On the ground near the entrance door lay a notice-board in three languages, with regulations as to fees and visiting; but it was half-buried under such an accumulation of dirt and weeds that it must have been in disuse many years. Evidently a tariff had proved unnecessary. I patiently awaited the appearance of my guide, who, I imagined, was refurbishing his neglected uniform and declining memory.

At length my guide approached. It was no uniformed cicerone with obsequious bow but a fat, white-bloused woman, with a smile on her olive-brown cheeks, who swelled with importance as she bore the key for the catacombs. I accompanied her to an outhouse where she got tapers and matches, and then she conducted me through a path bordering on vineyards to a red barred gate, which she opened and locked behind her. We descended a flight of steps to an oblong atrium, where we lighted our tapers; and my guide, hastily throwing a kerchief on her head, led the way into the bowels of the earth. Why she should have covered her head is a moot point: perhaps she regarded the catacombs a sacred place, perhaps she simply wished to protect her glossy hair from spiders.

The tunnel we had entered was about eight or nine foot high, and for the most part it was so narrow that we had to walk in single file. The soil was loose and slippery, and the wall, which I clutched for a moment as I missed my footing, was cold and clammy to the touch. There were horizontal cavities on either side, each large enough to contain a corpse, and arranged in three or four tiers. Most of them were quite empty, except for the soft black earth at the bottom; but in many of them was a whitish powder, which was all that had remained of human bones. Now and again, in the little white heap we discerned bits of bone and occasionally a solitary limb, a leg or an arm. In one of the tombs there was a part of the pelvis, and in two or three of them I espied a complete skull lying on one side. But the most ghastly sight of all was a full-sized skull placed erect in the middle of an upper tomb, and grinning at us full in the face. Some irreverent joker had evidently wished to give future visitors the shivers. Occasionally my guide pointed to a rather small niche, with the exclamation "*Bambino!*" and once, stopping near a hollow in the wall on a level with the ground, she exclaimed "*Sepher Torah*" (A Scroll of the Law)! The scrolls of the Law buried here must have been those rendered unfit for synagogue use. All that now remained of them were some white ash-like fragments, which crumbled at the touch.

A great number of the tombs had inscriptions on marble slabs, which have been fixed in the walls by modern hands. Most of the inscriptions were in Greek letters, though generally expressing Latin words, whilst some were in Latin characters too. They merely gave the name of the deceased but hardly ever the years of his life, while his occupation was stated only when it was of a religious character: the only two instances were *grammateus* (scribe) and *archon* (ruler). One inscription attracted my particular attention as the letters were in red, and on reading it I found that it was in memory of a proselyte, whose adoption of the ancient faith had won perpetual record though his mortal remains were now but a spoonful of ashes. The inscriptions were often embellished with artistic devices, the most frequent being the seven-branched candelabrum, which is an infallible sign that the tomb is Jewish as it is nowhere found in Christian catacombs. According to theologians the symbol is a reference to the Biblical verse, "The spirit of man is the candle of the Lord," but it may well be an allusion to the golden candlestick which Titus had taken from the Temple, and the loss of which was mourned by the pious Jews even unto death.

There were more elaborate decorations in the chambers which branched off from the main passage, and which were entered by narrow doorways. These were most probably family vaults of the rich, and they had cavities of different sizes in tiers on every side. Both on the ceiling and the walls there were primitive frescoes in crude colours, representing palms and citrons, peacocks and lambs. In the most spacious and grandiose of these chambers there was a picture of Adam and Eve in their native simplicity in the centre of the ceiling: thus were the fabled ancestors of mankind made to hold vigil in the vault of death. On one marble tablet I saw a design which looked like a lamb's head with a plum beside it; and on another there were two curious figures which resembled nothing so much as a pair of fighting-cocks.

The level of the floor descended once or twice, making us feel that we were burrowing still deeper into the bowels of the earth; but we were reminded of the sunlight above now and again by an air-hole, which seemed like a dismal, moss-covered tube. At length, after plodding and groping our way for half an hour in these subterranean passages, the gloom of which was only intensified by our flickering tapers, we came to another flight of steps, three times as long as that by which we descended, and marking the end of our explorations. The air seemed laden with unwonted warmth as I regained the path through the vineyards, and my portly guide, panting for breath, uncovered her head once more and fanned herself with her kerchief.

I left the Jewish Catacombs to return to their death-like stillness, but when I presently drove past those of St. Callixtus the crowd of carriages was still the same.

VI.—MUSINGS IN GENOA

There are dismal memories that haunt Genoa the Superb. Beautiful in situation and wealthy in commerce, the city may fascinate with a myriad charms. But its alluring beauty has always concealed a cold and cruel heart, its wealth was often amassed by deeds of violence, and though it has risen to be one of the great centres of the world's traffic, a gathering-place for ships from every clime, yet its charms cannot dispel the sombre memories that linger about its quay and its ancient narrow streets. It was known as the gateway of Italy in the legendary beginning of its history—a fancy perpetuated in its very name. But it was a gateway that opened outwards more readily than inwards, and it was jealously guarded against a possible foe or an unwelcome friend. It opened outwards to let its merchant adventurers sally forth upon their freebooting quest, or to speed the valiant Crusaders upon their mission, pretending piety unto heaven while practising plunder upon earth. It opened inwards only to welcome back its cut-throat corsairs, returning rich with captive galleons, or to receive the motley merchandise that was brought in vessels from every land. But if any storm-tossed refugee, fleeing from the terrors of the Spanish Inquisition, was driven to the sunlit gulf, the janitors of the gateway would pounce upon him and profit by his despair. For upon the posts of this ancient gateway was written in lurid letters the barbarous motto: "Greed and Cruelty". No stranger, however sharp of sight, could have seen those menacing words, for he was dazzled by the rays of the gladdening sun; but if only he approached near enough he felt their dread reality.

Memories of some of the dark passages in the city's annals came back to me as I wandered about the wharf, perchance on the very spot where, four hundred years ago, a band of ill-fated Jews from Spain had sought asylum. The New World had just been discovered, and hundreds of exiles, tired of the Old World and sickened by its civilisation and inhumanity, ventured forth across the Atlantic to seek a haven of peace. Thither have they been followed in this twentieth century by their kinsfolk, not in hundreds, but in thousands each year, and before the First World War even in hundreds of thousands. But most of the fugitives from the wrath of Ferdinand and Isabella were minded still to seek out a new home in the Old World, hoping that change of place would bring change of luck, according to the dictum of the ancient Rabbis. And so some went north to Holland, and others went east to Italy and Turkey, and one of the harbours whither they steered in quest of safety was that from which Columbus, of whom there is a statue in a square near by, had first gazed upon the alluring sea and dreamed his dreams of another world far, far beyond the waters around him. But in that harbour where the dreams of Columbus had been scoffed at, the fugitives who owed their fate to loyal faith could scarcely receive more unkindly treatment, for ideals were a ware which the Genoese held in light esteem. They had to crave permission to remain in the harbour until they could get their damaged ships repaired, and their own battered bodies restored to health, and while they were preparing to continue their journey winter came on and many of them died on the wharves. The short respite that they were allowed was withdrawn at the clamours of the jealous merchants and the fanatical priests, reinforced by the venomous sermons of Bernardino da Feltre; but the repeal was soon annulled in the hope that the fugitives might be lured from their faith. It was a vain hope, for only one man was tempted to adopt the creed of his persecutors. Other exiles, however, were even in worse plight, for they had lost their liberty to flee. They had been captured in the Mediterranean by corsairs and brought to Genoa to be sold as slaves. Their captors appreciated their marketable possibilities and the moral qualities of their brethren, for they knew that a Jewish prisoner would always be ransomed by his people. What suffering was wrought in those days of romance in the misused name of religion!

As I stood on the lofty wall overlooking one of the busiest parts of the harbour, the Mura della Malapaga, watching the bustling scene of the lading and unlading of ships, I recalled the moving martyrology written by Joseph Ha-

Cohen, physician and historian, who lived and suffered and died in this city in the sixteenth century. It is well named *The Vale of Tears*, for there is scarce a single page in the Hebrew narrative, couched in the pure diction of the Bible, which does not describe some episode of pathos and tragedy in the tribulations of Israel from the day of his dispersion. The most vivid pages are those which record the sufferings witnessed or experienced by the author himself, for although a man of distinction, esteemed both for his professional skill and his philanthropic zeal, he had to submit to the general decree of banishment launched against the Jews of Genoa. Twice was he exiled from the city in which all his childhood's memories were rooted, once as a young man of twenty, and again after a residence of twelve years, at the age of fifty-four. His first exile was spent in the neighbouring town of Novi, and the second at Voltaggio and Costeletto, whose townsfolk welcomed the medical skill which had excited the jealousy and hostility of the Genoese physicians. "A man of sorrows and acquainted with grief", he returned, bent and hoary, to live the last few years of his life in the city of commerce and cruelty, where on the verge of eighty he was gathered unto his forefathers.

The pen of Joseph Ha-Cohen was dipped in tears, and the heart that inspired it was laden with grief. His narrative is interspersed with the imprecation, "Perish the name of the wicked!"—for many were the deeds of wickedness he records, and the tragic stories that he tells always close with that agonised cry, reiterated unto despair, "How long, O Lord, how long?" He had his share of personal sorrow, for two of his children died in infancy and he mourned after them bitterly. His firstborn son was drowned while bathing in the river Reno, near Pieve, and the tragic loss moved him to write an elegy in which he uses all the classic lamentations of Holy Writ. "Let there be no dew upon Pieve, nor rain upon the land of Ferrara!" he exclaims; "let there be no fields of offerings, for there has fallen the most beautiful of youths. Would that I had died in thy stead, O my son, my son!" Disaster also overtook the family of his brother-in-law, Rabbi Moses Ha-Cohen—"may this month be solitary!"—for during his absence three miscreants from Pieve broke into his house and murdered his wife, his daughter, and two sons. The bodies were taken to Bologna for burial, and there "the whole community was seized with violent emotion, and raised its voice and wept."

But of all the happenings in this *Vale of Tears* perhaps the most striking, because it is suffused with an air of romance, is that concerning the family of a cantor who had lived in Spain, and who embarked on a ship for Italy when the decree of expulsion was issued. The cantor was accompanied by his wife, his son, and several daughters. One of the daughters—as the daughters of Israel often are—was beautiful and fair to look upon, and the captain of the ship fell in love with her. The mother was alarmed at the probable consequences, and, so strong was her religious zeal, she preferred that her daughter should die rather than be disgraced. So she threw her into the sea, and her other daughters after her, and then, seized with a frenzy of despair, hurled herself into the watery grave to be united with them. The sailors were stricken with horror and plunged into the waves to rescue them, but they only succeeded in saving one of the girls. How many other daughters of Israel, fleeing from the myrmidons of the Inquisition, must have captured the hearts of the captains who were bearing them to a harbour of safety! At least one other has her name immortalised in the annals of her people's history—Maria Nunez. She was the daughter of a Portuguese Marrano, and in order to escape the perils that encompassed her she set sail with her uncle and brother for Holland. But their vessel was captured by an English ship, and the captain, a nobleman of high degree, was deeply moved by the charms of Maria. He wooed her with ardour and lavished upon her promises of riches and happiness, but she steadfastly rejected his suit. And when the ship reached

England, Queen Elizabeth heard of Maria and her beauty and her staunch faith, whereupon, woman-like, she summoned her to court to see if she was as beautiful as rumour described her, and she was so enchanted with her that she drove with her in a royal carriage through the streets of London amid the admiring gaze of her applauding subjects. The Queen then allowed Maria to continue on her journey with her companions to Holland, and there she married one of her own people.

If Joseph Ha-Cohen had lived in Genoa to-day he would have had no occasion to compose a *Vale of Tears*, so far as the material lot of his brethren was concerned. But if he had witnessed the plight that has overtaken their spiritual welfare he would doubtless have dipped his pen in tears again and lamented the decline of faith. He would also have probably wondered why the only synagogue, situated on the Mura della Malapaga, is distinguished by no outward sign, so that a Jew from another land in quest of it might even pass it by unnoticed. Can it be that the local congregation are ashamed of their Judaism, or simply that, in true piety and humility of spirit, they disdain all external show? Whatever the reason, the stranger who merely sees an open doorway, with an unusually clean step, in a row of dilapidated houses, can hardly feel inspired to exclaim: "This is no other than the house of God!" Once you enter the doorway, however, you perceive a certain distinction, for the narrow staircase is all of marble.

At the top of the second flight you come to the synagogue, which the beadle, who lives on the premises, will readily open for you. I found him a most amiable man, unlike all the beadles I had ever met in Northern Europe. He had a grey beard of Imperial cut and wore a straw hat, while his slow measured step and his gentle voice gave him an air of dignity. He rather surprised me by his ability to speak Hebrew, and I began to wonder what his actual position was in relation to the house of prayer.

"Is my master a teacher of the Law?" I asked.

And he answered simply: "I am a *Shammash*" (beadle)!

He told me that he had come from Monticelli, near Cremona, where in his youth there was a thriving congregation, but now all its members were scattered and the synagogue was closed. He produced a little calendar from his pocket, containing particulars of all the Jewish communities of Italy, and he fingered it as though it were a marvellous mine of information. It certainly did contain some curious features, such as a chronology of the world from the time of its Creation and a calendar which gave the Jewish Sabbaths and Holydays on one side and a complete catalogue of the saints' days on the other. I thought it would make an interesting souvenir, but hesitated to ask for it, fearing it might be the only one within the precincts of the synagogue, and that its removal would throw the whole community into perplexity as to the time of the outgoing of the Sabbath or the date of the next fast. But the beadle told me that he was the local agent for the calendar, and I understood. I procured my souvenir and gave another in exchange.

Apart from the situation of the synagogue there is nothing remarkable about it. It is a small neat chamber, with a marble floor, and has a gallery for women. There is something remarkable, however, in the entrance. It is an ancient tablet with a Hebrew inscription on the wall, containing a warning to *Cohenim* (priests) not to defile themselves unwittingly by walking over the old cemetery, and giving minute topographical instructions as to its locality. That ancient tablet is the sole surviving monument of the piety of bygone times.

VII.—ADVENTURE IN TURIN

There is little in the city of Turin to inspire you. It has nothing to compare with the natural beauty of Venice, or

the artistic treasures of Florence, or the historic antiquity of
Rome, or the spirit of romance that still haunts the byways
of Genoa. The very disposition of the city robs it of any
latent charm or lurking mystery, for it is cut up like a
chessboard, flat, open, and bare. Its streets are straight lines,
at right angles to one another, forming square blocks of
buildings, which are locally known as "islands." Stand at
any of the cross-roads, and you can have an uninterrupted
view in four directions; no curving street or projecting building prevents the eye from scanning the horizon or discerning the peaks of the neighbouring Alps. You are reminded
of the spick-and-span look of Mannheim, which is also
intersected in chessboard style. Beneath a blue sky, shedding
its warmth and radiance around you, the monotony of the
streets and the drabness of the buildings might borrow a
reflected charm. But when the heavens rain down in
torrents, drenching the curious stranger and all his glowing
fancies, he must indeed be superhuman if he can wax
enthusiastic over so doleful a city or indite a eulogy to its
memory. The reminiscences of his visit are mingled with
the vision of a weeping umbrella and the chilly sensation
of soaking boots.

These unpleasant impressions, however, might have been
utterly banished if only my quest after the spirit of Jewry
had received an agreeable fulfilment, if only I had discovered
some token of pride in the glorious past, some earnest of
loyalty to the sacred traditions of ages. For here, too, in
days gone by the persecutor had reigned and raged, cooping
up the children of Israel in a Ghetto, decreeing that they
should wear upon their garments a red badge—a variant
from the usual yellow and a fitting symbol of the blood of
martyrdom. Caged within their squalid prison and expelled
from it, and from the confines of the city, too, at the bid-
ding of envious citizens, and then re-admitted to the gloom
of the Ghetto on payment of thousands of golden florins,
they were like a shuttlecock in the hands of the oppressor,
who lightly tossed them to and fro. But no tribulations were

so poignant as to make them waver in their faith; no temptations were so seductive as to lure them away from the Ark of God. But now the sturdy faith of old seemed to have yielded to complacency and indifference.

The spirit of Judaism might be sluggish here, but there was at least a great and ornate temple that could worthily enshrine a noble devotion. I reached it in the gloaming, after wearily wandering through an arcade of shops where I sought refuge from the pelting rain. It rises, bold and splendid, at the corner of a street, like an impregnable fortress of faith, its lofty turrets crowned with domes recalling the minarets of a mosque whence the muezzin summons the people to prayer—an Oriental fancy aroused by the rich display of arabesque and the threefold Moorish arch that forms the approach. The splendid exterior is matched by a beautiful and impressive interior, stately pillars and a floor of patterned marble and manifold seven-branched candlesticks being the prominent feature in the scheme of decoration. Only a few electric lamps were lit when I entered, for it was a week-day, the splendour of maximum illumination being reserved for Sabbaths and holy days; but the dimness that filled the lofty space above gave free play to the imagination, which conjured up the spirits of departed generations gazing pensively upon the cheerless scene below. The precentor was trolling away the evening service, and four other ministers in full canonicals—their hats adorned with gold braiding—were sitting on the bench to the left of the *Almemar*. The worshippers were few, mainly of the poorer class, and their sparseness gave a melancholy touch to the service. But what impressed me as curious was the presence at the lower end of the synagogue of three women, who followed the prayers attentively, for even in the dim light I could discern a substantial gallery which went round three sides of the building. But their presence in the section usually sacred to man was at least convenient for the beadle, who came round towards the close of the service with a pyx, which he vigorously rattled as he approached each worshipper to rouse the charitable instincts into immediate action.

When the service was over I went up to the *Rabbino Maggiore*, a little grey-bearded man, as he was entering the vestry room. He asked me to wait until he had solemnised another service. He doffed his robe and cap, and put on his silk hat; and the other ministers likewise resumed their ordinary attire. Five or six members of the congregation, with the beadle in the rear, followed us into the room. There was a muffled whispering between the old Rabbi and a young man, and more whispering among the rest of the men. The beadle closed the door and whispered to the Rabbi. I wondered what was the meaning of all this whispering and secrecy, and what was this service that could not be held in the synagogue but must be solemnised in the dim light of the vestry room. An eerie sensation came over me; my memory flitted back to the days of the Marranos who prayed in underground chambers to escape the doom of the Inquisition, and I wondered whether this was a local survival of a mediaeval practice, even though the last myrmidon of the Holy Office had long gone to render his final account. But as my mind was stirred by these fancies the Rabbi, holding a book beneath the solitary lamp, began a Hebrew invocation in slow and solemn accents in the language of the ritual of the Eve of Atonement Day:

With the permission of those who are gathered here and with the permission of all this congregation, and with the permission of all Israel, I hereby declare as null and void and utterly destitute of meaning and effect the oaths, curses, maledictions, and imprecations, by which Bilha, daughter of David, believes that she hath been cursed. They shall not be binding nor shall they have any power!

I thought that Bilha was the wife or child of the young man who was standing near the Rabbi, that she had indeed been cursed with a grievous curse, and that this was the prescribed ceremony for exorcising the devil. After a brief consultation with the young man, the Rabbi resumed:

Now inasmuch as her name hath been Bilha, daughter of David, her name in Israel shall be called Esther, daughter of David, and the curses that have been uttered against Bilha shall have no power or dominion over Esther; even as the name of Abraham our father was changed from Abram to Abraham. And may she find grace and favour in the eyes of the Lord!

The Rabbi concluded with the *Kaddish* (a prayer for the glorification of the Deity), shook the young man cordially by the hand, and the congregation departed as quietly as it had assembled. Then the Rabbi turned to me, and I accompanied him on the way to a Hebrew school where he held a class for adults for the study of the Mishnah. So the light of the Torah was not yet quenched here! I at once commented on the strange ceremony which he had performed.

"It is the rite of *Shinnui Hashem*—the change of name," he observed. "It is the first time that I have performed it in the four years that I have been here, and only twice before in my whole life have I been asked to do it. The custom is German, not Italian, and it is based upon superstition. That is why I do not wish to encourage it by giving it publicity in the temple."

"And who," I asked, "is the person concerned—the young man's wife or child? No doubt he wishes to prevent her being cut off in her youth by some terrible curse."

"It is the young man's grandmother, a lady of seventy-five," replied the Rabbi. "She is the mother of a Rabbi, and the widow of one, so she knows what the custom is."

"Is she suffering under the spell of any particular curse?"

"None that I know of," he returned with a shrewd smile. "She is ailing with bronchitis and probably has illusions. But she wishes to have her days prolonged. May she live to a hundred and twenty!"

" At any rate she is strongly attached to the synagogue. Is she typical of your flock? "

The Rabbi gravely shook his head. " It is not as in the days of our fathers. Few are they who come to the synagogue on the Sabbath, and they rest content with that as their whole duty. The poor are even worse than the rich; they come in the middle of the week when they hear that somebody is observing a *Jahrzeit* (death anniversary), expecting to receive alms, but not on the Sabbath, when no money is exchanged. The Jewish shops that are closed on the holy day—I could count them on the fingers of one hand. And as for those who eat kosher—very, very few. Yes, the situation is very sad. The present generation are throwing their Judaism behind their backs."

" Are intermarriages frequent? "

" Mostly among the poor—the wicked. But since I have been here there have been three proselytes, Christian women desirous of marrying Jews. I impressed upon them the difficulties of the Jewish faith and urged them to be cautious and deliberate. But their minds were made up. So I taught them Hebrew and the principles of our religion and the chief events in our history, and then they were married in the synagogue."

Then the Rabbi began to enquire about the religious conditions of the Jews in London. Were they conforming? Did they have a Sunday Sabbath, as in America? Did they have a Hebrew newspaper?

From England the conversation drifted back to Italy. The Rabbi recalled the great names of the past, Nathan of Rome, Immanuel, the friend of Dante, Azariah di Rossi, Kalonymos, Luzzatto, Reggio—scholars, theologians, poets, historians—who had shed their lustre on the pages of our history. But now? *Ichabod*, the glory had departed.

There was a grave look in his eyes when I bade him farewell.

Not far from the synagogue there is a tall, striking building, with a Corinthian portico of granite, surmounted by a corridor of granite columns. A high tower and bold cupola rear their heads to the skies. The building impresses you at the first sight, even before you know aught of its history or purpose; and when you learn these you examine it a little more closely, and from observation you turn to reflection. For the building was designed as a synagogue in 1863, modelled on the plan of the Temple of Herod, and it was then converted to a National History Museum in commemoration of Italian unity. The strange irony of things! . . . Will a day yet come when the synagogue whose Rabbi bemoaned the decadence of Judaism will succumb to the fate of this other building, and likewise become a museum of antiquities?

VIII.—A POST-WAR DIARY

It was with mingled emotions that I set out again on a journey to Florence, for it was forty years since I had first stayed there, and later visits had increased the store of my early memories. I always associated Jewish life in the city with the scholarly figure of Dr. S. H. Margulies, who was Chief Rabbi of the community for many years. He was also Principal of a Rabbinical Seminary, at which his assistant, before the First World War, was Dr. Hirsch Chajes, who afterwards won fame and popularity as the Chief Rabbi of Vienna. It was at his house too that I first met a young Falasha, who had been brought from his home in Abyssinia by the traveller, Dr. Jacques Faitlovitch, to be trained as a teacher for his people.

Before leaving London I was told by a friend who had just come back from Florence, that the handsome synagogue, which had been regarded with pride and veneration by Jews, and at least with admiration by non-Jews, had been destroyed by the Nazis, and that the remnant of local Jewry met for religious worship in a small synagogue in the Via dell' Ocche near the Cathedral. As I did not know the address of this little bethel, I called at the British Consulate to inquire where I could find the Rabbi. To my astonishment, an official told me that he would doubtless be at the principal synagogue, which, he assured me, despite reports and rumours, still existed as before. So I hastened to the Via Farini, where I was relieved to see, a few hundred yards behind tall iron railings, the familiar Moorish contour of the majestic fane, with its dominating cupola and the twin turrets rising on either side of the façade. As I entered the spacious forecourt I heard the singing of children and the tinkling of a piano from a kindergarten, and a workman showed me the way to the office of the Rabbi.

The new spiritual leader of the community, Dr. Mashiach, verbally confirmed my ocular observation that the synagogue still stood, but hastened to add that it had been seriously and wantonly damaged inside. The Germans had laid mines to blow up the building before they retreated, but fortunately the explosives were defective and the structure was spared. On entering it, I saw extensive evidence of the vandalism that the Nazis had perpetrated, although workmen had been occupied on the task of restoration for the past twelve months. There was scaffolding supporting the women's galleries, which had been wrecked; most of the wooden benches were battered and broken; the Menorahs in front of the Ark had been uprooted from their marble bases; the artistically designed pulpit had disappeared; and the arabesque decorations on the walls had been hideously defaced and disfigured. The Scrolls of the Law and most of the prayer-books had been looted or burned, but others had been obtained from more fortunate synagogues.

I asked Rabbi Mashiach whether the report was true, that the Municipality of Florence had generously undertaken to pay for the cost of restoration. He replied that he had never heard of this, and that the community itself, although sadly reduced in numbers, was covering the entire expense itself. About three hundred Jews had been deported by the Nazis, and only a handful returned, but there were nevertheless about 1,500 Jews still in the city. Before the occupation he had been Rabbi in the little town of Vercelli, midway between Turin and Milan: he then escaped to Florence, where he was hidden and protected by a Christian friend until the liberation.

On Friday evening my wife and I attended the Sabbath service, which was conducted by a young cantor, whose resonant tenor voice filled the vast spaces of the sacred but sorrowful-looking shrine. There were about a score of people present, a rather small percentage of the surviving community, but I recollected that even in the former years of peace and tranquillity the congregation was generally meagre. What the worshippers lacked in numbers, however, they made up in devotion, and all united in singing *Hashkivenu*[1] to the tune of *Hatikvah*[2] with melodious vigour. The attendance on the following morning was somewhat larger, but scarcely exceeded three dozen, apart from a handful of women in the central gallery. I had the honour of being called up to the Law as *Cohen* and recalled in the absence of a Levite.

After the service, when the congregants were exchanging greetings in the sun-drenched forecourt, the Rabbi, who had worn a black gown and tall black hexagonal hat, emerged in a brown lounge suit and white straw hat and introduced me to some of them. Among them were relatives of old friends of mine, who had been living in Palestine since the beginning of the war and had come back to retrieve what they could of their former possessions.

* * * * *

I was surprised at the number of people from Palestine whom I came across at different times and in different places, and at hearing snatches of Hebrew in open-air cafés. Sitting one evening in the garden restaurant on the roof of my hotel, with all the wonders of the city spread out below, I overheard some talk at a neighbouring table between a man and a girl, which alternated between English, Yiddish, and Hebrew. Owing to our proximity it was not long before

[1] A prayer for peace and security.   [2] The Jewish national anthem.

Interior of Synagogue in Florence

Scene in the Ghetto Vecchio in Venice at the Reopening of the Synagogues

conversation became general, and I learned that the man—a South African Jew—was on the way with his wife and daughter to Jerusalem, and the girl—a friend of his daughter—had been living in Tel-Aviv for some years.

The difficulties of entering Palestine were a frequent theme of discussion, and I gathered that there were more ways than one of "illicit" immigration. A well-to-do Jewess from a Balkan country who had been living in Jerusalem some years was anxious that her only daughter should join her. All her efforts to obtain a permit were in vain. She therefore hit upon an ingenious idea, although one of doubtful morality. Since the girl could not be got into the country as a Jewess, why should she not be brought in as a non-Jewess? So with the co-operation of a Government employee in Palestine and of another official in the Balkan country, who testified that the girl's original identity papers had been lost in the war, she was furnished with new papers and thus obtained the long-sought permit. This irregular procedure cost the mother about a thousand pounds, but she thought the price trifling for the happiness of being reunited with her only child. It also cost the Government employee his job, though the loss was compensated in some measure by the monetary inducement. The moral of the story—if that term may be used—is that there were no limits to the devices conceived to circumvent the British Government's White Paper, which restricted immigration so drastically and unjustly.

On returning to my hotel one day, I was given by the porter a large envelope addressed to me, bearing the printed superscription: *Bolletino di Scienze Semitiche*, with the sub-title *Rivista Illustrata fondata nel* 1944. At first I thought it contained a scholarly review and wondered why the Rabbi had not told me of this manifestation of a cultural revival. But on opening the envelope I found in it two publications of the "Irgun Zvai Leumi"[1]—a large-

---

[1] " National Military Organisation," a dissident body which used violence in its struggle to secure independence for the Jews in Palestine.

sized brochure of forty pages with an attractive blue cover bearing the Zionist flag, and a four-page newspaper entitled *La Risposta dei patrioti ebrei*. The former, which was attractively got up, with numerous illustrations, contained a Memorandum addressed to the United Nations Special Committee on Palestine and an account of the aims and activities of the I.Z.L. in English and French, and facsimile reproductions from the Irgun press and propaganda material. The newspaper, which also had many illustrations (including portraits of Garibaldi, Washington, Pilsudski, De Valera, Smuts, and others, all described as fore-runners of the Jewish terrorists), was printed entirely in Italian. There was no attempt to conceal or disguise the origin of these publications, as the brochure bore an address in Rome and the newspaper one in Florence.

* * * * *

Some friends who had motored from Stresa to Milan told me on their return that as they drove along the shore of Lake Maggiore they noticed a large portrait of Herzl on the front of an imposing mansion. So, on the following day, we set out on a journey of discovery, and after some twenty minutes along the Lake, we beheld the familiar pensive head high up on the façade of a palazzo in Palladian style. It was so large and conspicuous that it was obviously intended to attract, and on either side of it were rather smaller and barely distinguishable portraits of Jabotinsky and Trumpeldor. On the sloping lawn, about twenty feet above the main road, there was a large floral Menorah, which could also be seen quite easily as we approached. We got out of the car and began to ascend.

As we made our way up a rough path we drank in the scent of lime-trees mingled with that of pines, and found ourselves in the midst of an abundance of sub-tropical vegetation, richly coloured with hibiscus, bougainvillaea, and huge pink and blue hydrangeas. Suddenly a bronzed youth in shorts came nimbly down the hill-side and led us to the level path above that ran the length of the mansion.

At the foot of the hilly slope was an upright memorial tablet in marble to an unknown soldier, with a brief inscription in Hebrew and Italian, and the date, " May 8th, 1947." On the lawn itself, worked out in marble chippings of different colours and black soil, was a map of biblical Palestine, and on either side of it were two Hebrew legends also inscribed in marble chippings: " In blood and fire Judah fell" and "In blood and fire Judah will arise." Near by was a tall flag-staff with the Zionist banner, the blue colour having been bleached by the strong sunlight.

Presently a few other young men, also tanned and in shorts, appeared upon the scene, and one of them, acting as our guide, explained to us the purpose of the establishment. The mansion, with its extensive grounds, had formerly been the property of a Marchese. It was rented two years previously by the American Jewish Joint Distribution Committee to serve as a *Kibbutz*—a training centre for young Jewish refugees and "displaced persons" who intended settling in Palestine. There were about two hundred persons, including a smaller number of young women and girls, ranging in age from eight to forty. They had come here, after thrilling adventures, from all the countries of Central and Eastern Europe, the majority hailing from Poland, Rumania, Lithuania, and Czechoslovakia. Most of them had been in concentration or extermination camps; many had fought among the partisans in their respective countries: and some had been prisoners in Siberia. All of them had undergone perilous experiences in their wanderings, which many had accomplished largely on foot, and had to smuggle their way across successive frontiers before reaching this lake-side mansion, with its beautiful surroundings and magnificent view. But on reaching Italy their troubles were over. They were given official permission to remain in the country and were on the best of terms with the local authorities and the neighbouring populace.

In the main hall there were striking texts in Hebrew, mostly of a militant sort, such as: " The choice before us is war or destruction." Some of the walls were covered with many written sheets containing articles, sketches and poems in Yiddish (for most of the young people were not yet sufficiently acquainted with Hebrew, though they had lessons in the language every day). A new wall newspaper was produced every week, and there was much competition to contribute to it. The writers had certainly had terrible experiences, for most of them were the sole survivors of their families.

There was an expert agronomist in the *Kibbutz* who trained most of the members of the little community in the growing of vegetables, fruit, and vines. Other occupations that were practised were those of joiners, tin-smiths, tailors and shoe-makers. They also had their own doctor, who had helped at the birth of the first child born on the estate—now a sturdy youngster of a few months. But before settling down to these various crafts, they had all to devote much time and labour to making the house habitable, for it had been empty for eight years and the grounds needed much clearing and tidying-up.

I did not inquire how, coming from different places separated by thousands of miles, they had all found their way to this pleasaunce. I doubt whether they would have told me. It was sufficient to realise that they had all been gripped and guided by the same elemental force that was directing them to the self-same goal. One hundred of their comrades had already gone to Palestine, and they were all patiently and confidently awaiting their turn.

One of the *Halutzim*[1] accompanied us about half-a-mile farther on the main road to show us a memorial of Nazi barbarity and Italian humanity. It was a grey marble tablet fixed against the wall, bearing the names of fifteen Jews who had been murdered by the Nazis in April, 1943, and thrown into the Lake. The victims, several of whom were named Mosseri and others Fernandez, had formed three families, the entire Jewish community of the townlet of

[1] Pioneers for Palestine.

Meina. They had been popular with their Italian neighbours, and as soon as the Germans retreated the Italians had the tablet placed on the spot from where the dead bodies had been flung into the water. Flowers were regularly laid at the foot of the memorial by the people of the district, and the *Halutzim*, too, often brought some from their garden.

"We shall look after it until we leave," said our guide. "*Lehitraot ba-aretz!*"[1]

[1] "*Au revoir* in the Land of Israel."

Chapter XX

EVENINGS IN PARIS

I.—A GHETTO RESTAURANT

THE GHETTO begins just where the long and fashionable Rue de Rivoli fades away into frowsiness. It starts abruptly from the Rue des Rosiers, which, but for an occasional French accent that strikes the ear, might have been in Whitechapel, or off the Nalevki in Warsaw. Little grocery shops, with their exotic wares in dusty disarray, were still open and busy, though all other trading establishments in the neighbourhood were long wrapped in darkness. The windows were cluttered up with white twisted loaves besprinkled with seed, and elongated brown loaves, with little bags of rice and beans, bottles of olives, Palestine wine, and suspended sausages. The butchers' shops were adorned with the sprawled legend in Yiddish lettering: "*Strictly Kosher*," whilst the booksellers displayed Yiddish books and newspapers and gramophone records of famous cantors. The walls were plastered over with numerous posters in Yiddish, among which a notice announcing the performance of *The Dybbuk* in French stood out conspicuously in large, bold type. A boy rushed along calling out "*Pariser Haint!*"—a local replica of the once popular Warsaw daily—and a pathetic Yiddish melody came floating from some open window aloft.

The decade following the First World War witnessed the growth of a new Jewish colony in the French capital, consisting partly of refugees from Soviet Russia and partly of immigrants from Poland and other regions of Eastern Europe. The hospitality to foreigners that Paris then showed, as though out of gratitude to the many distinguished foreigners who had assembled in her midst to make the Peace, was so alluring that Oriental Jews too, from such distant cities as Salonika and Smyrna, economically distressed and politically despairing, as well as Russian Jews who found the anti-Semitic outbursts in Berlin and Munich little change from their former oppression, migrated to the metropolis of gaiety and fashion. And from the beginning of the Nazi terror in 1933, Jews from Germany also fled to Paris. The establishment in its midst of the "Comité des Délégations Juives," devoted to the furtherance of the civil and political interests of all the Jewries in Central and Eastern Europe, had doubtless also played its part in attracting Jews in search of a haven of refuge situated not too far away. Altogether, over seventy thousand immigrant Jews were computed to have settled in Paris since the end of the First War, including five thousand from Salonika alone and twenty thousand from Germany.

We entered a restaurant, whose windows and glass door shed a flood of light in the surrounding gloom. The interior presented a bright and homely scene, the diners being engaged in animated discussion, which was not confined to any one table but ranged freely from one table to another. Hardly a word of French was spoken, most of the conversation being carried on in Yiddish and in English with strong American accent. Some young men, having apparently sated themselves with a good bourgeois dinner, were discussing the merits of Communism.

"It's a new religion," said one of them, with a projecting forelock and a gesticulating forefinger.

"A religion for *gazlonim* [1]" retorted another, puffing a cigarette. "It's a plague and a curse."

From a neighbouring table a prosperous-looking American Jew, who was devouring a roast chicken in partnership with his buxom spouse, called out: "I know you. You are all Communists until it touches your pocket. Do you think

[1] Robbers.

295

that Communism can ever be of any benefit to a country? Wait till you are a few years older, and you'll get a little more sense. There's nothing like work, hard work, properly paid."

Our waiter, in a shabby dress-suit, whispered to us that the American was a millionaire, certainly in francs and perhaps in dollars, and that he was going back to his native town in Lithuania to see how things had changed since he left it thirty years ago, and also to distribute a little charity. "Ah, won't they be pleased to see him!" he said, rubbing his hands and shaking his head with anticipatory glee. Suddenly he was called away by a new arrival, a ruddy-cheeked greybeard, and then we heard him cry down the food-lift: "*Eine Suppe mit a Kreppel mehr!*" Evidently the old gourmet had a weakness for meat-patties in his soup.

A diversion was created by the entry of a fiddler, a hungry-looking fellow with a two days' growth of beard and a tartan muffler round his neck. He began to tune up, when one of the protagonists of Communism called out: "No Yiddish tunes for us: they're too sad. We want opera."

"Opera?" exclaimed the swarthy proprietor. "Then I shall have to charge you extra, with a tax *de luxe*."

A guffaw of laughter burst from the young men. But the melancholy fiddler, anxious not to spoil the harmony of the scene, at once struck up an aria from "Bajazzo," to which the whole company paid silent and critical attention. The performance over, I called for our bill, which the waiter reckoned up first in Yiddish and then, rather haltingly, in French.

"Why repeat it in French?" I asked.

"Because I must improve my French, so I practise it on the Yiddish customers," he replied apologetically. "A year ago I was a bath attendant in Lemberg, but that was no *Tachliss*.[1] And some day I hope to have my own restaurant on one of the grand boulevards. Then I shall be a real *Franzose*."

[1] Aim in life.

II.—A TALMUDICAL STUDENT'S EVOLUTION

We went to the Café de la Paix, that famous hub of the capital, where strangers from all lands sit at the marble-topped tables in the open air and watch the endless procession of variegated humanity. But I found my companion as interesting as any of the multifarious types that promenaded before us, and besides I felt that he had a story. He was a student at the Sorbonne and was dressed rather smartly, with a soft blue collar and gaily-patterned socks.

"How do you keep yourself?" I asked, after the waiter had brought us our coffee.

"By giving lessons in Talmud and Hebrew. My first lesson is at eight in the morning."

"Where did you learn Talmud?" I inquired, a little astonished.

"At the Slobodka *Yeshiva*,[1] near Kovno, where I was for a few years. Before that I was at Tels, but I was expelled owing to its becoming known that I read modern books. At Slobodka I studied Talmud all day long, and was not allowed to read anything else. The most striking thing in the day's programme was the lecture or exhortation that the head of the *Yeshiva* gave us just before sunset. He called it *Musar*—moral instruction—and he talked about devils and demons, Satan and Lilith, and all sorts of superstitions, and he worked so much upon the feelings of the students, especially in the growing darkness, that he made them grimace, stare, clench their fists, tear their hair, shout, dance, and jump—in short, it was a perfect pandemonium.

"It was noticed that I didn't attend prayers in the morning regularly, and I was suspected of not putting *tefillin*[2] on and also of studying modern books. Spies used to go about at night, peeping into windows to see if anybody was reading; and as we pored over the Talmud long enough all day and had our fill, anybody who was caught reading

[1] Seminary.   [2] Phylacteries.

at night was naturally suspected of studying a modern book. My father, who lived at Kovno, was a fearful fanatic, and threatened that if he caught me writing on the Sabbath he would kill me."

The quondam student of the Talmud allowed his eyes to wander for a moment after a tall mincing damsel in a flaming red frock, and then continued:

"So I was transferred to a *Klaus*, a smaller Talmudical school, at Chelm. Chelm is a mere village, situated many miles from any town, where the students are entirely isolated. They were all *Perushim*, that is, separated from their wives. I was the only *Bachur*.[1] Our mode of living was extremely strict. From seven to nine we had morning prayer, which was fearfully drawn out with all sorts of extra meditations and supplications. From nine to ten we had breakfast, then we settled down to study for five long hours without a break. At three we had afternoon prayer, and then dinner. At half-past four we sat down again to drone over the Talmud and continued without a pause until nine. Then we had evening prayer, followed by *Musar*, which lasted until eleven. By then, as you can imagine, we were quite worn out, but no sooner did I get back to my room than I began reading some forbidden book—a Yiddish translation of Shakespeare or Schopenhauer, or a book in German, such as Heine's *Reisebilder*.

"I was lodged with a very pious student, a perfect *Tsaddick*,[2] who was expected to keep me in the path of righteousness. But I argued with him night after night until he yielded to my influence, and then he also started reading modern books. I stood this mode of life for eighteen months, but then I could bear it no longer and escaped to Kovno. There I hid from my parents, who would have sent me back to Chelm, and I was helped by friends until I passed my *Arbiturium*[3] examination. At last I was able to leave the country: it was like release from a prison. I went to

[1] Bachelor.   [2] Pietist.   [3] Matriculation.

Berlin, from where I wrote the news to my parents, and then to Basle, where I hoped to find a friendly welcome. But owing to the difficulties put in the way of foreign students I passed on to Strasbourg, and after earning a little money by giving lessons I came to Paris. Here I am studying *lettres*."

"How do you account for your loss of faith?" I asked.

"I'm afraid I can't give you any definite explanation. I had already lost my faith before I entered the *Yeshiva*. It was partly due to my reading and partly to a romance."

"What romance?" I enquired.

"My own romance," he replied, lowering his eyes and blushing like a girl.

He glanced at his watch and found that it was nearly midnight. "You will pardon me," he said, as he rose, "but I have to give a lesson at eight in the morning." And so we parted until the next day, and as he went I marvelled at the inscrutable workings of assimilation.

III.—A LITERARY EVENING

There was a Jewish literary gathering at a fashionable hall the following night, and I was advised that it was an event that one should not miss. It was a manifestation of the national cultural revival that had taken place in French Jewry after the First World War, a revival that formed a healthy reaction from the apathy and ossification that had seized upon such large sections of the native community. The Dreyfus affair, whilst firing many a sluggish soul with pride of race, had driven thousands of timid children of Israel underground, and it was left for a later generation, consisting of younger and bolder men, to raise the flag of Judah aloft in the citadel of assimilation. The renaissance had been marked by a growing regard for religious traditions and by an intelligent cultivation of Jewish lore. It

had been animated, if not dominated, by the Zionist idea,
and it was furthered by a number of agencies working in
fruitful collaboration—the influx of the Eastern European
element with its strong Jewish consciousness, the rise of a
number of writers who had devoted themselves to a sympathetic revelation of Israel's spiritual treasures, and the
activity of the "Union Universelle de la Jeunesse Juive,"
commonly called the "U.U.J.J."

It was under the auspices of this last-named organisation,
which had branches not only in France but also in the
French-speaking countries of North Africa, as well as in
Italy and the Balkans, that the literary gathering was held.
There was a small charge for admission—the surest sign
that the organisers felt confident of a satisfactory audience;
and, indeed, the intellectual fare offered fully warranted
the charge. The programme consisted of an address on
Rachel and a symposium on Edmond Fleg's little book
L'Enfant Prophète, and it attracted as large and representative an assembly as though it were an important social
function. A vivid and critical account of the famous actress
was given by the poet Ernst-Charles, who paid an eloquent
tribute to the genius and the Jewish spirit of Rachel. Then
came an interval during which the audience were invited to
purchase copies of M. Fleg's book, which was to form the
theme of the symposium, and, as an additional inducement,
there was the author himself, with a large black butterfly
bow, willing to autograph any copy bought within that
limited time.

The three speakers in the symposium were a Rabbinical
aspirant, a Catholic writer, and M. Aimé Pallière. *L'Enfant
Prophète* is the poetically written story of a Jewish boy,
who, brought up by parents indifferent to Judaism, is spas-
modically attracted through his love for a Christian girl to
Christianity, and then comes to learn of the teachings of
his ancestral faith to which he is won over, though he experiences a mental conflict in reflecting on the purely

religious and the national conceptions of Judaism presented to him in turn by a conventional Rabbi and a Zionist student.

Of the three addresses by far the most penetrating, the most illuminating, and the most elevating was that of Aimé Pallière, that remarkable convert from Catholicism to Judaism, whom I saw for the first time. A lean, ascetic figure, with clean-shaven cheeks of waxen pallor, and thin sensuous lips which he closed tightly at the end of each sentence, he seemed to cast a spell over his audience as he discussed the main ideas in the book and described the torment which the Jewish soul in the maelstrom of the Western world underwent in its quest for a Jewish salvation. Having himself groped his way from the mystical recesses of the Catholic Church to the luminous path of the Torah, and realised the necessity of Israel's national revival, he was able to depict more clearly and forcibly than either Catholic or Jew the peculiar spiritual problems of " the child prophet." And his hearers—half belonging to that section of Parisian Jewry whose interest in Jewish matters had almost become moribund, and half to the East European and Palestinian element—drank in his words with an avidity that was the sincerest form of flattery. It " gave one furiously to think " to see this righteous proselyte, with his saint-like simplicity, acting as a " guide of the perplexed " to a generation that had given such little heed to the teaching of its own Rabbis—perhaps because that teaching itself had somewhat strayed from the traditions and aspirations of the Jewish people. He reminded me of another remarkable figure, Father Ignatius, an eloquent monk who, in the early days of Herzl's crusade, sought to move the multitudes of London Jewry with his passionate appeals for the rebuilding of Zion, though his fervour would have been more fittingly, and perhaps more fruitfully spent, in launching a philippic against Christendom to Christianise itself.

After the meeting my companion took me to a café in

the Latin Quarter, telling me on the way of the hundreds
of Jewish students who had drifted in recent years to Paris
from those intolerant lands—mainly Poland, Rumania,
Hungary, and Germany—that would not allow Jews un-
restricted access to their universities, lest they became too
clever and too influential in the professions and public
affairs, and who were studying here law, letters, and philosophy, with only a vague idea of what they would afterwards do with their diplomas and doctorates. He also told
me of the scores of other Jewish students, men and women,
from Western countries, even the United States and Canada,
who had come here to study painting, sculpture and music,
fired perchance by the ambitious hope of contributing to
the world some new artistic creation, some epoch-making
product of the imagination.

We had scarcely been seated more than a few minutes,
during which my companion pointed out some of the
bizarre types among the medley of Bohemians of all ages
gossiping and smoking amid the blare and jangle of the
jazz band, than who should enter but M. Aimé Pallière
himself. My companion immediately rose and brought him
to our table. I suppressed the instinctive question, how such
a spiritually-minded man could be prompted to beguile his
time in such a worldly haunt, as I reflected that even if he
did not seek any diversion (and who was so ultra-human
as to dispense with it?) he doubtless found here many a
serious theme for contemplation and cogitation. I compli-
mented him on his contribution to the evening's symposium, but he made light of the matter.

"I simply repeated, or recapitulated, the ideas that I have
been expounding for so many years," he said. "*L'Enfant
Prophète* was just the text of my discourse."

And then he spoke of his travels in various lands, in
which he had addressed Jews from pulpit and platform on
their spiritual heritage, warning them of the evils of assimilation, and exhorting them to be faithful to their traditions.
He had recently been on a tour through the Jewish com-

munities of Algeria and Tunis, and his advocacy of the
Zionist cause among them had made such an impression
that the leaders of the "Alliance Israélite Universelle," forgetting the original idea underlying their own foundation,
had been moved to express their displeasure. The Jews of
Algeria and Tunis might become too Jewish!

We left the café together and had not walked more than
a dozen yards when we came to a large bookshop with wide-
open doors. Whoever might think of Paris as wholly given
up to pleasure at night must have received here a pleasant
shock. We passed in: the long walls were lined with books
on all subjects, and students old and young were browsing
over them at leisure, the sympathetic shop-assistant making
no attempt to coax a purchase. Presently I came across *Le
Sanctuaire Inconnu*, and as I showed M. Pallière my
acquisition the author's pride could not suppress a smile of
gratification.

IV.—AT A MUSIC-HALL

The following night, by way of a change, I was taken to
a Jewish theatre of varieties.

"Would you like to see Breitbart, the strong man?"
asked my devoted guide.

"I thought that Breitbart was dead," I replied. "Didn't
he die of poisoning by a rusty nail in Berlin some years
ago?"

"That was Siegfried Breitbart, whose exploits as a strong
man in Germany evoked the admiration of everybody, while
it aroused the envy of the Anti-Semites. But here we have
his younger brother, Joseph, who is said to be even more
wonderful."

The theatre was a rather simple establishment: a
medium-sized hall with a stage, garishly decorated and
half-filled with a working-class audience, who munched
sausage and bread or oranges to sustain them during the
performance. The prevailing language, both on the stage

and among the onlookers, was Yiddish, spoken with various accents ranging from the Lithuanian to the Bessarabian, and interspersed with occasional French idioms sadly mutilated. The first part of the programme consisted of a revue, in which an Indian prince, magnificently attired, sang sentimental ditties with a Galician accent, and various comic characters exchanged humorous patter and danced fox-trots.

But the star of the evening was the strong man, Joseph Breitbart. He was a debonair young fellow, with laughing eyes, who came to the footlights in a costume reminiscent of both a Roman athlete and warrior—buskins on his legs and a gleaming helmet on his head. An impresario described his phenomenal physical gifts in Yiddish, French, English, and Russian, so that all members of the audience might understand, and the youthful Samson displayed his many golden teeth, which had doubtless replaced the ravages caused by his athletic feats. The orchestra emphasised every sentence of laudatory explanation with a vigorous arpeggio, the expectancy of the audience was keyed up to the pitch of excitement, and the hero doffed his helmet, exhibited his swelling muscles, and began his performance.

He took some bars of iron, which he first dropped on to the stage, so that their resounding thud dispelled any suspicion of their genuineness, and then bent them with his hands into fanciful shapes as though they were of clay. He took a long iron rod, which he twisted and bent on his knee until he fashioned it into a " Shield of David," which he held up to the astonished enthusiasm of the public. Then, lying on his back, a small platform was placed across his breast, and on it stood three men holding in position a piano, on which a musician played the opening bars of " Hatikvah." Breitbart emerged from the ordeal apparently as unaffected as if a child had sat on his chest, and the rafters rang with repeated applause. But the most sensational feat was to follow. He lay with his bare back on a board studded with nails, whilst on his breast were placed three huge blocks of stone, on which two men struck alternately with sledge-hammers. It seemed as though he would be pounded to pulp, but he lithely jumped to his feet, smiled with his golden teeth, and then, turning round, showed his back riddled with punctures but utterly free even from a spot of blood. The storm of applause reached its climax: never was a prima donna at the Opera awarded such a tumultuous and prolonged ovation.

"Now you shall all see for yourselves," exclaimed the impresario. "Breitbart will walk down one gangway and up the other, and you will all be able to look at his back. But do not touch him, as that might set up infection." And the warning was repeated in the three other languages.

The strong man—he seemed little more than a youth—nimbly stepped along among the audience, with a smile right across his face, and displayed his back to all eyes. But he was a susceptible youth, or an obliging one, for, encouraged by the admiring glances and the inviting lips of some young ladies, he kissed them with an unrestrained gusto, the like of which had surely never been seen on that side of the footlights in any Parisian theatre. And when he returned to the stage, to the strain of "See the Conquering Hero Comes!" the impresario offered for sale the various iron objects wrought and fashioned by his skill and strength as souvenirs of the momentous evening.

V.—AN ELDER STATESMAN IN ISRAEL

In a secluded office in an upper floor of a building in the Avenue de la Grande Armée sat a little man, with a grizzled beard, peering through his spectacles at all the lands in which the Jews still suffered oppression or disabilities. Whether it was a brutal pogrom or an act of persecution disguised as an economic enactment, whether it was an anti-Semitic speech delivered in a Parliament or a menacing article published in a semi-official organ, he was immediately in possession of the facts and began to deliberate what counter-measures should be taken to redress the evil done or prevent the impending wrong. He was always feeling the pulse of Israel and prescribing for its maladies, and he certainly rendered great service, in a life-time devoted to the welfare of his people, in helping to alleviate its ills. He was the President of the "Comité des Délégations Juives," a body which he was instrumental in founding in the spring of 1919, when delegations from all the Jewish communities in Central and Eastern Europe came to Paris in order to take counsel together and make concerted representations to the Peace Conference on behalf of those Jews who were not yet emancipated or who had been transferred from the jurisdiction of one State to that of another. The movement represented the wish of the millions of Jews who had been oppressed before the First World War to formulate and advance their own demands, instead of entrusting them to the old-established organisations of Western Jewry which had hitherto figured as their protectors and champions; and at its head was Leo Motzkin,[1] who, before the War, had played a doughty part in revealing and broadcasting the barbarities committed in "Darkest Russia."

I found him at his desk, poring over some reports on the latest outrages in Rumania. I was rather fortunate to meet him, for his movements were somewhat erratic and his absences from Paris rather frequent. Associated with all the big Jewish philanthropic organisations engaged in the regulation of Jewish emigration from the East to the West (bodies that were styled for convenience by eclectic abbreviations, such as "Emigdirekt" and "Hicem"), and likewise with non-Jewish organisations devoted to objects subserving Jewish interests, such as the Federation of the League of Nations Unions and the Congress of National Minorities, he was such a conscientious member of their various councils, committees, and sub-committees, that no meeting or

[1] Died 6th November, 1933.

conference was complete without him, and whether it was
held in Brussels or Berne, in Vienna or Geneva, he was
always there, ever active and vocal. Add to his activities in
connection with these various bodies his duties and functions
as Chairman of the General Council of the World Zionist
Oganisation, over whose animated deliberations—often
protracted into the small hours of the morning—he presided with the imperturbability of a Buddha and the alert-
ness of a Speaker of the House of Commons (unlike whom
he really was a speaker), and you will be able to form some
idea not only of his indefatigable energy but also of the
fact that his official engagements covered a great proportion of the calendar and caused him to flit from one city
on the Continent to another.

His office was a clearing-house of intelligence on all
Jewish questions of the day. Whether it was the *numerus
clausus* or Stateless Jews, anti-Shechita legislation or Sunday closing regulations, restrictions on emigration or on
immigration, colonisation projects in Siberia or Peru;
whether you wished to learn of the latest developments in
Poland or Persia, in Hungary or Estonia, he could furnish
you readily with reliable data, factual and statistical,
docketed and documented. He conducted an extensive correspondence in various languages with many countries, he
received and read the newspapers of a still larger number
of territories, and his archives were a storehouse of classified
information on the political and social conditions of present-
day Jewry. He was, moreover, sought by every Jew from
a foreign land who had a story to unfold about either his
own sufferings or those of his people, like an Elder Statesman in Israel, and his waiting-room always re-echoed with
strange tongues.

After we had chatted for a while there was ushered in a
cadaverous young man with a slight dark beard, wearing
the black blouse of a Russian student. He was a Zionist
who had escaped from the torments of the Solovetski
Islands, whither he had been banished by the Soviet

oligarchy for his devotion to the Jewish national idea. He told us of the privations that he and hundreds of his comrades had suffered in the gaols of Russia, of the inhuman treatment to which they had been subjected, of the persistent and tempting efforts to lure them from their faith, of the agony he had endured in his final place of captivity, and then of the cunning and daring of his escape. He paused now and again as though to conjure up the vision of the incidents he related, and when he had finished it was clear that he had much more to say than he had told us.

After the Russian refugee had gone, with a warm-hearted invitation to return the next morning, Mr. Motzkin glanced at his watch and brought our conversation to an end. "Quick," he said, "I have a meeting in twenty minutes, and it will take me all that time to get there. Where I am chairman the meeting must begin punctually."

VI.—SABBATH EVE AT SYNAGOGUE

I had heard so much about the religious laxity of Parisian Jewry that when I wended my way to the synagogue in the Rue de la Victoire one Friday evening I expected to find there only a handful of worshippers, consisting mainly of retired greybeards and American tourists. The bustle on the boulevards and multifarious allurements of the gay city, to which the setting sun gave a roseate glow, seemed to smother any impulse to join in a sacred ritual that was outwardly alien to its Western environment. All the greater, therefore, was my surprise when I found a concourse of men and women streaming into the house of prayer, many of them having come in private cars. The synagogue is inconveniently situated, for owing to the narrowness of the street and the neighbouring buildings it is unable to impress you with its dignified and imposing fabric as it surely would in an open square.

In the spacious and lofty vestibule a beadle with the

cocked hat of an admiral and the resplendent chain of a
mayor paced to and fro with a charity-box, which he offered
to each arrival, a sign that here at least you were not expected
to observe the orthodox rule of leaving your purse at home
when going to meet the Sabbath bride.

Within, the synagogue, vast and lofty, presents a scene
of ornate and overwhelming grandeur: with its tall marble
pillars, its galleries with vaulted arches, its celestial cupola,
its stained-glass rose-windows, and the brilliant illumination
of its towering multi-branched candelabras, it is suggestive,
both in the magnitude of its proportions and the beauty of
its design, of a cathedral, but is free from the all-pervading
gloom that depresses the interior of so many minsters. An
enormous dais at the upper end, approached by a series of
easy steps, is occupied by the *Almemar*[1] and, on a higher
level, with the Ark of the Law, and on it are situated also
the seats of the Rabbinate. On the left, in their pews, were
the Chief Rabbi of Paris and an assistant Rabbi, and on
the right, in solitary dignity, the Chief Rabbi of France,
with the red ribbon of the Legion of Honour conspicuous
on his long black soutane—all three wearing round flattish
hats like French priests. (In matters of assimilation I have
found in all my travels that no Jews are so assimilated as the
Rabbis in their professional garb.) But what astonished me
more than anything was the size of the congregation, for
there must have been more than a thousand people, the men
occupying all the middle benches, and the women, dressed
mostly in black, filling the galleries on either side of the
ground floor. A little army of uniformed beadles, in cocked
hats and chains, strutted along the various aisles, and the
decorum was beyond reproach.

The service was intoned by a cantor, with a loud, resonant
voice, whose melodious roulades filled the sanctuary, the
responses coming from a choir perched in a lofty gallery
facing the Ark, but most of the congregation seemed content
to leave the praying to the tuneful precentor. And after the

[1] Cantor's platform.

recital of the *Kiddush*[1] a Rabbi slowly descended from his elevated pew, advanced to the lectern at the middle of the balustrade which surrounded the *Almemar*, and delivered a sermon. He read it word for word from a book in which his manuscript was placed, or perhaps from the book itself, and he spoke on the week's portion of the Law, *Parashath Shekalim*, explaining the purpose of the Shekel in ancient days, which was needed for the maintenance of the Temple.

" As we have no Temple nowadays," he discoursed, " the synagogue service is all the more necessary. If the Almighty should grant that the Temple be rebuilt, O what a thrill would course through the veins of all the faithful children of Israel, what gratitude they would feel, what happiness, what edification, and how they would vie with one another in contributing towards its support and beautification."

He became almost dithyrambic as he read out this passage, scarce raising his eyes from the page. But although he had such a suitable text for descanting on the work of Jewish revival that was progressing in Palestine, he did not refer to it by so much as a syllable. It might have been a sermon in the seventeenth century, or even the seventh. For this Rabbi apparently nothing had happened since the downfall of Judea except perhaps the erection of this magnificent sanctuary, in which he was concerned with the attachment only of his own particular flock. I wondered whether such a jejune discourse could secure their attachment or evoke in their breast even an ephemeral response.

As we streamed out into the vestibule, the air in which was as heavily charged with the pungent perfumes of the ladies as in the foyer of a theatre, the beadles urged us to pass out quickly—heedless of the traditional rule that one should leave the presence of God reluctantly and lingeringly. The worshippers were soon swallowed up in the cars that lined the narrow street or disappeared among the crowd, and within a few moments the huge iron gates were locked and bolted, and all was in darkness.

[1] Sanctification of the Sabbath.

Chapter XXI

WAYFARING IN PROVENCE

I.—MEMORIES OF AVIGNON

O F ALL the hosts of seekers after pleasure or fortune who stream through Avignon on their way to the famed resorts of the Riviera, comparatively few even note the name of the city as the night train from Paris rumbles into it in the early morning, when they are either still wrapt in slumber or too weary from lack of it to be concerned about anything but the end of their journey. Even those who may be awake are hardly likely to recall the historic importance of the city, unless in their youth they were made to study the annals of the Popes, or in their middle age they have pored over the literature of tourist agencies. And even of those who appreciate the part played by Avignon in mediaeval Europe, few are tempted to make a halt and explore the wealth of mediaeval memorials that still exists both within and without its imposing ramparts. Yet such a visit of inquiry will richly repay the traveller in the store of romantic interest and charm that he will find, whether it be in pacing the impressive chambers of the Papal Palace, which swayed the Catholic world for seventy years, or in contemplating from a pleasant garden restaurant on the Rhône the old broken bridge that is glorified in song, or simply in watching the military bugler, posted on the modern bridge, sound a shrill blast whenever he espies a barge come steaming down the swirling river, which reverberates for miles through the peaceful country, or just sitting at an open-air cafè in the old market-square and ruminating on the associations with the city of personalities so varied as the poet Petrarch, the tribune Rienzi, and the economist Stuart Mill. And if the traveller be a Jew, his mind will be stirred by memories of the tribulations of his own people, who have been settled here—so it is believed—for eighteen hundred years, and whose chequered story inevitably provokes a train of reflections.

The first settlement of the Jews is reputed to have been on a site on the bank of the Rhône, facing the Papal Palace, whence so many intolerant edicts were later launched against them, although they were so useful to the Popes as treasurers and stewards; but since the thirteenth century their communal life has been centred in the heart of the city, close to a square that is named, fitly enough, "Place Jerusalem." It was there that they had their Ghetto, known as "Carrière," shut off from the outer world by two ponderous gates, and within which they exercised a form of autonomy, assessing themselves in taxes not only for the maintenance of their own institutions but still more to meet the rapacious demands of the Popes and all their covetous satellites and servitors. The archway leading to the Ghetto is still preserved, but of the synagogue that was built in the thirteenth century, and in which the Jews were compelled to listen to conversionist sermons on the Sabbath by Jesuits or Dominican monks, there is now unfortunately no trace, as it was burnt down in 1844. In its place, and on its site, there is another shrine, which some of the local Jews actually believe to date from the thirteenth century, describing it simply as "restored." In point of exterior, it is the most un-Jewish-looking place of worship that I have ever seen. It is an unimposing corner-building of stone, square and squat in design, and with a single cupola in the form of an undersized cylinder—a style that I saw repeated in one or two other parts of the city. It has two doors facing the street, but these are very rarely opened, admittance being obtained through another door at the side.

It was a Friday evening when we approached, curious as to whether there would be any sign of life. I pulled a bell, and after a few minutes there emerged a little grey-haired woman in black. She was so small and frail, and yet so graceful, that she almost looked like a doll, except that dolls have no grey hair. In response to our request she readily opened the side-door, and we entered the house of prayer. The interior was a strange contrast to the exterior, for it was absolutely circular, the ladies' gallery resting on fourteen equidistant pillars, and the roof being supported by a similar number. Apart from these features there was nothing particularly noteworthy, the *Almemar* [1] being in the centre, and a pulpit of modern design facing it from the left. But on one of the pillars was pasted a written notice stating that conversation was forbidden, as it disturbed the prayers; whence it was permissible to conclude that worshippers still assembled here.

Suddenly there entered the figure of a young priest. At least, I would have thought from his attire that it was a priest, had I not been told a few moments before by the little dame that the Rabbi would be coming very shortly, for, except that he had no cross, he was clad exactly like a Catholic cleric—with a long black soutane reaching to his feet, a black silk sash round his waist, a flat black billy-cock on his head, and a square jabot of beautiful lace on his breast. Evidently the writ of the *Shulchan Aruch*,[2] in the matter of eschewing the garb of Gentiles, did not run in Provence, nor, as I found later, in other matters too. But the face of the minister, with its fringe of beard, and especially his nose, were unmistakably Jewish.

We exchanged greetings, and he told us something about himself and his community. He came from Nice, was trained at the Rabbinical Seminary in Paris, and had been here for the last two years. Formerly Avignon had been a large and famous community: now, owing to the exodus of the Jews following the decline of the city's greatness, it numbered some sixty families, but only few of them were loyal to the tenets and rites of their faith. Service was held

[1] Cantor's dais.   [2] Religious code of law.

every Sabbath, but not always with a *Minyan*.[1] His apologetic tone seemed to suggest that the attendance of the prescribed quorum was rather the exception than the rule. Until some time ago—it was not clear how recently or how long ago—there had been a *Shochet*[2] in the town, but the provision of *kosher* meat was now impossible. My mind flitted instinctively to a moribund congregation in New Zealand, where there was also a minister but no ritual slaughterer, and where in consequence laxity of observance was fomented through knowledge of the minister's own nonconformity.

I expressed curiosity concerning the Ark of the Law and its contents, and he at once opened it. It was similar in design to the Ark that I had seen in a Calcutta synagogue, though by no means as large. The scrolls for immediate use were in a small cabinet in front, whilst behind this was a semi-circular chamber with a shelf on which reposed a number of others, there being thirteen in all. Meanwhile some worshippers had come in—men, women, and children —all of whom sat in the body of the synagogue. As they entered they stretched out their right hand in the direction of the Ark, touched each eyebrow with their forefingers, and then placed the latter on their lips. The movement was done so quickly that it almost looked like making the sign of the cross. A little girl of about eight who came in with a younger brother made him repeat the rite to her satisfaction. Most of them had the typical Provencal features— blue eyes, short nose, and broad face of fairish tint—which was not surprising in view of the many centuries during which physical assimilation had been able to take place; but, withal, they had not shed the inherited trait of restlessness in worship. For the Rabbi, retaining his ordinary headgear, and merely donning a *talith*, began the evening service, and soon various members of the small congregation were strolling to and fro and exchanging remarks, in defiance of the written prohibition posted up. The Portuguese ritual

[1] Quorum of ten.   [2] Ritual slaughter.   [3] Prayer-shawl.

was followed, and the prayer-book that I was given stated on its title-page that it had been compiled in conformity with the decision of the " sages and judges of Carpentras." The Rabbi pitched his voice unnecessarily high for his scanty flock, though its loftiness may have been accentuated by being thrown up to the cupola.

The service over, I asked the Rabbi about " the sages and judges of Carpentras."

" They are no longer there," he replied, " and there are very few Jews there altogether. But there is a very interesting synagogue which I would advise you to go and see. It has been closed for some years, but the key is kept by a Jewish woman at a bootshop in the Place de l'Hotel de Ville, and she will be very glad to let you in. There is a diligence that will take you from Avignon to Carpentras in an hour."

" There is a *Matzo*[1] factory there too," added a member of the congregation. " But it is no longer used."

"Then where do you get your *Matzos*? " I asked.

A faint smile flickered on the face of the Rabbi: " From some other place—Marseilles," he said. " Judaism here is no longer what it was when the Jews of Avignon formed with those of Carpentras, Lisle, and Cavaillon the four communities—the *Arba-Kehilloth*, as they were styled—in which alone Jews were tolerated in French Papal territory. They had a special liturgy called Comtadin, the name formerly borne by this province, to distinguish it from the Portuguese ritual. Judaism, alas, is dying out here and in other parts of Provence. When Jews were compelled to listen to Christian sermons in this synagogue and in others, they clung to the yoke of Judaism. Now that they are free, they have cast aside the Jewish yoke too."

And he heaved a sigh of philosophic resignation amid the nods of assent of his diminishing flock. They were the staunch remnant of a community that had crumbled beneath the assaults of centuries upon its religious loyalty,

[1] Unleavened bread for Passover.

and yet betrayed only too clearly that their own powers of resistance were also ebbing away.

II.—THE DOOM OF CARPENTRAS

We took our seats early in the motor diligence that was to leave from Avignon station in the afternoon, for we were warned that it usually filled up some time before the appointed hour of departure. Most of the passengers were simple country folk, middle-aged men and women in quaint native dress, who had come into the town in the morning to shop and had regaled themselves with sandwiches in the park, where they could quaff freely from the purling fountain. They were burdened with panniers and packages of all kinds, which rested on knees or were stowed away under the seats, whilst heavier loads were secured on the roof. The vehicle was soon crammed, so that perspiring latecomers were left panting and disappointed. From behind us we overheard some muffled criticism about this diligence not being intended for tourists, but we were unaware of any such restriction. I considered the purpose of our journey at least as legitimate, if not as necessary, as that of our fellow-passengers, and wondered what these good folk would think if I explained to them that we were going to Carpentras to see the old synagogue. But I doubted whether they knew what a synagogue was, and as the buzzing gossip around us soon fed upon other themes I deemed it wisest to hold my peace.

Presently the lumbering vehicle throbbed and snorted with unsuspected energy, and we left the ramparts of Avignon behind us. The road along which we travelled was lined with plane trees, which formed a picturesque avenue against the deep-blue sky, diversified here and there by trees laden with figs and by sprawling vines with their luscious fruit. Fortunately there was little traffic, so that our progress was speedy and uninterrupted, except for an occasional halt to enable some people to alight and others to take their place, and for one or two stops in the high streets of the townlets on our way. It was the road that the Jews of Avignon must have trodden generations ago, when an edict of expulsion compelled them to seek a temporary asylum within the more hospitable borders of Carpentras. It led through the hamlet of Monteux, beneath whose soil must be mouldering the bones of the seventeenth century poet, Joseph ben Abraham, whose additions to the ritual of Provencal Jewry in the form of *piyutim* [1] were welcomed by his contemporaries, and whose son, Saul, followed in his father's poetic footsteps. The whole region was rich with the names of scholars, poets and physicians, who illumined the annals of French Jewry for some hundreds of years, and whose intellectual activity has been followed by an era of spiritual stagnation.

An air of lassitude seemed to possess the streets of Carpentras, as we inquired our way to the Place de l'Hotel de Ville. The square was silent and for the most part deserted as we approached the first bootshop and asked for the lady who had the key to the synagogue. We were shown to another shop further on, in front of which sat three women knitting stockings. They had distinct Jewish features and represented three generations, and but for their needles they might have symbolised the Three Fates presiding over the doom of Carpentras Jewry.

I explained the object of our visit, whereupon the youngest, of the trio hastened away, returning presently with a short middle-aged man. He was a simple-looking person, with a dark moustache tinged with grey, whose shabby dress and cloth cap gave him a plebeian appearance, but the bunch of keys in his hand proclaimed that in him was vested the responsible office of sole guardian and controller of all that was left of Jewish memorials in this ancient city.

" You wish to see the synagogue? " he queried. " And I suppose you have come a big distance. Strange, the Jews who live here don't want to see it at all."

[1] Hymns.

" How many Jews are there here now? " I asked.

" About twenty altogether," he replied, as he conducted us across the square to the opposite corner. " But they are mostly bad Jews: they keep nothing at all—*rien, rien.*"

We stopped in front of a tall, well-preserved building, with three tiers of windows, which was not distinguished by the slightest visible token suggestive of a Jewish house of prayer. Our guide unlocked the great door, and we ascended a wide stone staircase, at the head of which was a landing leading to the body of the synagogue, and disclosing a further flight that wound its way to the women's gallery.

Within all was sombre and forlorn. The air was stuffy and musty as in a sepulchre, the light of the perpetual lamp was extinct, and the dingy tone of the walls and the various appurtenances, with the door of the Ark undraped, gave to the whole interior a dreary and melancholy hue. It was a lofty structure, built after the manner of one of the old synagogues in the Ghetto of Venice. There was a yawning emptiness in the centre, as all the benches were ranged round the walls, whilst the *Almemar* was situated immediately above the entrance, on a level with the gallery, access being gained from below by a winding wooden staircase on either side. The panelling on both sides of the Ark and the pillars supporting the *Almemar* had the grain and colouring of terra-cotta marble, but a rap with the knuckles evoked the unmistakable sound of common timber. But of all the curious features of the shrine, perhaps the most striking was a miniature chair perched aloft in a niche on the right of the Ark.

" That chair is a real Louis Quatorze," said the guardian of the sanctuary. " It is called the 'Chair of Elijah', and used to be taken to every house where there was a circumcision, but of course it is too small for anyone to sit in. The Ark has twenty-eight scrolls of the Torah, including those from the synagogue of Cavaillon, which is also closed."

We followed him up the staircase to the *Almemar*, and

as I turned over the sere and yellow pages of a ponderous prayer-book on the Reader's desk, he explained that the building dated from the middle of the eighteenth century and had been restored about the beginning of the present one. It stood on the same site as the first synagogue, which was built in the thirteenth century, when the Jews signed an agreement in which they acknowledged themselves as vassals of the Bishop and pledged themselves not only to pay all sorts of taxes and tallages but also to provide sheets for the Bishop's guest-beds and to give him all the tongues of the cattle that they might kill. Despite their punctilious observance of the contract, the Jews were expelled in the following century and the synagogue was replaced by a church; but after an interval of twenty years another Bishop allowed them to build a new shrine in return for a yearly contribution of six pounds of spices, three pounds of ginger, and three pounds of pepper. These condiments, however, were not acceptable to a later lord of the episcopal see, who demanded an annual tribute in money, and the Jews were obliged to continue paying episcopal imposts until the liberation brought by the French Revolution.

"We are free now from all such taxes," said our guide and philosopher, "and you see the result," with an eloquent sweep of the hand through the musty air. "It is six years now since we have had any service here. There is a *Mikvah*[1] in the basement, but I don't remember when it was used last. The Jewish population has dwindled little by little, and most of those who have remained do not care. For *Yom Kippur*[2] we used to go to Avignon, but I am thinking this year of calling together the few who still have a spark of Judaism and holding a service again—with myself as cantor."

He took us into an adjoining room, in which there was a small library of modern Jewish literature, mostly in French, and showed us a number of documents relating to episodes in the history of the community; and then we followed him

[1] Ritual bath.   [2] Day of Atonement.

to another chamber on the ground-floor, where there was a motley collection of Hebrew prayer-books and Bibles, many of which had been printed in Carpentras in a more religious age, together with some phylacteries rotting in their little bags. Most of the books were faded, stained and tattered, and lay about in a state of confusion, but when I asked if I could take one—or even buy one—of which there were duplicates, he bristled with zealous vigilance. "No, I cannot let anything go," he said firmly. "There is a complete inventory, and I am responsible. Once I lent a couple of books to an American Rabbi who was here and promised to return them, but so far he has not sent them back."

"Does not the Grand Rabbi interest himself in this synagogue?" I inquired.

"No," was the reply, with a disparaging shake of the head. "He is interested only in celebrating rich marriages. I closed the synagogue some time ago in Cavaillon and brought the scrolls of the Torah here. Now I am wondering what may happen when I am no longer here to look after this synagogue. Perhaps it may become a museum."

He conducted us down the stairs and out into the street, and locked the great door behind us; and as we passed out of the square we caught a final glimpse of the three women who, sitting so grave and unperturbed, seemed, in the distance, to be more suggestive than ever of the Three Fates.

III.—A MARSEILLES KALEIDOSCOPE

The port of Marseilles had always appeared to me to be a place of transit through which one rushed to catch a ship for some far-off land, rather than a city in which to stay and saunter for its own sake; but this was a mere prejudice, probably shared by many, of which I soon was cured. For apart from gazing at the ingenious hanging bridge, which can transport half-a-dozen motor charabancs and their human freight gently over the water dividing the old town from the new, and the more amazing achievement of a tunnel bored through the bowels of the foreland to let vessels pass straight into the waters of the Rhône, and apart from being thrilled by the romance of the sea-girt isle of the Chateau d'Iff, sacred to the memory of Monte Cristo, I had only to watch the ceaseless flow of variegated traffic and found intellectual refreshment enough to tickle even the most jaded palate.

Seated at one of the cafés in the tumultuous Cannebière, opposite the Bourse, we saw a veritable kaleidoscope of humanity unroll before us on the margin of pavement left free for its use. Men and women of all nations, of all creeds and climes, who had landed for a few idle hours until their ship was ready to bear them hence again, strolled along in endless procession. Brawny Argentinians and dapper Japs, dusky Cingalese and flaxen-haired Swedes, Greeks and Malays, Algerians and Americans—they filed along in every variety of colour and costume, of physique and physiognomy, of speech and gesture, some lingering, others hurrying, but all gazing around in indolent curiosity.

Presently, in the midst of all this motley parade, there emerged a strangely familiar figure—a bearded old Jew, shuffling along with bowed head and weary limbs. I seemed to have seen him often before and in different places—in the crowded Ghettos of Vilna and Warsaw, of Kovno and Riga, of Vienna and Bucharest; but in all those cities he was at home, and his face bore a look of resignation, if not of contentment. Here he trudged along as an alien, friendless and forlorn, not an idle sight-seer like all the other people around him, but a woebegone wanderer, without any goal in view. Our eyes met for a fleeting spell, as though attracted by some strange telepathic impulse, and then he was swallowed up in the swirling throng.

The next day, being the solemn day of New Year, we wended our way to the synagogue. It is a modern and imposing building, standing back a little from the narrow

street in which it is situated, the space between the entrance
and the tall railings forming a convenient exercise-ground
for the little knots of worshippers who came out in quest
of fresh air. The French flag fluttered aloft from either
gate in honour of the great day, and a policeman was on
duty to see that fervour of devotion did not bubble over
perchance into some emotional outburst. Within there was
a large and animated congregation, which showed that
though Jewish life was decaying in the interior of Provence
it was still fairly vigorous in what the mediaeval traveller,
Benjamin of Tudela, described as " a city of princely and
wise citizens." Not only the body of the shrine but the
two women's galleries were filled, and as the day was warm
and few windows were open the air was oppressive. The men
presented a strange contrast to their co-religionists in any
English synagogue, not so much in appearance—although
there were many Algerians and Tunisians among them—as
in attire, for among the whole of that devout assembly there
was not a single silk hat. There were all kinds of other
headgear—bowlers of London pattern, trilbies of different
hue, straw-hats, cloth caps, even the peaked hats of two or
three Jewish soldiers, and the quaint cylinders of the
cantors, but though I scanned every row of worshippers from
the entrance-doors to the Ark my eye did not light upon
the sheen of a single top-hat. Even the president who
occupied an elevated pew near the Ark bravely sported a
circular hat of straw!

The most distinguished-looking hats of all were those
on the heads of the beadles. They were magnificent
structures, shaped like the cocked hats of a Lord Lieutenant,
and adorned with a white and red cockade, whilst the rest
of the attire of those functionaries was in keeping, consisting of black coat-tails, white tie, and a silver shield on the
breast suspended by a chain round the neck. Not even the
Marshal of the City of London could have stalked with a
prouder bearing than the senior beadle, as he headed the
procession of the cantors and the scrolls of the Torah

through the thronged aisles to the Ark, which was draped, not with a curtain of symbolic white, as in England, but with a brocade of palish brown. And the Rabbi, clad from head to foot exactly like a padre, must have felt a little thrill of pride as he saw the flock crowding round the scrolls, which they were so eagerly anxious to touch, if not with their lips, with the corner of their *talith*, whilst the women high above, many of them with a dark lace mantilla over the head, threw out their hands in an imaginary caress, and kissed the tips of their fingers.

The assistant cantor blew the *Shofar* [1] with ease and vigour, and also with unusual rapidity, which was due to his reading the notes himself instead of having them called out by his colleague, but he had scarce concluded the last blast when there was a cry and a disturbance. A man had fallen in a fainting fit and was immediately lifted up and taken out into the fresh air.

My neighbour, glad to welcome a stranger, told me that this was the only synagogue in the city, and that the Jewish community had grown since the War of 1914–18 owing to the arrival of many Jews from the other side of the Mediterranean as well as, to a smaller extent, from Russia and Poland. The community followed the Portuguese rite, to which the immigrants from Eastern Europe could not easily adapt themselves, and the latter were therefore allowed to hold a service of their own in the vestry-room. Would I like to see it?

The Ashkenazi congregation was a typical Polish *Chevrah*.[2] There were about three dozen men and women, with a sprinkling of children, in a small room entered from the courtyard. The door was wide open owing to the heat, the worshippers were following listlessly the fervid roulades of an amateur precentor, and every now and then one of them would walk out to cool his perspiring brow. I looked on from the doorway, restrained from entering by the oppressive atmosphere, when suddenly I perceived my old

---

[1] Ram's horn trumpet.   [2] Small synagogue.

man of the previous day. He came shuffling out with heavy tread.

"*Shalom!*"[1] I greeted him. "Whence comes a Jew?"

"From Berditchev," he replied wearily. "From the land of misery and bondage, where Jews are treated as in Egypt in olden times."

"And *wohin?*" I asked.

"Only the Most High alone knows," he said wistfully. "I have five children in different parts of the world, and I am waiting for the means to go and join one of them. I have one son in Chicago, another in Buenos Aires, a daughter in Montreal, a third son in Johannesburg, and a fourth in *Eretz Israel*. I have written to all of them to send me money to buy a shipping ticket, so that I can go away from here. Whichever child sends me the money first, to that land I shall go. At present I know not whether I am going to the east or to the west, or to the south—or how long I have yet to remain here."

"And is it all the same to you to what land you go?" I asked.

"What a question!" he answered, in a tone of righteous reproach. "The nearest land is to me also the dearest. I always dream that my son in Rishon-le-Zion will come to my help first."

"May your dream soon come true," I said.

The piercing blast of the *Shofar* resounded through the courtyard, and the old man shuffled back to resume his prayers.

IV.—AN OUTLAW AT JUAN-LES-PINS

Midway between the fashionable attraction of Cannes and Nice there is a more modest pleasure resort on the Riviera, which basks just as freely in the burning sunshine, and which can be frequented even by those who do not belong to the plutocracy. It abounds in pine-trees, which

[1] Peace.

have given it part of its distinctive name, but whether it is called Juan by reason of the legendary sojourn in its vicinity of Don Juan, or of the actual domicile in its midst of some modern disciples of that amorous adventurer, is a question one need not trouble to answer. As one surveys the happy, laughing crowd on the beach, some splashing in the shimmering waters, and others disporting their bronzed bodies on the golden sand, one would think that this was the last place in the world where one would hear an echo of the *Judenschmerz* or be tempted to discuss any phase of the complicated Jewish question. And yet it was in these exhilarating surroundings that I came into contact with a person whose career exemplified some of the hardships and paradoxes of Jewish life.

She was a young woman who came down to the beach every morning with a novel of Marcel Proust in the original, over which she pored, through smoked glasses, with religious devotion. That in itself, and on that particular shore, would not have aroused either my curiosity or my notice. But she spoke with an unmistakable American accent, and that was sufficient to mark her out as a rare phenomenon, for even if it were usual for an American woman to read Proust in French, it was rather uncommon for her to stay in any place on the Continent for more than forty-eight hours. And this American lady, so I heard, had already been here over a month, as the scorched skin of her arms and neck testified only too well. But as soon as conversation was started, after the unconventional preliminaries of strand etiquette, I was surprised to find that she was not a real American after all.

"I have lived in America ever since I was a little child," she said. "That accounts for my accent."

"But aren't you an American citizen?" I asked.

"I was," she replied hesitatingly. "But what I am now I really cannot say."

After a little diplomatic manoeuvring she became somewhat more communicative.

"The fact is, I was born in Kharkoff of Jewish parents. I was married to an American and left New York with an American passport. But as I didn't get my passport renewed within twelve months after leaving the States it is no longer valid."

"But how does that deprive you of your American citizenship?" I urged.

There was a momentary embarrassment, and then the explanation was given. She had divorced her husband some months ago, and that act, together with the expiry of her passport, had deprived her for the nonce both of citizenship and of all political protection. She could not resume her Russian nationality, for she had no birth-certificate to attest her origin, nor could she speak a single word of the tongue of her native land. She was, in fact, an outlaw.

She laughed as though she had not a care in the world, and yet her position was embarrassing. She could not go back to the country in which she had spent the greater part of her life, and which had moulded her into her present personality. Nor, without a passport, could she go to any other country either. She could not obtain such a document from the Soviet Government without some proof that she was entitled to it, and if she did obtain it and wished to return to America she would be subject to the Russion quota fixed by the American Government and have to wait years before her turn came.

"What about Palestine?" she asked, with a flash of hope. "I confess I am not a nationalist, but then——. You undersand."

"I am afraid that to go there you must also have a passport, even if it's only the kind of passport given to refugees."

"But I'm not a refugee," she said despairingly. "I'm only an outlaw."

And she sought distraction in the enthralling pages of Marcel Proust.

V.—RELICS AT NARBONNE

Of the countless Jewish communities that enjoyed importance and even fame in the Middle Ages, but were later doomed to fade away to a mere memory, few have received such scant attention in our days as that which existed in Narbonne for close upon a thousand years. For Jews lived in that city of Provence from the fifth to the fourteenth century; they flourished as traders through the commerce which they carried on with all the lands that enclosed the Mediterranean Sea, and also with some of the Orient; and they boasted of celebrated Rabbinical scholars whose authority was acknowledged far beyond the frontiers of France itself. The foundations of their fortune were laid in the eighth century, probably by Charlemagne, who is said to have bestowed favours and privileges upon them as a reward for helping him to conquer the city, for, according to some historians, he divided Narbonne into three lordships, one for the bishop, another for a Frankish lord, and the third for the Jews. Not content with ensuring the material security and welfare of the Jews, he also took steps to promote their cultural advancement, although the latter measure may have been prompted by the desire to make his Jewish subjects independent of the Talmudical colleges of Babylon, to which they were wont to send tribute. He brought from Lucca the learned Rabbi Kalonymos and his son Moses, and gave them a considerable area in the city as their permanent property. Kalonymos was accorded the deference paid to a prince. Indeed, he and his descendants and followers bore the title of *Nasi*, which was maintained until the expulsion of the Jews from France at the end of the fourteenth century. The part of the city that they inhabited was called "La Cour du Roi des Juifs" (the Court of the King of the Jews), a name that has been preserved for the locality until the present day, except for the words "des Juifs", which have been dropped. Within their prescribed district the Jews were allowed to govern themselves: they elected two consuls, who administered the community's affairs in accordance with the municipal ordinances issued by the city's consuls.

The Jewish community of Narbonne owed its fame much more to the Hebrew learning that flourished in its midst than to its privilege of autonomy, for it had a Talmudical college headed by a succession of eminent scholars for some centuries, and other savants too were attracted to it from time to time. The head of the College in the days of Charlemagne was Rabbi Machir, a scholar from Babylon. In the early half of the eleventh century the principal of the college was the Biblical exegete and Talmudical authority, Rabbi Moses Hadarshan ("The Preacher"), whose father, grandfather, and great-grandfather had all occupied that position before him. Early in the following century Narbonne had a Jewish population of 2,000, but owing to a war between the city and the Count of Toulouse so many Jews emigrated to other provinces that when the famous traveller, Benjamin of Tudela, visited the city in 1166 he found that there were only 300 there. Even so, he writes of it as " a city pre-eminent for learning: thence the Torah goes forth to all countries. Sages and great and illustrious men abide here." He had been preceded by that roving scholar, author, poet, grammarian, mathematician and wit, Abraham Ibn Ezra, whose wanderings extended from Jerusalem to London, and who paid two visits to Narbonne, first in 1139 and secondly in 1160, when he translated there an astronomical work from Arabic into Hebrew.

It was in the twelfth and thirteen centuries that the distinction of Narbonne as a centre of Jewish scholarship reached its height, an eminence to which it was then raised by the Kimchi family. Joseph ben Isaac Kimchi, who immigrated from the south of Spain, transplanted the Judaeo-Arabic scholarship of that country to the south of France. He translated Bahya's philosophical work from Arabic into Hebrew, wrote commentaries on various books of the Bible, composed liturgical hymns, and also wrote Hebrew grammars. His elder son, Moses, was also a Biblical commentator and the author of a Hebrew grammar, which proved particularly useful for the study of Hebrew by non-Jews and was translated into Latin. His younger son, David, commonly known from his initials as " ReDaK ", lived all his life in Narbonne, from his birth in 1160 until his death in 1233. He is the most famous of the trio, thanks to his mastery and originality as Hebrew grammarian and lexicographer, as the author of Biblical commentaries (which became popular in Christian circles through Latin translations) and as religious controversialist. In the vehement dispute that raged between the supporters of the views of Maimonides and his antagonists, David Kimchi, like other scholars of his community, sided energetically with the former, and even travelled to Spain at an advanced age to win over the opposition. In the fourteenth century the most important figure was Moses Narboni, also called Maestro Vidal, who divided his admiration between the two philosophers, Maimonides and Averroes, on whose works he wrote commentaries.

So much must be told about Narbonne to make clear its position and importance in Jewish history, and yet it is the barest skeleton of a rich and voluminous record, which has been chronicled in meticulous detail by a French scholar, Jean Regné, in a book of a few hundred pages (" Étude sur la Condition des Juifs de Narbonne du Ve au XIVe Siècle "). But it should suffice to explain why, when I was returning from Barcelona to Paris and had to pass through Narbonne, I decided to make a brief halt in the city. I was anxious not merely to recall on the spot memories of the men who had rendered such enduring services to Jewish traditional lore and Hebrew scholarship, but also to find out what visible traces of the mediaeval community still remained. As I arrived on a Sunday morning and had to leave again in the evening, I was afraid that my quest would be fruitless, but fortunately my fears were falsified.

I had been told by a friend in Paris that there was still a "Rue aux Juifs" in Narbonne, and, therefore, before leaving my hotel to set out on my search, I asked the manager where the street was. "Rue aux Juifs?" he echoed incredulously, looking at the porter. "Rue aux Juifs?" repeated the porter with a blank stare. And then both vigorously shook their heads: "No, there is no street here of that name."

So I went to the General Post Office and put the same question to the only official on duty, a matron lady selling stamps. "Rue aux Juifs?" she re-echoed. "No, there isn't one. I should know." I thereupon asked her if the Municipal Library was open, as I had been advised that, if anybody, the Director of that institution would be helpful to me. No, the Library was always closed on Sundays. Therefore, there remained nothing else to do but to track down the Director in his home and to hope that he would be able and willing to furnish me with the desired information. She told me his name, M. Philippe Helena, and explained in detail how I could reach him.

After walking through a succession of quiet, deserted streets, and over some old bridges, where the only traffic consisted of some motor lorries with empty barrels, which were lumbering to the vineyards in the neighbouring country to bring back loads of ripe grapes, I found myself in the tastefully furnished home of M. Helena. He was a tall, intellectual-looking man, with a scholar's stoop, and he and his wife gave me a friendly welcome, despite my unannounced irruption into their Sunday repose, and as though this were a normal occurrence. M. Helena readily offered to accompany me to the Museum, which was open, and also to unlock the Library for me, so as to show me the few objects of Jewish interest which had survived since mediaeval and even early mediaeval times.

In the Museum, established over a hundred years ago, in a large and impressive building which was originally an Archbishop's Palace, there was a varied collection of works of ceramic art from Etruria, France, Spain, Greece, and other lands, as well as a large exhibition of pictures by French, Flemish, Italian, and other painters. It also comprised a gallery of Narbonese antiquities, among which M. Helena pointed to five exhibits of Jewish origin. The most interesting was a tombstone with the oldest known Jewish inscription in France. It was dated 668 c.e., was marked with a Menorah, and inscribed in Latin except for three Hebrew words. It read as follows:—

"Here rest in peace the three children of blessed memory, of master (*dominus*) Parator son of the late master Sapaudus, namely, Justus, Matrona, and Dulciorella, who lived, Justus thirty years, Matrona twenty years, Dulciorella nine years. *Shalom al Yisrael.* They died in the second year of our lord, King Egicanus."

Parator, the Greek for " consoler ", stands for Menahem, while Justus is the Latin equivalent of Zadok or perhaps Joseph, and Dulciorella is the same as Naomi.

The other three inscriptions on tablets were in Hebrew. The longest, recording the dedication of a synagogue in the year 1239 or 1240, was as follows:—

"The permission to build a Synagogue, a Holy Ark, and an enclosure on the eastern side, was granted in the year 5000, in the month of Tebet. The Lord hath given us the Sabbath and placed a limit to our dispersion, as it is written (Deuteronomy, XXX, 3): 'The Lord thy God will turn thy captivity, and have compassion upon thee, and will return and gather thee from all the peoples, whither the Lord thy God hath scattered thee.' "

Of the other two tombstones, one read:

"This inscription, incised with an iron pen [chisel] testifies and says that David was hidden in our midst. He was buried two days after the death of his young wife."

The other tombstone, which was that of a " son of Rabbi Joseph," was short and mutilated.

The fifth inscription, headed by the seven-branched candlestick, recorded the persecutions and massacres inflicted by the Visigoth kings upon the Jews—by Recared (586), Sisebut (612), Chintilla (636), Receswinthe (653), Ervige (680), and Egicanus (687). The ages of the victims, whose names are inscribed on the marble tablet, and some Hebrew characters, furtively engraved at the end of the penultimate line, meaning "Peace upon Israel!" leave no doubt as to their fate.

Thus, the only memorials of the mediaeval Jewish community that had survived after five and a half centuries related to some obscure and unknown individuals and to a synagogue of which there was otherwise not the smallest trace. There was no reminder of the scholars and sages whose light had once gone forth to the Jewries of France and other lands. But there was still a reminder of the *Nasi* or "King of the Jews," who had held his court here in former times, and M. Helena kindly conducted me to it. It consisted of a small courtyard, which we entered through a narrow alley leading from a business thoroughfare, the Rue de l'Ancien Courrier. It was cobble-stoned, as it had probably been for generations, and it was surrounded by tall shabby tenements with mouldering walls. That courtyard, which had originally been called "Cour du Roi des Juifs," was now known simply as "Cour du Roi," and probably few of the local inhabitants knew the origin of the name. No attempt had ever been made in modern times to restore the once famous community, and the two or three shopkeepers, the only representatives of Israel now living there, seemed hardly likely to form the promising nucleus of a real revival.

Chapter XXII

A SPANISH TOUR

I.—ISOLATION IN MADRID

W HEN the late Señor Antonio Pulido Fernandez launched his movement before the First World War for the return of the Sephardic Jews to Spain, it was generally thought that advantage would be taken of the policy of hospitality upon which it was based, at least by those who did not feel contented in the lands in which they were domiciled. In particular, it was expected that the Jews of Salonika, who had flourished under centuries of Turkish rule but chafed under the more repressive régime of the Greeks, would avail themselves of the offer. The spirit of tolerance that had animated the Spanish authorities then found generous expression in the creation of a special Chair for the Hebrew language and literature, to which Professor A. S. Yahuda was appointed, and it was believed that this furtherance of Hebrew studies would serve the twofold purpose of promoting a better understanding between Spaniards and Jews and encouraging the resettlement of the Sephardim in the country from which they had been expelled over 400 years ago. Unfortunately, neither the liberal-minded campaign of Pulido Fernandez nor the lectures of Professor Yahuda produced any lasting effects, and there was even perceptible a change of attitude towards the Jews on the part of some sections of the population.

This change was particularly noticeable before the Civil War. Fortunately it was not shared in Government circles, but was confined to political elements who had obviously been influenced by the Nazi gospel, and also to certain

Catholic quarters. Anti-Semitic articles had been making
a disquieting appearance in such papers as *A.B.C.* and *La
Nación*, which were prone to attribute to the Jews all the
troubles and disturbances of recent years. During a
general election there were posters with caricatures of Jews,
Freemasons, Marxists and Catalans, as those jointly responsible for all revolutionary disorder. More than one edition
of the notorious *Protocols of the Elders of Zion* had been
published in Madrid, and, curiously enough, the publisher
was a Spaniard who had a Jewish wife. To what extent
anti-Semitism had been fomented by Nazi propagandists, it
was rather difficult to determine; but the fact was that, for
some years before the Second World War, there was a large
German colony in Madrid, many book-shops contained a
big display of Nazi literature, and concerts were held under
the patronage of the German Embassy for the benefit of the
" Winter-Hilfe " in Germany. That Hitler had his Spanish
admirers was shown by the creation of the party called the
" Falange Española " (or Spanish Phalanx), which was
distinguished by a blue shirt and by the usual symbols and
salutes characteristic of the Nazis, under the leadership of
the son of the late Primo de Rivera.

The manifestations of anti-Semitism could not find an
excuse either in the numbers or the influence of the Jews in
Madrid or in Spain generally, for their numbers were trifling
and their influence was non-existent. The total number of
registered members of the Jewish congregation in Madrid
was only forty-five.[1] There were, of course, more Jews than
that in this city, but most of them did not wish to be
associated with the synagogue and many did not wish even
to be known as Jews. They lived in seclusion and isolation.
So invisible were they that a Polish Jew told me that he
had been living in the city three years before he acciden-
tally came across some fellow-Jews, his discovery being due
to overhearing some persons behind him in a cinema talking

[1] Before the Second World War. The number increased later
(see " Barcelona Revisited ").

Yiddish. Cases of intermarriage were frequent, and it was difficult sometimes to know whether a man was to be regarded as a Jew or not. There were certain families of which some members were openly Jewish, while the others professed either Protestanism or Catholicism. In any case, even if we included the converted Jews and the *Confessionslos* ("religion-less") the total number was insignificant.

It was rather curious that the language mostly spoken among the Jews in Madrid was German, due to the fact that the majority had come either from Germany or from other parts of Central and Eastern Europe, such as Austria, Hungary, Poland and Rumania. Most of them were settled there before Hitler came into power, and although a certain number of refugees from Germany found their way there afterwards, most of them had gone away again—some having settled in Barcelona or else left the country altogether. A committee for the relief of German refugees was in existence there, but the cases with which it was called upon to deal were comparatively few until after the outbreak of the Second World War, when the number of refugees, including many from France, greatly increased. Among the Germans who had settled there, some had established a one-price store called "Sepu", in the important business thoroughfare, Alcala. The opening of this establishment proved very popular, despite the attempt to boycott it engineered by a Catholic Bishop, who issued a confidential circular among his aristocratic followers, exhorting them to withhold their patronage. But while the Spanish ladies who received the circular might not shop at "Sepu", they had no compunction in sending their maids there on their behalf.

The heterogeneous character of the local Jewish community was one of the reasons responsible for its slow and struggling growth. The congregation was founded during the latter period of the First War, but could not be said to have made any progress. After an existence of about twenty years, it had neither Rabbi nor cantor, nor could it afford to keep either, even with the most slender salary. The synagogue consisted of a couple of rooms on the second floor of some premises in a busy business street near the famous Puerta del Sol, but there was not the least sign or symbol to indicate the approach to the only place of Jewish worship in the capital of Spain. Before arriving at the synagogue, you had to mount some seventy steps of a narrow staircase (for there was no lift), an ordeal that was probably sufficient to ward off some of the more weak-kneed members of the community, and even then there was no emblem or inscription of any kind to mark the entrance to the house of prayer. The door was closed even during the Sabbath morning service, and such silence reigned on the stairs that one might be forgiven if one thought that the place was deserted. But on pressing an electric button the door was opened by one of the worshippers and then you found yourself in the midst of the small congregation of the faithful. The large room was the synagogue proper with the Ark and a simple *Almemar*,[1] and a number of chairs, whilst the adjoining room was occupied by women. On one side of the Ark was a small brass *Menorah*[2] affixed to the wall, and on one of the walls was a printed sheet with diagrams showing how *Tephillin*[3] were laid; but as the service was held only on Sabbaths and Festivals when phylacteries were not used, that sheet was intended to serve a purely decorative purpose. Although most of the worshippers were Ashkenazim, the ritual followed was Sephardic, which was perhaps only natural in the land of Sepharad.

The congregation has had a very serious struggle for existence owing to the fact that those Jews who were in the best position to maintain the synagogue were the least concerned about it. For a number of years almost the whole of the communal budget had been covered by Señor Ignacio Bauer, but when he experienced a reverse of fortune it became necessary for all members to bear their

[1] Reader's desk.   [2] Seven-branched candlestick.   [3] Phylacteries.

Site of Mediæval Ghetto in Cordova
with Jews' Street (Judios) on the left

proper share of the burden. Even so, the income only just sufficed to cover the rent and the modest wages of the beadle. The Municipality had provided the community with land for a cemetery, but whenever there was a burial, a payment of 40 pesetas (about £11) had to be made to the Municipality, and the committee did not always find it easy to raise this sum in the case of the funeral of a poor person. The task would, of course, have been greatly lightened if only there had been a stronger sense of solidarity and Jewish consciousness among the Jews of Madrid. Even Dr. Max Nordau, when he lived in this city during the war, and although he was generally regarded as a free-thinker, used to worship in this synagogue and wear a silk hat for the occasion; but there were far lesser lights who considered it beneath them to be associated with it.

If only the means could have been raised to provide a more suitable and dignified place of worship, there was no doubt that the congregation would have increased, and communal life would have received an impetus. It was, perhaps, the recognition of this need that prompted a certain Jewish adventurer from Hungary several years ago to make a proposal to the committee. Claiming that he was a Rabbi, although he could furnish no proof of his claim, he proposed to the committee that they should appoint him as Rabbi without a salary. In return for this sacrifice all that he wanted was a liberal supply of finely printed note-paper bearing his official title, with which he proposed to appeal to pious philanthropists in various parts of the world for contributions to the building of a synagogue, of which forty per cent should go to the synagogue and the balance of sixty per cent should be retained by him as commission! His offer was declined, so he went off to Barcelona, where he was said to have met with greater favour, and when last heard of he was engaged in his money-raising campaign somewhere in America, in the interests of a synagogue in the capital of Catalonia.

II.—CORDOVA: PAST AND PRESENT

The glamour with which the ancient capital of Andalusia had been invested for me so long was rudely dissipated as the train in which I was travelling from Seville careered through the night and the deluge of rain came beating against the rattling windows. It was the first downpour that I had experienced after three weeks of cloudless, deep-blue sky, and the dim light in the long, sombre-hued carriage— which reminded me somewhat of the cars I had known in Canada—was such as to produce a depressing effect even upon the jauntiest of spirits. It was impossible to read in such semi-gloom, while the combined noise of the roaring train and the raging storm made it difficult even to think consecutively.

It was with a feeling of relief, therefore, that I clambered down from the train when we at length drew up in the cavernous station of Cordova, and found my way to a dilapidated carriage drawn by a doleful and venerable nag. The streets were dark, deserted and silent as we splashed along. We seemed to be plunging right into the Middle Ages, and it was now easy to conjure up the vision of the Jews who had both flourished and suffered in the days when the southern half of Spain was under the sway of the Moors.

But the spell was immediately broken when I entered the hotel and filled in the usual questionnaire, which sought detailed personal information from the date of my birth. There were only a few guests present, which seemed to testify that this romantic city was also a victim of the slump, and that the expected throng of pilgrims to the birth-place of Maimonides had not yet begun to arrive.

Sleep was rather difficult to woo in the lofty bed-chamber to which I was assigned, so inevitably I fell to thinking of some of the men whose memories were for ever bound up with the city—above all, of that remarkable statesman, financier, physician and patron of Talmudical scholars,

Hasdai ibn Shaprut, whose adventurous spirit brought him into communication with the ruler of the almost fabulous Jewish Kingdom of the Hazars. There followed in fancy the figure of that strange captive from Babylon, Moses ben Hanoch, reputed to have been brought by a sea-captain to the slave-market of Cordova and redeemed by his Jewish brethren, who soon discovered in the tattered stranger a master of the Talmud destined to establish in their midst a Rabbinical school that vied with all the glories of Sura and Pumbaditha.

Cordova was then a city of magnificence, of pride and pomp, with half-a-million inhabitants, three thousand mosques, and three hundred public baths, gay with palaces and gardens, and yielding in size and splendour only to Bagdad, with which its citizens loved to compare it. Strange that all the world was now reminded of it only as the birth-place of Maimonides, though the budding philosopher left it as a boy of thirteen—a fugitive with his family from the fury of the fanatical Almohades—and probably gave it but scanty thought in the days of his manhood and his fame in Egypt.

How much or how little of all these memories of mediaeval times, I wondered, could there still be traced? And musing on the chequered annals of the past, on the scenes of barbarism that alternated with periods of peace and comfort, I was soon transported to the realm of dreams, wherein the figures of history jostled in kaleidoscopic confusion against the more familiar personages of my own acquaintance.

Happily the morning brought a surcease of rain, so that I was able to set out on my journey of inquiry. I wended my way first, as all visitors do, towards the Cathedral, which was originally the great Mosque of Cordova, when I was accosted by some vendors of lottery tickets, who are more plentiful in the streets of Spain than newspaper-sellers, and far more vocal and pertinacious. After emerging safely from their solicitations I was approached by a neatly-dressed individual, who addressed me deferentially in an American accent and offered his services as a guide. He had been a waiter for some years in New York, but since his return to his native Cordova he had found it more lucrative to show foreigners round the city than to minister to their wants in hotels. I accepted his services with little persuasion, partly because it would facilitate my quest, and partly because I was thus rendered immune from further molestation.

We soon reached "La Mezquita", the imposing and rather forbidding-looking edifice, which took two centuries to build as a shrine for Moslems, and which passed under Christian control in the thirteenth century to be transformed ingeniously into a Christian place of worship. From without it looked like anything but an ecclesiastical structure, surrounded as it was by a massive battlemented wall, fortified by solid buttresses, whilst within one was bewildered by a veritable forest of columns—over eight hundred in number—of all kinds of marble, jasper and porphyry, varied in style, and symmetrically divided by over forty arched aisles.

First we paced through some of the aisles from north to south, and then from east to west, my guide calling my attention every now and again to some surprising vista, conducting me to the elaborate choir stalls and carved pulpits, and glibly pouring forth a torrent of historical lore, abounding in names and dates. He would have liked to make me explore every avenue and admire every aspect, perhaps out of a conscientious conception of his duty, perhaps with a view to a richer reward, but I was anxious to pass on to the site of the mediaeval Jewish quarter. We had not far to go, for after threading our way through two or three streets we came to a little quiet cobble-paved square, at one corner of which, on the wall, was inscribed in large bold letters the name: "Plazuela de Maimonides". This square my guide informed me was formerly called "Plaza de las Bulas."

It was the market place in mediaeval times, where Jewish housewives bought their fish and vegetables, but it is now silent and deserted, except for the occasional shouts of children who find it a convenient playground. It has only recently been renamed in honour of Maimonides, whilst the long narrow straggling lane beginning from the square, which used to be called " Calle Maimonides ", because in it was reputed to be the birthplace of the philosopher, now bears the name of " Judios ".

It is the main thoroughfare of the mediaeval Ghetto, and it is so narrow that my guide and I could not enter it until a horse-drawn cart that entirely blocked its width had creakily emerged into the square. It is flanked on either side by low, whitewashed houses, whose shabby exteriors belie the attractive homesteads within, for when the door opens one has a glimpse of a picturesque Moorish patio, gaily patterned with flowers, and of slender pillars supporting surrounding balconies. It is in this street, about midway, that there stands the only authentic memorial of mediaeval times—a synagogue.

From without one cannot detect the least sign of it. The entry is through a simple doorway, which is hardly distinguishable from all the other doorways in the street, and which is opened by a caretaker in response to a bell. The synagogue is a rather small chamber designed in Moorish style, very much smaller than either of the two surviving synagogues in Toledo and not so well preserved. It is almost cubical in shape, and the light comes through a window in the upper part of one of the walls and through an aperture that was added later. On the eastern side there is a recess that once contained the Ark of the Law, whilst in the upper part of the south wall there is a balcony where the women were wont to pray, discreetly secluded from the gaze of their menfolk. The decorations on the walls, florid arabesques with regular patterns, are still in a good state despite the lapse of over six centuries, and one can easily discern the familiar motifs of the " Shield of David ", the palm-leaf and the tree of life.

Above the recess, in a narrow frieze, are verses from the

Psalms in Hebrew, whilst on the sides of it is an inscription, likewise in Hebrew, presenting a modest record of the origin of the building. It reads as follows:

> "*A little sanctuary and a house of testimony which was built by Isaac Mehab, son of the wealthy Ephraim. Erected in the year 75 (1315) as a temporary structure. Arise, O Lord, and hasten to rebuild Jerusalem.*"

The unmistakable date prevented me from indulging in the momentary fancy that Maimonides had ever worshipped there as a boy (as he died in 1204), although it was not impossible that he had prayed in a synagogue of similar appearance and design on the self-same site. The temporary character of the shrine had far surpassed the anticipations of its founder, although its purpose was forgotten in later centuries, and it was for a time in the possession of a Shoemakers' Guild. But its original function was discovered by two academicians in 1884, and it was thenceforth preserved as a national monument, forming now the principal goal of pilgrimage of all who are drawn to the city as the birthplace of Rabbi Moses ben Maimon.

Threading my way once more through the narrow lane, which had certainly been traversed countless times by the youthful Moses and all his family until the moment of their enforced exile in 1148, I came to an old Moorish gateway at the other end, the Puerta de Almodovar, which had been the entrance to the ancient Ghetto. But now there is no Jewish quarter, nor even a single Jew in this city. Not many yards farther off stood an electric tram-car, patiently awaiting passengers, and as I took a seat in it and was sped back to my hotel I was transported once more from the scenes of mediaevalism to drab modernity.

III.—REFUGEES IN BARCELONA

The city of Barcelona has proved a much more attractive place of refuge to Jews than any other city in Spain, thanks

partly to its convenient geographical situation and partly to
the extensive economic opportunities that it provides. Not
only is it the most important commercial and industrial
centre in the country, but it is easily reached both by land
and sea, and, besides, it has a wonderful climate throughout
the year. Jews began to establish themselves there over forty
years ago, but it was not until after the First World War
that their number appreciably increased, while the Nazi
persecution brought a comparatively large influx. According to official figures the number of Germans who had
settled there since 1933 was 3,000, of whom by far the
majority were Jews, but many of them left in the following
years.

The Jewish population was derived from so many different
parts of the world that its heterogeneous character presented
a serious problem. Not only were there Jews from Germany,
Poland and Rumania, but also from Holland, France and
Switzerland, from Greece and Turkey, from Morocco and
Egypt, and even from Guatemala. Among these manifold
diverse elements it was difficult to establish unity, not only
because of their own differences of social status and religious
and cultural outlook, but also because of the fear that still
deterred very many Jews there from openly avowing their
Judaism. The anti-Semitic prejudice that had been fostered
for centuries, mainly by the Catholic clergy, had influenced
very large sections of the Spanish people against the Jews,
who had literally been represented as monsters with horns
and a tail. I was told by a Jew who had been living there
for about ten years that on one occasion a Catholic priest
visited the school attended by his son and asked the boys in
his class to what nationality they belonged. On receiving
from this Jewish boy the reply that he was a Jew, the priest
exclaimed: "That is impossible. Where are your horns and
your tail?" Whether the priest really believed in the
existence of such a mythical monster or not, his comment at
least showed that he wanted the children to go on believing
in it. When I was in Gibraltar I found confirmation of

this strange belief among the Spanish lower classes. A Spanish maid-servant asked her Jewish mistress to show her her tail, and when the latter attached a fur boa to her person so that one end dangled between her legs the maid immediately crossed herself. Her mistress then removed her fur boa so as to show her maid the stupidity of her belief.

It was owing to the fear that their economic interests might suffer, and partly to sheer indifference, that a very large number of the Jews in this city held strictly aloof from the synagogue and refused to identify themselves with any form of Jewish activity. An anti-Semitic article in a Catalan paper caused a little uneasiness. The consequence was that the religious congregation, which had about two hundred members, had a difficulty in maintaining itself. The synagogue that I saw on my first visit to the city was established some thirty years ago on the ground floor of a large private house. It was a more commodious and attractive place of worship than the one in Madrid, and its interior fittings were much more in accordance with traditional and ritual requirements. There was a raised *Almemar* with a small Menorah on either side and there was also a perpetual lamp; the men occupied chairs between the *Almemar* and the Ark, while the women sat in the rear. For many years the Sephardi ritual was regularly followed, but owing to the influx of Ashkenazim in recent years, the wishes of the latter were met by arranging that the Sabbath service should be conducted according to the Ashkenazi rite on alternate week-ends.

Externally, religious life in Barcelona was certainly healthier than in Madrid. Not only was service held every day in the week, but there was always a *Minyan*[1] in the evening as well as in the morning. The Sabbath service was attended by over thirty people and was over by a quarter to ten, and when I asked what was the reason for holding the service so early I was told that it was because everybody wanted to go to business. Unlike Gibraltar, where every Jew

[1] Quorum of ten.

kept his shop or office closed on the Sabbath, the Jews in Barcelona all attended to their occupations on the Sabbath as usual, including the burly beadle, who doffed his official uniform and peaked cap before betaking himself to his secular business. The only exceptions were the *Hazan*,[1] who wore a tall black hat and a scarlet band round his black robe while officiating, the *Shochet*,[2] who still sported his big round Galician hat, and one or two lay members, who were wealthy enough to be able to live on their incomes. The *Shochet* was one of the many German refugees who had succeeded in finding a position here. The office was, indeed, already occupied on his arrival, but as he possessed superior qualifications to those of the older incumbent, the latter was induced to relinquish the appointment in return for monetary compensation.

The wave of German immigration brought quite a number of cantors and ritual slaughterers to Barcelona, sufficient to satisfy the requirements of a score of congregations, but as soon as they realised that there was no opening for them they either tried to engage in some secular calling or went off to some other community. The position had greatly changed from what it was some years previously, when eight months elapsed without any Jewish male infant being circumcised. As soon as a newly arrived member of the community from Czernowitz realised the state of affairs he arranged for a visit of a *Mohel*,[3] who performed the rite on fifteen infants, whose ages ranged from eight days to eight months, on one and the same day. That was, indeed, a day of rejoicing in Barcelona Jewry.

I learned something more in Barcelona about the Hungarian adventurer of whom I had previously heard in Madrid. He hailed from the Hungarian part of Czechoslovakia, and he came to Barcelona from The Hague without any invitation. When he offered himself for the position of Rabbi, the leaders of the community wrote to the late Chief Rabbi of Holland for information, and as a result of

[1] Cantor.   [2] Ritual slaughterer.   [3] Circumciser.

the advice received they decided to have nothing to do with him. Thereupon the latter threatened that he would establish his own community. He got together a handful of German and Polish Jews and conducted a separate service, and then drew up a memorandum to the first President of the Catalonian Republic, Dr. Macia, asking for permission to found a new synagogue. The memorandum bore the signatures of his little band of followers, some of whom were said to have been paid for their signatures, and the result was that President Macia issued an official document approving of the establishment of a new place of worship. That document proved exceedingly valuable to its recipient, who, by means of it, was estimated to have raised some thousands of pounds. He received little money in Spain itself, but carried on a systematic campaign in other countries, ranging from Egypt to the United States, and he was believed to be still living in America. His collection was on behalf of an Ashkenazi congregation in Barcelona, which did not exist. He had an account at the local bank in the name of the congregation, of which he had the sole and absolute control, so that sympathetic subscribers abroad who gave him cheques payable to the Ashkenazi congregation innocently believed that the money would be devoted to its declared purpose. The leaders of the Barcelona community had been trying for years to enlighten the heads of foreign communities about the swindling activities of the so-called "Chief Rabbi", but so far he had managed to elude their pursuit.

In consequence of the German influx a society called "Ezra" was established to furnish advice and relief to needy immigrants. Its office was situated in the same building and on the same floor as the synagogue. The society was maintained partly by local subscriptions and partly by a grant from a Jewish organisation in Paris. Most of the refugees had started businesses of their own or secured agencies for foreign firms, as they had a legal difficulty in obtaining employment, and a new "German quarter" had grown up near the Calle Muntaner. The wealthier members of the community had a club under the neutral name of the "Union Club", while many of them foregathered on Saturday evenings in the Café "Maison Dorée", which was nicknamed "Maison Isidorée." A Zionist society also existed for a short time, but it proved a casualty of the Second World War.

IV.—BARCELONA REVISITED

It was sixteen years since I had last been in Barcelona, and I therefore looked forward with eagerness and curiosity to seeing what changes had taken place in the Jewish community. I received my first Jewish greeting soon after leaving the French frontier, for, on stepping out of the train at Port Bou, the first station in Spain, for the passport and customs formalities, or rather ordeal, I was welcomed by the Jewish uniformed representative of a well-known tourist agency, who told me with pride that he was also the local representative of the American Joint Committee and the "Ambassador of Israel". As I needed his help in the scrimmage that was taking place, I did not dispute the titles that he had assumed or remind him that there were no diplomatic relations between Spain and Israel, but simply expressed pleasure at the privilege of meeting him.

I had not been in the Catalonian capital long before I realised that there had indeed been changes since my previous visit, owing partly to the Spanish Civil War and partly to the World War. The former synagogue premises in the Calle Provenza had been demolished during the Civil War, and the Scrolls of the Law torn into shreds; but as soon as the conflict was over the Government allowed the resumption of Jewish religious services. The Jewish community, however, was at no time suppressed. It was first legalised in 1902, and had an unbroken history since then.

On Sabbath morning I went to the Synagogue in Calle de Roma, 153a. This is a tall, aristocratic-looking apartment-house in a prosperous residential street, without any external sign that it contains a Jewish place of worship. Nor is there any such sign or symbol on the staircase within. On reaching the first floor and finding that there was a flat on either side, without any distinguishing plates, I asked a maid who was sweeping the stairs where the Synagogue was. She tapped at a door, which was opened by a man wearing a *talith* and a beret. He ushered me into a room in which about two dozen men of various ages were seated decorously on chairs against the walls. Facing them stood a *Hazan* at a simple *Almemar*, and as his Sephardi chant struck my ears I asked the man acting as beadle whether there was also an Ashkenazi service. I was thereupon conducted to a smaller room on the other side of the passage, where there were about a dozen men all praying aloud, some shaking themselves, and a few strolling to and fro. There were no women there, and my wife, who was with me, was provided with a chair in the passage. The Ark was draped with a dark-red plush curtain adorned with some Hebrew lettering and the *Magen David* (Shield of David), and near by stood a tall brass Menorah. Both the service and the reading of the Law were rendered by volunteers, the *Baal Koreh* (cantillator) being a recent immigrant from Hungary, who was by trade a tailor. My visit proved very welcome, as there was no other *Cohen* present that morning. The rate of *schnodering* (offering) was rather low, as I heard more than one amount offered of five pesetas (less than a shilling).

When the service was over a member of the congregation, Mr. Hausmann, invited us to his home, and on the way told me something about local conditions. Although the Ashkenazim and Sephardim held separate services, they formed one congregation, but they did not mix socially.

After *Kiddush* (blessing on wine) Mr. Hausmann related a rather interesting story of his experiences on the Island of Ivica, the smallest of the Balearic Islands, where he came into contact with the " Chuetas " ("pork-eaters") as the local descendants of Marranos are called. He was at a pension together with another Jew, and they washed their hands before meals and said grace afterwards. A couple of days later a fellow-guest who had watched them approached Mr. Hausmann and asked him if he was a Jew. Upon being told that he was, the stranger embraced him and said, in a state of deep emotion; "You are my brother!" He was one of the "Chuetas." He took Mr. Hausmann to a café, where, after seating themselves in a corner, he spoke softly and timorously, turning round repeatedly to make sure that nobody was listening. He told him that there were quite a number of "Chuetas" on the island, and that a local Catholic priest acted secretly also as a Rabbi. They performed the rite of circumcision in the privacy of a cellar. They observed the Sabbath by lighting a couple of candles, which they immediately threw into the fire, thus following the custom of their Marrano ancestors, who used to throw the candles into the fire for fear of being discovered by an informer. On Sabbath afternoon, several leading personalities, including the priest, the Chief of Police, lawyers, doctors, pharmacists, and other professional people and intellectuals usually met for an hour to discuss Jewish matters and then dispersed.

The next day I visited Mr. Chaim Glantzmann, the head of the Ashkenazi community, who reminded me that he had presided at the Zionist meeting that I had addressed in Barcelona sixteen years ago. He furnished me with some interesting data about the Jews in Barcelona and in other cities in Spain. He was in regular communication with the other communities and had a complete register of the Jews in the country, which showed that it was necessary to revise the generally accepted estimate of the Jewish population. According to his lists the numbers were as follows:

Barcelona .... 296 families, about 1,200 souls
Madrid   between 60 and 70 families, about 250–300 souls
Seville ....,...... 4 families, about 16 souls
Valencia .... 10 families, about 40 souls

Total about 1,556 souls

He did not know of any Jews in any other city in Spain, and did not believe that there were any.

All the adult Jews in Barcelona were immigrants and had settled there during the past fifty years. They had no Rabbi, but only a Sephardi *Hazan*, Mayer Melul, who came to them from Morocco two years ago. The latter, who lived on the synagogue premises, was also a *Shochet*. The city authorities allowed them to kill one ox per week, so that all who wanted *Kosher* meat could get it. The President of the community was Señor Enrique Benaroya, a merchant, who had migrated from the Orient a few years previously. They had no school of their own. Most of the Jewish children went to the French school, where permission had been secured by Mr. Glantzmann's son, a doctor, for Hebrew instruction to be given to them for three hours a week. At first Dr. Glantzmann acted as the Hebrew teacher, and he was succeeded by another instructor—both giving their services gratuitously. The children who did not go to the French school received Hebrew instruction from the *Hazan*. No communal functions took place, apart from Chanukah and Purim balls, which were held in a public hall and were very well attended. For the High Festivals the Sephardim, who were the more numerous, left the Synagogue entirely to the Ashkenazim and hired a cinema for themselves. Most of their religious and ritual requisites were obtained from Israel, but they also had prayer-books printed in Frankfort and Casablanca.

Mr. Glantzmann emphasised the friendly attitude of the Spanish authorities throughout the World War. There was no interference with the Jews who were residents. Hundreds of others, who had fled from Holland and Belgium as well as France, smuggled themselves over the frontier and arrived without identity papers or money; they were first of all sent to a camp outside Barcelona and later released through the intervention of the American Joint Distribution Committee's representative. Some of them went to Madrid or Lisbon, and others sailed direct to Palestine.

As for the occupations of the local Jewry, 25 per cent were merchants, and 10 per cent manufacturers, while there were four doctors, two dentists, and three engineers. Most of the rest were artisans and craftsmen. There were no Jews in any branch of the public or municipal service. Since the establishment of the State of Israel a keen desire had been manifested among some members of the community to settle there, and of those who had lived in Barcelona before the war at least 150 had already left with the help of the Joint Committee to make their homes there.

Probably few Jews now domiciled in the capital of Catalonia ever pause to reflect upon the vicissitudes of the mediaeval Jewish community, which had enjoyed fame for a few hundred years as a centre of Talmudical learning and also great material prosperity before being subjected to a terrible massacre at the end of the fourteenth century and compelled to go into exile a century later. But there are still visible reminders of those affluent yet tragic times. On the southern side of the city there towers the lofty eminence known as the Montjuich (or "Jews' Mount"), where the Jews once owned a great deal of landed estate (or perhaps had their cemetery). In the frowsy labyrinth of narrow streets off the Ramblas, that crowded thoroughfare lined with kiosks, which once formed the Jewish quarter, as indicated by the Calle del Call (abbreviation of *Kahal*), there can be seen at the corner of Calle de Marlet and Calle del Arco de San Ramon, embedded in the wall and rather high up, a stone about eighteen inches square, with a Hebrew inscription, which was the tombstone of "the martyr Rabbi Samuel of Sard." And in the Ayuntamiento (Town Hall) there are several interesting Hebrew manuscripts, about eight hundred years old, which were signed agreements made between the heads of the Jewish communities in Aragon and Castile with the Kings of those provinces, stipulating that the Jews would help their respective sovereign in his war against his neighbour on condition that the Jews who fought under the other king were spared in the event of his defeat.

Chapter XXIII

ESCAPE *VIA* LISBON

THE JEWS OF LISBON, who constantly pass through the busy square known as Rossio, probably seldom pause to reflect upon the *autos da fé* that used to be enacted there, except perhaps when a foreign traveller emerges from the railway station near by and is immediately enlightened by welcoming friends regarding its sinister historic memories. For now there reigns perfect civil equality for Jew and Gentile, a position that has been affirmed more than once since the beginning of the nineteenth century and especially in recent years. The mediaeval edict of expulsion has been formally rescinded, and no question has ever been raised about the rights of the Jews to settle in the land ever since they began returning in small numbers in the first or second decade of the nineteenth century. The resettlement has always been on a modest scale—at least it was so until the end of the First World War—and the total number of Jews in Lisbon even now is estimated at less than 2,000, of whom the majority are not Sephardim.

The earliest settlers came partly from Morocco and partly from Gibraltar, and in the latter case several immigrated *via* the Azores, where they had lived for a number of years. A few prominent members of the Sephardi community can still recall the stories they heard from their grandfathers, who, after having engaged in trade in the Azores for a time, decided to transfer themselves to Lisbon and to foster commercial relations with "the islands". Several of the pioneers, having been born in Gibraltar, felt secure as British subjects against any attempt to interfere with their settling in a land that had once proved so inhospitable. It is in the British cemetery that there can be found the oldest tombstones of the Jews of Lisbon, and it was a part of that cemetery that was subsequently acquired by the Sephardi community as its own burial-ground. Some years before the First World War Jews from Central and Eastern Europe, especially from Germany and Poland, began to find their way to the Portuguese capital, and after 1918 their number continued to increase, until it is now estimated that there are more Ashkenazim than Sephardim. The rivalry that exists between the two sections is undoubtedly one of the most interesting features of the Jewish life in Lisbon.

The paucity of the Sephardi community is due to the prevalence of inter-marriage between its members and Portuguese Catholics, a process that is still going on almost irresistibly. The frequency of these mixed marriages is explained as being due to the lack of choice open to Jewish young men and women in search of a life's partner, while another factor has doubtless consisted in the inadequate religious education provided and the lack of any spiritual guidance. Religious worship has been regularly maintained for about a century, and two synagogues were built, of which only the later one—a small and pleasant sanctuary not far from the beautiful Avenida da Liberdad—is now used. This synagogue was erected over forty years ago, and it is characteristic of the conditions of the time that it has no façade to the street but lies back somewhat discreetly, without any external design or inscription to indicate its character. It has no Rabbi or Haham and its services are conducted by two cantors, one of whom is a Sephardi from Tangiers and the other an Ashkenazi from Vienna. As for the worshippers, they attend in respectable numbers, and several of them even wear silk hats on the Sabbath.

There are no striking differences that distinguish the Portuguese Jews from the members of the Ashkenazi community. Many of them have a house at Estoril, the fashionable pleasure resort on the coast, in addition to a house in Lisbon, and some even have a third establishment in the country. There have been many marriages between Sephardim and Ashkenazim, thus helping to unite the community.

Despite their paucity the Portuguese Jews of Lisbon have produced some notable scholars and scientists, such as Dr. Alfred Bensaude, who established a scientific college; Senhor Joaquin Bensaude, who has published works on the history of Portuguese nautical astronomers; and Professor Alfred Benarus, who was once President of the local Zionist organisation. Professor M. B. Amzalak combines an unusual range of activities. He is both economist and Oriental scholar, as well as Vice-Rector of the Technical University, and was formerly part-proprietor and co-editor of the leading daily, *O Seculo*. He is the author of an imposing list of books and monographs, and has lectured in England and France.

The Ashkenazi section, largely consisting of Polish Jews who have settled here at various intervals during the past thirty years, have established themselves in a different part of the city and have their own place of worship, which is on private premises. The upkeep of their separate religious organisation is cheerfully borne by the Polish Jews, who impart a vigorous impulse to Jewish life in general. Before the recent war Professor Benarus founded a Jewish day school, combining general with Jewish education, which is attended by nearly a hundred children.

The centre of Jewish social life consisted of a club that was founded over twenty years ago, under the name of "Hehaber," by a young Polish Jew from Breslau. The premises comprised a reading room (where Jewish papers in various languages could be found), a room for games, a buffet, and a hall for concerts, lectures and dances. This club, with a membership of a few hundred, was open every night and played an important part in the communal life of Lisbon Jewry. On the other hand, the community was not so fortunate with its little hospital, which had to be closed some time ago owing to inadequate support.

The Jewish community in Lisbon appeared to take little interest in the Marranos in Oporto and in the other places in the north of the country. It was the general view that the organisation set up in Oporto for the revival of Judaism among the Marranos would fail of its purpose, owing to the head of the Seminary being unqualified for such a position, and also to the fact that the students were not afforded the opportunity of being brought up in a truly Jewish milieu. "The Marranos are all right for the Jews abroad," was the general comment, in which one could perceive a blend of cynicism and disillusionment.

From the time that the Nazi persecution in Germany began, Lisbon became a coveted asylum for many thousands of its Jewish victims, who hoped to be able to be transported from there to some safe destination beyond the seas, and a considerable proportion succeeded in reaching it. After the outbreak of war large numbers came over from France, braving all the dangers of the Pyrenees, after having fled from the Lowlands, and the problem that they presented was one with which the local community alone was utterly unable to cope. A few hundred of these refugees were the descendants of Jews exiled from Portugal in the sixteenth century, and, fortunately for them, their claim to Portuguese nationality was recognised by both the German and the Portuguese Governments, so that no hindrance was placed in the way of their journey to Lisbon. An even larger number of Jews claiming Spanish nationality from their exiled forefathers were permitted to enter Spain and stay there. Realising the urgency of this refugee problem, the Jewish Agency for Palestine and the American Jewish Joint Distribution Committee took what steps they could to deal with it. They sent special representatives to Lisbon to open offices and to select refugees suitable for settlement in Palestine or America, and provided the requisite funds to cover the cost of their transport. The task of selection was by no means easy, and the procuring of ships amid the hazards and perils of war was a harassing and tantalising business as it involved protracted negotiations with all sorts of authorities and agencies. But, by dint of perseverance, and with their patience nearly exhausted, some thousands of Jews, who had at first despaired of ever being able to reach a safe destination, and who felt and feared that they were being daily spied upon by the myrmidons of the Nazi Government, at last succeeded in sailing from Lisbon to new homes. Some left before the end of the war and the rest when it was over, some for the land of Israel and the rest for other parts of the world.

INDEX

INDEX